Clinical Delegation Skills

A Handbook for Nurses

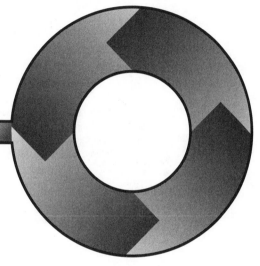

Ruth I. Hansten, MBA, BSN
Principal
Hansten and Washburn
Bainbridge Island, Washington

Marilynn J. Washburn, MA, BSN
Principal
Hansten and Washburn
Bainbridge Island, Washington

An Aspen Publication®
Aspen Publishers, Inc.
Gaithersburg, Maryland
1994

Library of Congress Cataloging-in-Publication Data

Hansten, Ruth I.
Clinical delegation skills : a handbook for nurses /
Ruth I. Hansten and Marilynn J. Washburn.
p.   cm.
Includes bibliographical references and index.
ISBN 0-8342-0603-X
1. Nursing services—Personnel management. 2. Delegation of
authority. 3. Differentiated nursing practice. I. Washburn, Marilynn. II. Title.
[DNLM: 1. Nursing, Supervisory—organization & administration. 2. Nursing Services—
organization & administration. 3. Decision Making—nurses' instruction. 4.
Interprofessional Relations—nurses' instruction.   WY 105 H251c 1994]
RT89.3.H36   1994
362.1'73'068—dc20
DNLM/DLC
for Library of Congress
94-18669
CIP

Editorial Resources: Jane Colilla

Library of Congress Catalog Card Number: 94-18669
ISBN: 0-8342-0603-X

Printed in the United States of America

3   4   5

To the thousands of staff nurses, students, and managers who have struggled with the issues we discuss in this book; to our wonderful mentors, countless nurses from our past who were excellent examples of expert delegation; to all the assistive personnel from our past who taught us, supported us, and helped us learn our professional role. You all helped us discover that caring and scientific knowledge can be combined to make healing magic!

Table of Contents

About the Authors

Ruth I. Hansten, MBA, BSN, and **Marilynn J. Washburn, MA, BSN,** are accomplished national consultants, speakers, and seminar leaders, offering a unique team approach, blending the inspirational with the practical, and humor with skill development; drawing from their years of experience in staff, middle manager, and executive positions in hospitals and other health care settings. You'll see their work widely published in nursing and management journals. Their first book, *I Light the Lamp,* is a motivational gift book for and by nurses, offering quotes, poems, and observations about the issues most central to the nursing profession (published in 1990 by Applied Therapeutics in Vancouver, Washington). Their second book, *The Nurse Manager's Answer Book,* was published in 1993 by Aspen Publishers in Gaithersburg, Maryland. This indispensable resource answers the toughest everyday challenges experienced by nursing leaders and managers, contributing realistic, workable solutions, step-by-step advice, and essential tips.

Clinical Delegation Skills: A Handbook for Nurses is based on experiences gained while Hansten and Washburn have conducted seminars and consulted nationally with nurses undergoing care delivery redesign across the health care continuum. A workshop was developed in 1990 by Loretta O'Neill, MN, RN, (author of Chapter 8) and Hansten and Washburn at the request of the Washington Organization of Nurse Executives. This portable workshop continues to be updated and is individualized to the needs of the hosting health care organization. For more information about the workshop, please contact the Washington Organization of Nurses Executives' Executive Director, Karen Haase-Herrick, MN, RN, (author of Chapter 2) at 190 Queen Anne Ave. North, Seattle, WA 98109, or 206-285-0102.

Hansten and Washburn also consult on care delivery systems change and work redesign from a nursing and interdisciplinary perspective. For more information, contact them at:

Hansten and Washburn
4643 Blakely Avenue N.E.
Bainbridge Island, WA 98110
Telephone 206-842-1189, or 206-842-0912
Voice Mail 206-999-1640
FAX 206-842-9921

Contributors

Karen S. Haase-Herrick, MN, RN
Executive Director
Washington Organization of Nurse Executives
Seattle, Washington

Karen A. McGrath, RN
Associate Executive Director
Washington State Nurses Association
Seattle, Washington

Loretta O'Neill, MN, RN
Faculty
St. Joseph's School of Nursing
Lancaster, Pennsylvania

Foreword

In today's health care environment, there are many issues which challenge us to become more effective, creative, and productive, and give us an opportunity to learn and grow in our professional practice. *Clinical Delegation Skills: A Handbook for Nurses* is a timely resource for the development of delegation skills that are required of professional nurses in a changing delivery system. The skills and knowledge needed to care for patients in every health care setting along the continuum of care will be required of nurses. We must, however, develop the ability to work through and with other people. We have just educated a generation of nurses who are not comfortable with the concept of delegation in their practice, yet these nurses delegate many things in the course of their private lives. In an effort to translate these personal delegation skills to professional practice, there are some easily adapted knowledge and associated discussion sources available. I believe this book captures the essence of the knowledge and strategies necessary to assist in this transformation.

A professional nurse must understand the law regulating our practice (i.e., State Nurse Practice Act), the scopes of practice of both the registered nurse and the licensed practical nurse, and the functions and roles of each. A nurse must understand what can be delegated and what must be retained as professional responsibility—those functions of assessment, evaluation, and nursing judgment. A nurse must recognize and understand what the responsibility of supervision is, and must know how to recognize and validate competence in the individual to whom tasks are delegated. To achieve some confidence and comfort level with delegation, a nurse must also understand the risks and liability associated with this professional function. With this knowledge and understanding will come the development of the skill of clinical delegation. This book offers a very comprehensive discussion and analysis of the concerns, barriers, and opportunities, along with the available resources to build important skills for professional nurses. Every school of nursing and each nurse manager will find it a helpful tool in broadening the nurse's role as we position ourselves to take a leadership role in health care reform.

Mrs. Margaret O. Jobes, RN, MS
Associate Administrator, Maryvale Samaritan Medical Center
Member, Arizona State Board of Nursing
Chair, Task Force on Unlicensed Personnel
Phoenix, Arizona

Acknowledgments

We express special appreciation to Karen Haase-Herrick, MN, RN, Executive Director of the Washington Organization of Nurse Executives (WONE); Loretta O'Neill, MN, RN, and the Washington Organization of Nurse Executives for being involved in this writing project. This handbook is based on the workshop developed by WONE, Ruth Hansten, Marilynn Washburn, and Loretta O'Neill at the request of the nurse executives in Washington State. Since 1990, Hansten, Washburn, and O'Neill have presented this workshop throughout the United States to thousands of nurses (and nursing students) in acute care, long-term care, and community health. In conjunction with the workshops, Hansten and Washburn have been involved in consulting projects related to care delivery system changes. The material in this book is based on the experiences they have enjoyed as a result of these interactive seminars. Ms. Herrick contributed to Chapter 2, and Ms. O'Neill wrote Chapter 8.

"Clinical Delegation Skills: Patient Care Management Skills for the Nineties . . . and Beyond" has continued to be an extremely popular and practical presentation. Call the WONE office at 206-285-0102 (190 Queen Anne Avenue North, Seattle 98109) for more information regarding having this seminar presented at your facility.

We also thank Karen McGrath, RN, who serves as the Associate Executive Director of the Washington State Nurses Association and has considerable expertise in the area of collective bargaining, for her contribution to Chapter 4 describing the role of unions in care delivery changes and delegation. Although we recognize that RN unions are not present in all locales, they are an important factor to consider in all organizations that have union representation.

Randall DeJong, MSN, RN, CCRN, a clinical educator at Providence Hospital in Everett, Washington, has been kind enough to share with us his copyrighted pictorial care pathways as illustrated in Chapters 2 and 6. We also extend our heartfelt appreciation to Carolyn Bonner and the home care group at Community Home Health Care, Seattle, Washington, who have permitted us to publish the changes they have made in their organizational chart as a result of their restructuring efforts.

We also extend our thanks and appreciation to Dennis Burnside. His creativity, patience, and impressive ability to transfer our visual images into reality will be an added benefit to all visual learners (like us!).

Chapter 1

The Overall Process
of Delegation

Ruth I. Hansten and Marilynn J. Washburn

"All this talk about delegation—we seem to be going in circles. First you're by yourself, then you're in a team trying to do everything with everybody else, and then primary nursing comes along. Nursing assistants come and go depending on what the budget looks like—why should I bother to learn about delegation? Tomorrow it will be something different anyway."

There's no doubt about it, nursing has tried on many different styles of delivering care, and no doubt will continue to do so in the future. But it is apparent to us that we must better understand how to work with other members of the health care team in order to provide the safest and most effective care to our patients. If nurses are to assume their rightful position as coordinators of care, systematically implementing the holistic approach that is the foundation of our profession, then we must be certain of the process necessary for this coordination.

THE DEFINITION

Just as a surgeon establishes anatomical boundaries before he or she operates, we need to establish boundaries, in the form of a definition, when delegating to other personnel.

> Delegation: "Transferring to a competent individual authority to perform a selected nursing task in a selected situation."

We cite the operational definition adopted by the National Council of State Boards of Nursing (1990, p. 1) in their *Concept Paper on Delegation*, and will use this as the basis of our discussion throughout the book. It is important to note the generic approach of this definition, which certainly allows the practicing nurse a great deal of freedom in selecting the task and the individual to perform that task. As we will note in some detail in future chapters, the primary ingredient of this concept is that the nurse ensures the competency of the individual to whom he or she is delegating. To some, this is an added dimension of responsibility, and one that is not always willingly adopted. The challenges for nurses in this area are apparent since many do not feel they are adequately prepared to teach individuals to perform tasks that have been a part of their own scope of practice.

To practice clinical delegation effectively requires the development of a skill that has not appeared to "belong" to nursing and that consequently many nurses have not been taught or had the time or interest to pursue. This book will assist in developing that skill by applying a process that is very familiar to all of us: the nursing process. By following the four major steps of the nursing process, we can systematically analyze what is necessary for any practicing professional nurse to know in order to develop a skill that will be a fundamental of practice.

THE MODEL: THE KEY TO DELEGATION

The activities of delegation, like those of the nursing process itself, are cyclical, beginning with a gathering of data, continuing with the utilization of those data as plans are made and carried out, and concluding with the analysis of the activity; the cycle then repeats itself. We have developed a key model that illustrates this process (Figure 1–1) and will refer to the sequence of events often to make our point that this is not a singular process. The ongoing cycle of events will be the result of your ability to connect one component with the other until you have an integrated skill that allows you to perform many of the fundamentals concurrently. We will isolate each step for the purpose of our study and allow you to focus your attention on the areas of the process in which you determine you need the most skill building.

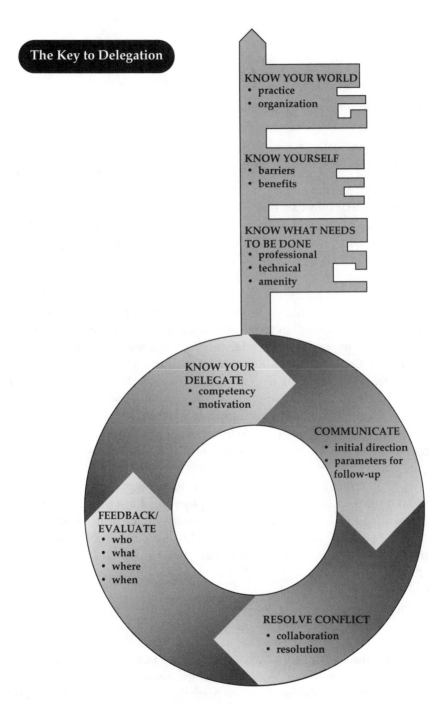

Figure 1–1 The Key to Delegation

Assessment

- Know Your World
- Know Your Organization
- Know Your Practice
- Know Yourself
- Know Your Delegate

A foundation must be laid upon which to build the decision making that is implied in the concept of delegation. Selecting the right task for the right individual sounds a little like the job of the personnel manager and is foreign to many of us. We must do a certain amount of assessment, as we would in any situation in which we were determining the best course of action for the patient.

Assessment implies knowledge: an overview of the total picture of factors that are affecting the current condition. Such a review will help us to understand how best to respond and to plan for the future of health care. "Knowing your world" in terms of demographics, economics, and social changes will be essential in understanding why we are pursuing a skill that many believe is outside the domain of our profession. Analyzing these factors will help us to prepare for changes ahead and to position nursing as a profession to lead the way instead of following a path determined by others as a reaction to health care reform.

Knowledge of the nurse practice act, including the numerous regulatory changes that are being made as a result of the changes in care delivery systems, cannot be overemphasized. The responses of the individual boards of nursing, as they strive to protect the public by setting up ground rules for the changes in nursing personnel, have been significant. Many nurses feel at risk, voicing their concerns in the heartfelt statement, "I'm not putting my license on the line!" Knowledge of the practice act, the statutes and rules that govern nursing practice, and the policies of the employing institution will help the nurse to allay those fears and to practice more professionally.

The knowledge of the organization in which we work, its mission and values, will help nurses to assess the attributes of their environment in terms of its support of nursing practice. What is the plan for quality? What are the policies for working with other personnel? Is nursing directly involved with the decision making regarding the changes in care delivery systems, whether they are occurring in a community setting or in the acute care arena? Answers to such questions will prepare the nurse for the decisions to be made regarding how she or he practices and delegates clinically.

Knowledge of our own attitudes and beliefs is an area that each of us must explore if we are to fully develop the skill of delegation. What personal barriers make it difficult for me to work with someone else? What do I do best that makes working with others the most reasonable choice? And what benefits can I get from this whole thing, anyway? Often we find that nurses know the fundamentals of delegation and appreciate the principles but that they just aren't buying it. There is no substitute for attitude, which will make all the difference in how successful you are in your practice with others.

Speaking of others, it is also necessary to assess the delegates. Who are these people that you are being asked to share your practice with? Individuals with gifts and challenges like the rest of us, delegates have their own strengths, weaknesses, preferences, motivations, and cultural backgrounds. Since the basic tenet of safe delegation is the insurance of the competency of the delegate, a careful assessment of this individual is an absolute necessity. We will ask you to refocus your thinking, however, by first emphasizing the strengths of your delegate and optimizing the resources you have available, rather than focusing on all of the tasks she or he cannot do. We will ask you to examine these areas of weakness as potential growth areas and to determine what can be done to overcome an apparent inability to perform a procedure—is more teaching necessary, or is this task truly beyond the scope of the individual?

Having completed an assessment of the external environment, the internal environment (that's you), and the delegates with whom you are asked to work, you are ready to proceed to the next step of the cycle. The foundation of knowledge you have developed in your assessment will allow you to plan the best use of resources and coordinate a high-performance team.

Plan

- Know What Needs To Be Done

The first step in planning involves gathering the knowledge of what needs to be done. You have some latitude here: as a practicing professional coordinating a plan of care, you are in the position to prioritize which outcomes are the most important to attain. Notice that we are talking about outcomes; we will continue to ask you to focus your attention in this direction. Before you can plan anything or determine who will carry out the plan, you must think in terms of outcomes, the goals that you and your patient want to achieve from this experience. For many, thinking in terms of outcomes will be an unwelcome experience, and you will seek to return to the comfort of a task list, which quantifies the amount of "work" you have done and certainly gives a sense of accomplishment. Often tasks are done for the sake of work, and very little thought is spent on the analysis of what the performance of these tasks contributes to the bottom line (and we don't mean budgets!).

In Chapter 6, we will look at a model of nursing that divides our work into three areas of focus: the professional, the technical, and the amenities aspects of nursing care. From this "PTA model" we will be able to determine the emphasis of our care and those parts of our practice that may be performed by others.

Intervene

- Prioritize, and Match the Job to the Delegate
- Know How To Communicate
- Know How To Resolve Conflict

Continuing our cycle, we arrive at the point where the majority of delegation takes place. Procedures and tasks may be taught to unlicensed personnel, but the critical components of the remainder of the nursing process rely on the knowledge and experience of a professional licensed nurse. Herein lies one of our greatest challenges, for we are faced with the need to determine which parts of our practice to "let go" of, and we often find that some of those direct care tasks may be what we have found the most personally satisfying. Once again, according to the operational definition of delegation, the registered nurse is selecting the tasks and the appropriate situation in which to delegate. Matching the job to the delegate then becomes a decision we can control, and we must continue to make the choice wisely, based on sound judgment. Numerous studies have demonstrated that the nurse spends considerable time performing tasks that can more easily and efficiently be done by someone else. We owe it to ourselves and to our patients to free up this time so that we may do what we were educated to provide. Although we may strongly voice our concerns about the quality of care when someone else is performing the task, we must assume control of the decision and make the best choice by mastering the skill of delegation and directing the process.

Working successfully with others requires communication. This skill is one we perform quite readily in interactions with our patients; we need to transfer that skill to the directing and supervising of our delegates. Clearly outlining the expectations we have, giving complete and concise directions for implementation, and providing parameters for following up with the nurse are essential ingredients to successful communication. Being able to be assertive without being aggressive when the response is not the eager and willing "yes" that we would like is also part of the skill of effective delegation.

We have implied that the response given by the delegate may not be enthusiastic, and indeed it may be an absolute refusal. Knowing how to resolve conflict when the members of the health care team do not agree is fundamental to a successful working relationship. Passivity and a strong desire to avoid conflict will not lead to the desired outcome of a high-performing partnership with your delegates. Knowing when to take the lead and assuming a calm but assertive stance will assist you in clarifying the work to be done and by whom.

Evaluation

- Know How To Give Feedback
- Evaluate and Problem Solve

The final step of the process is one to which we are held accountable by law, yet it is the one area that we do not often find time for and that we willingly shift to management. However, the contract of delegation carries with it the legal expectation that you will be supervising the delegate. Once again, an operational definition is provided by the National Council of State Boards of Nursing (1990, p. 2):

> **Supervision: "Provision of guidance by a qualified nurse for the accomplishment of a nursing task or activity with initial direction of the task or activity and periodic inspection of the actual act of accomplishing the task or activity."**

Periodic inspection of the activity means that you oversee the performance (again, you determine the frequency of this observation) and offer feedback to the delegate in terms of an appraisal of his or her performance. This is certainly part of your obligation of ensuring competency of the individual, as well as closing the loop by giving the delegate an evaluation of how things are going. Rules and statutes will tell us that the supervising nurse (that's you any time you delegate) will be held accountable for the correction of any error made by the delegate. Whether you choose to pass that on to the manager for resolution or take action yourself by directly discussing the situation with the delegate, corrective action must take place.

Feedback and follow-up may be as simple as a thank you for a job well done or as formal as the documentation of an unusual occurrence form accompanied by a lengthy investigation. Whatever the situation calls for, you must be prepared to provide it. Just as you provide a thoughtful appraisal of the patient you have just taught to perform his own central line catheter care, you will need to evaluate the progress of the home health aide who is performing range of motion on an elderly patient with impaired mobility.

THE SKILL

You have probably determined by now that the majority of the components of the delegation process are not new to you. In fact, you are performing many of them continually as you plan and implement your care for your patients. What will be required, then, is not the development of new knowledge but the transfer of skills that you have already developed. Assessment of the patient is a skill that you have developed and practiced all of your professional life and is no different in technique when you transfer that attention to the new delegate who arrives at your work setting ready and eager to do his or her job. The teaching that you do with each of your patients requires planning, clear communication, and evaluation to complete the process, and is similar to the planning, communication, and evaluation you will do with delegates.

Throughout this book we will focus on fundamentals, offering exercises for you to check your knowledge and to apply any new material. There will be repetition (we warn you) since this is a basic principle of learning. Our goal, our *planned outcome* for you, is to develop your ability to implement the process of clinical delegation with confidence and completeness so that you have the time to do what you do best. Using this book will help open the door to growth in professional nursing.

REFERENCE

National Council of State Boards of Nursing. 1990. *Concept paper on delegation.* Chicago.

Chapter 2

Know Your World: Why Are These Changes in My Practice Happening to Me?

WHAT IN THE WORLD IS GOING ON?

Karen Haase-Herrick

Wherever you look today, one theme continues to surface—our world of work is changing rapidly and in ways we don't yet understand. Even the work world in Japan and Germany is undergoing significant change. A colleague recently said, "It used to be that we had periods of change followed by periods of stability. Now change seems to be the only stable factor!"

For registered nurses, the biggest area of change involves the giving of care through others—the delegation of some traditional nursing tasks to others (Blegen et al., 1992). You are switching from a model of nursing care delivery in which the RN provides all the care to a model in which you delegate to others some of the tasks involved in the care of patients. You are being asked to work on teams and/or in partnership with another person. You are sometimes being asked to work with caregivers about whom you know nothing and in whom you have little or no trust. Later on in this book, you'll be asked to fully explore your own personal barriers to the use of clinical delegation skills. To get to a point where you are ready to fully explore the why and how of clinical delegation skills for the management of patient care, however, you must first know the world in which you are working so that you will understand the driving forces

9

behind this change. The purpose of this chapter is not to provide you with new information so much as to bring to the fore of your thinking those environmental factors that are influencing the world in which you work or are about to work. You know that all of these things are happening. What you may not have done up to this point is to link all of them together into an assessment of why you are now in such a period of change in your work life.

Let's do an environmental assessment. Take a few minutes to think about things that are going on around you—what do you hear in the news? What articles in nursing journals have you read recently about changes in patient care delivery? What programs and systems has your facility initiated over the last five years? How many businesses in your area have laid off employees in the last five years? What is happening to your own health care costs? What are you seeing with respect to the length of time patients remain in an acute care facility? What types of patients are you now caring for in the home or in residential long-term care facilities whom you did not see five or ten years ago? What about the age of your patients? What about the knowledge level of your patients? In all honesty now, what have you and your coworkers said about your workloads over the past five years? How many times have you been able to do all the necessary patient and family education prior to discharge, especially when the discharge is from an acute care facility?

Now, list at least five things that you think are shaping this change that ask you, as a professional nurse, to use clinical delegation skills in the management of patient care:

1. _____
2. _____
3. _____
4. _____
5. _____

Your list of five will most likely fit into one of the following six categories:

1. Influence of the 1980s nursing shortage
2. Health care reform
3. Demographic trends
4. Health care delivery trends
5. Changing nature of work
6. Maturing of the nursing profession

INFLUENCE OF THE 1980s NURSE SHORTAGE

Vacancy rates for nursing personnel began to soar in the late 1980s. Hospitals across the country reported persistent vacancies; nursing school enrollments dropped. A devastating nursing shortage had developed very quickly. Positions were going unfilled for over a year in many rural facilities. And yet patients were in hospitals and needed care. Home care agencies had growing caseloads. Long-term care facilities were full and needed RNs. Public health agencies, schools, and prisons all had need of RNs. And schools of nursing had vacant faculty positions. States across the country set up commissions to study the nursing shortage and identify ways in which to address and resolve the issue. The American Medical Association proposed the use of a registered care technologist, or RCT, a suggestion that sent shock waves through the nursing profession because the RCT was not truly part of the nursing care delivery team.

Otis R. Bowen, Secretary of the U.S. Department of Health and Human Services, established the Secretary's Commission on Nursing in December 1987. The commission, which became known as the Bowen Commission, delivered its final report with recommendations in 1988. The Bowen Commission held hearings across the country to hear firsthand from RNs what issues were contributing to the current shortage. The conclusion reached was that the nursing shortage was primarily the result of rapidly escalating demand for RNs. The Final Report of the Bowen Commission contained 16 specific recommendations that were grouped according to the following issues:

1. Utilization of nursing resources
2. Nurse compensation
3. Health care financing
4. Nurse decision making
5. Development of nursing resources
6. Maintenance of nursing resources

Recommendations in the "utilization of nursing resources" category called on employers of nurses to develop innovative models of care delivery that would use scarce RN resources efficiently and effectively (U.S. Dept. of Health and Human Services, 1988).

Meanwhile, back at the site of care delivery, especially for acute care patients, nursing leaders had already begun to develop innovative ways in which to provide the needed care with the resources available. Nurse managers and staff nurses began talking about new ways to "get the job done." Out of this evolved the increased use of clinical delegation skills. However, the evolution of these innovative care delivery models was shaped by other environmental influences as well.

HEALTH CARE REFORM

During the 1992 presidential campaign, the public became intimately aware that 37 million Americans had no health care coverage. Long before the campaign, however, health care professionals in all disciplines were talking about health care reform. Starting in the late 1980s, American business leaders began talking in the press about the costs of health care and their impact on the ability of American business to compete in a global economy. What brought the need for health care reform to the forum of public discussion?

Most Americans thought very little about the cost of health care for a long time. However, in the 1960s, when Medicare was passed, government became a major purchaser of health care services for one segment of the American people—the elderly. As this group grew in size, the amount of money paid out by the government increased. At the same time, federal and state governments were paying for additional health care services for the poor through the Medicaid program. The number of people served by Medicaid had also grown, adding to the percentage of federal dollars purchasing health care for certain groups of Americans. In efforts to hold down the amount of federal money spent for Medicare, prospective payment in the form of diagnostic-related groups (DRGs) was introduced in the early 1980s. Medicaid budgets were also tightened. Consequently the amount the government reimbursed providers for Medicare and Medicaid patients ceased being equal to the amount the care cost. That reimbursement figure has run as low as 60 cents for every dollar of costs (ProPac, 1993).

The costs of providing the care did not go down. Salary costs, building costs, new equipment costs, and expanding technology all contributed to skyrocketing health care costs. Providers had to secure additional revenue to continue to operate. Cost shifting to payers other than the government became the means by which to secure the additional revenue. The "payer other than the government" was most often a health care insurance plan. Insurance premiums had to rise to cover these increased costs.

Premium increases of 15 percent for one year became common. Employers who provided health care insurance for their employees saw their costs of providing this benefit increasing annually and increasing the costs of producing whatever widget or commodity they made. The options for businesses were to hold down the cost of the health care insurance benefit, discontinue the benefit, increase the price of the product, or allow for declining profits. The only real choice to businesses became holding down the cost of the health care insurance coverage they provided employees (Smith, 1988).

Insurance companies began developing innovative ways to curb the growth of premium increases. Managed care, securing discounts from providers, and narrowing the scope of coverage were methods employed. Preventive services were deleted. Experimental procedures were seldom covered. Providers were still delivering these services, however. The costs to deliver the services continued to escalate because of increased demand for services due to increasing life spans, increasing birth rate, the AIDS epidemic, new technology, supply cost increases, and personnel and structural costs. The result of this cost spiral has been an increase in health care expenditures that exceeds the rate of inflation by three times ("Rising Health Spending," 1994). Individuals are also finding that the amount they must pay out of their own income for health care is increasing through increased copays and deductibles, increased contributions to insurance premiums, wage caps related to maintaining health care coverage at the desired levels, and limited choice. The percentage of our Gross Domestic Product (or goods and services produced by the U.S. economy, GDP) that is health care continues to grow. Internationally, GDP figures are used to assess the economic viability of a country. Continuing increases in the percentage of health care dollars in the GDP are having an adverse impact on the global competitiveness of this country. Coupled with the shame of no health care coverage for 37 million Americans and poor infant health standings internationally, the call by business and individuals to hold down health care costs has become a mandate for health care reform.

DEMOGRAPHIC TRENDS

The above discussion of the driving forces for health care reform mentioned several demographic changes.

CHECKPOINT 2–1

List the two demographic trends that are influencing the changes in patient care delivery models just mentioned in the discussion of health care reform.

1. _____

2. _____

See the end of the chapter for the answers.

Multiple demographic trends are influencing how we deliver health and wellness care to the American people.

Age

A growing percentage of our population is above the age of 65, and the greatest percentage increase will be in the over-85 group (Kaufman, 1993). This trend means there are more people with chronic and debilitating conditions who require more care than ever before. This demand for services means increases not only in total health care expenditures but in every type of expenditure in every category: more long-term care, more home care, more support services, more unique, community-based wellness services, more health education services (Bergman, 1993), and more training for family members to provide care.

Poverty

Anyone who reads a newspaper or listens to national news coverage hears that the number of poor in this country continues to increase, as has been the case since the so-called Decade of Greed, the 1980s. It is not as necessary to delineate why this is happening as to look at what it means for health care. The poor tend to wait longer to seek health care services and are thus sicker when they do come for care, so they end up utilizing more services. They tend to suffer more violent crime, so they end up utilizing more services. They tend to have more children born to mothers with substance abuse problems, so they end up utilizing more services.

They tend to avoid engaging in preventive health activities because they don't have the money to pay for such care, because they don't know about such measures, and because they don't have the time to engage in such measures, so they end up utilizing more services. Community-based services jointly developed by community and health care individuals are increasing in an effort to create healthier communities (Lumsdon, 1993).

Consumer Involvement

As in every other facet of their lives, the majority of Americans are becoming more involved in their health status. They are engaging in healthier behaviors related to smoking, eating, exercise, and stress management. They are also exploring the use of alternative medicine with increasing zeal. Congress, in 1992, passed benchmark legislation that directed the National Institutes of Health to study the effectiveness of alternative medicine therapies.

As consumers increase their involvement in health care decisions, they are becoming more involved in the way health care services are provided in their communities. They are also demanding more information about health care so they can make informed decisions. All of this increased consumer involvement is driving a need for more health teaching and advocacy services from the health care discipline that has claimed accountability for delivering this aspect of wellness care—professional nursing. Thus the need for expanded services from nurses, but with a relatively stable pool of nurses from which to draw, is increasing.

Value Orientation of the Consumer

The American consumer switched horses in midstream, so to speak, in the early 1990s. Business and news magazines as well as news broadcasts highlight this change quite often. Rather than spending for the most expensive item, consumers now want value for the dollar. This doesn't mean they won't spend money for something. But they will only spend to the level necessary to get the value they want. And they are demanding that producers of goods and providers of services deliver increasing value at less or at least stable cost. Health care providers are facing this consumer demand as much as Rubbermaid, IBM, or any of the U.S. auto makers.

Trends in RN Supply

Baby boomers, the biggest age group of this century, aren't getting any younger. As they age, they will also retire from the workforce. This won't happen until at least 15 years from now. And, of course, then they will enter that high-usage group called the elderly.

Meanwhile, as college enrollments in nursing programs appear to be stabilizing and increasing in some areas, or at least not precipitously falling, many of those entering nursing now are in their middle adulthood rather than early adulthood. That means they will retire sooner from the RN workforce.

Forecasts by the federal government on RN supply and demand seem to vary yearly, so there is no clear documented trend. The need for more nurses with education at the BSN and higher levels is a generally accepted trend. But with smaller age groups coming up, the largest age group soon to retire, and trends forecasting an increased demand for nursing services, one can safely intuit that demand may outstrip the supply of nurses in the not-too-distant future. Clearly, this means professional nurses must continue to develop and refine efficient and effective patient care delivery models that appropriately use varying skill levels.

HEALTH CARE DELIVERY TRENDS

To continue to deliver increasing health care services for minimal cost-increase prices, providers have been forced to find ever increasingly efficient ways to do so. Now we are moving to a discussion of environmental factors with which you are intimately familiar. Even without health care reform legislation at the federal level, health care providers and insurers are creating reforms of their own in an effort to deliver services at much lower rates of increase or even at the same cost. Providers knew that the economy of the United States simply could not sustain the spiraling health care costs of the 1970s and 1980s.

More and more businesses are offering employees options of health maintenance organizations (HMOs) or managed care plans for their health care insurance coverage. In either of these settings, the need to deliver services at a lower cost than previously thought possible is forcing many providers, especially hospitals, to rethink how they deliver care. Hospitals often must accept significant discounting on their costs to be included in a managed care plan offered by a major employer in a given area. The number of HMOs nationwide is increasing annually. Although HMO premiums are usually higher, they deliver preventive services often not available through traditional health care insurance coverage. But to be competitive in the eyes of the consumer, they also must find a way to deliver their services at a discounted cost. The good news about this is the inclusion of staff personnel in the planning and discussions on how to deliver the same quality care for a lower cost.

Another key trend is the change in the length of stay in acute care facilities. New technologies have enabled the ambulatory care setting to provide more and more services previously only done in a hospital. The same growth in technology often means patients suffer less trauma from invasive procedures that are done in the hospital and are able to go home faster. In addition to technological advances that have shortened the length of stay for many types of hospital patients, the advent of managing the costs of care has led to shorter and shorter lengths of stay for those patients who still require hospitalization. The patients in hospitals are sicker than 15 years ago, stay a shorter length of time, and require more care while they are in the hospital. A look into the future, however, indicates that hospitals as they are known today may not even exist due to decreasing need for surgical interventions and the technology to treat patients in a community-based setting (Bergman, 1993).

Patients still require nonacute care after these shortened lengths of stay, and this means that home and home health care, long-term care, hospice care, and other community-based care will continue to grow. As our population ages, more preventive and/or community-based services for the elderly will be needed (Bergman, 1993). In addition to the changes described above, nursing case management strategies are being employed for health care delivery all across the country. Nurses are learning to work in different ways as case managers—through others and as part of multidisciplinary teams—to provide continuity of care (Sherer, 1993). The growth in nursing jobs will come not in acute care but in community-based nursing, case management, and advanced practice nursing.

CHANGING NATURE OF WORK

This chapter started by painting a picture of rapid change in the work environment in the world today. Now it is time to put it in the context of your work world in health care. The 1990–1991 recession and the cuts in defense spending brought about an increase in unemployment across the country. Several things are different about this surge of job cuts nationwide, however. Managers and professionals are losing jobs at a rate that has alarmed even the most previously secure professionals—health care professionals. Job security now seems to be a thing of the past in all sectors of the economy in America. This bad news comes as companies and organizations flatten their structures in attempts to get rid of the hierarchy. Concomitant with this flattening is the expectation that all workers will play a more active role in decision making in the organization. (That's the good news!) We call this empowerment—and it strikes fear in the hearts of some who feel ill prepared to make those decisions they are now called upon to make (Duck, 1993). The trend toward empowering staff has evidenced itself in nursing departments through shared governance, implementation of quality programs, and the movement toward self-managed units (Wake, 1990).

Restructuring and redesign lessons first implemented in industry are being employed in health care organizations across the country (McManis, 1993). In an effort to find more efficient and effective ways to deliver patient care, many organizations are employing the concept of process redesign or reengineering. Other organizations are looking at patient-focused restructuring. It does not really matter which avenue for this process change is taken. What matters is what is happening. The traditional boundaries of organizations are falling down. Indeed, in the reformed health care environment, our whole concept of what constitutes an "organization" will change as we implement systems thinking to redesign care delivery across the continuum of care (Bergman, 1993). The delivery of care to patients is being accomplished by networks—or teams—of professionals, not individuals, and is a clear indication of the environment in which we will work into the next century (Kiechel, 1993).

CHECKPOINT 2–2

Think back to the section on "Demographic Trends." List the two trends discussed in that section that relate to the use of Total Quality Management (TQM) or Continuous Quality Improvement (CQI) programs in health care organizations.

1. _____

2. _____

See the end of the chapter for the answers.

Inextricably linked with the introduction of process redesign and changing organizational structures into your work world has been the implementation of TQM or CQI programs in health care organizations ("The Quality March," 1993, p. 6). Often it is not clear which has come first. The use of TQM and CQI, or any other formalized program to ensure the implementation of a full quality system in an organization, is driven by the increased involvement of consumers/clients/patients in purchasing and utilizing health care services. These consumers, who constitute communities, are demanding increasing value for their health care dollars. The use of TQM and CQI has opened the door for nurses to identify more effective and efficient means by which to provide high-quality, high-value care to their patients. Some are choosing multiskilled workers; some are choosing care partners; some are choosing new forms of old teams. Nurses are being asked in quality meetings to clearly articulate their contributions to the outcomes for the patients and communities they serve. They are being asked to find ways to improve or maintain outcomes for patients or clients without increasing the costs of achieving those outcomes. Nurses are being challenged daily to use their holistic, systems-focused knowledge base to create the continually changing environment in which they work to provide care for individuals as well as communities. Sister Rosemary Donley was exceedingly prophetic in forecasting what the nurse's future work world would look like when she wrote, "Third wave nurses will be recruited into positions not for what they do but for what they control, manage, and decide." She goes on to say that nurses in 2000 A.D. "will not be supertechnicians but professionals who establish parameters of assessment and use information to make clinical decisions" (Donley, 1984, p. 6).

MATURING OF THE NURSING PROFESSION

This involvement of nurses in creating their new world of work has led to another environmental trend that actually bridges all the other trends. More than any other trend, it has brought about the increased focus on clinical delegation skills for the management of patient care. It has brought about the maturing of the nursing profession—the movement from adolescence to young adulthood.

Consider this fictional vignette for a moment:

Sara, the baby-buster new graduate on her fourth day at work, sat down to join Pat, the 50-something philosopher on the staff; Kathy, the leading-edge-of-the-baby-boomers thinker; and Kim, the not-quite-boomer-not-quite-buster staff idealist for lunch.

"I just don't feel comfortable delegating to my partner," sighed Sara.

Kim growled and said, "If you ask me, none of us should have to delegate. After all, nursing should be providing total care to the patient. Delegating means I am just supervising others doing the work I spent four years of college learning to do."

"I don't know. This sort of feels like the team nursing I did in my college days, and yet. . . there is something different about it. I do like having the time to spend teaching my patients these days. I just feel like we're on to something new here and it rather excites me! I mean, there are days when I feel as though I have really used my knowledge to its fullest," rejoined Kathy.

Pat chuckled and said comfortingly, "Sara, don't give up. It will make sense to you. First, though, you have to feel comfortable with your technical skills. But Kathy is right. She seems to catch on to these new ideas so fast. This is different from the team nursing we did 20 years ago. I didn't like it. But this new system. . . I think it fits with all the changes we are seeing in the world today."

What this should demonstrate to each of you is that at various stages of our lives we perceive things differently. Those perceptions are filtered through generationally grouped values and beliefs. A profession also goes through these stages of development. The corollary runs something like this: As the nursing profession developed, it moved into adolescence, most likely during the mid-1970s. The focus was on establishing an identity as a profession. The profession was greatly influenced by peer behavior, but it was also quite intensely inward-looking and unsure of itself. Primary nursing, interpreted by many to mean that the RN did everything for a patient, was perfect for this phase of development. The search for a unique body of nursing knowledge and the quest for autonomy of practice coalesce under the adolescent struggle for identity (Rodgers, 1981).

Now, however, nursing has moved to young adulthood. The profession is fairly certain who it is. Nursing has a set of values and is ready to test them out in the "real world" on its own. Nurses have come to realize that doing tasks is not the essence of nursing. The nursing process, which requires thinking as well as doing, is part of the profession's set of values, as are holism and systems thinking. But the profession is still learning. It is learning to work with others. Nursing has discovered it is not a lone profession caring for patients while at the same time fine-tuning its understanding of what exactly professional practice means to nurses. The profession is learning respect for the values and perspectives of other professions and for others who may help perform those tasks that constitute the "doing" part of nursing.

In this learning, nursing is growing more and more understanding of its own identity. In discussing her concept of primary nursing, Manthey recently stated, "The all-RN staff became very popular. That was never part of the original work nor was that ever a requirement" (Villaire, 1993, p. 102). RNs are able to work with other disciplines and other workers on quality teams and task forces and develop new ways to shape their world of work. They are focused less on their own autonomy and more on their patients and communities. They are out there as a young adult profession bringing to life the identity established during adolescence.

As the profession ages further, who knows what changes in practice will develop or what exactly professional practice will come to mean? The vibrancy of the nursing profession's young adulthood allows it to continue learning and shapes the understanding it will bring to this learning in years to come. All of this means that more change is yet to come in your work world—change that will be shaped by you as professional nurses, based on the needs of patients and communities. Who knows where virtual reality and the information superhighway will take nursing in its "middle age." That is your world to know and to create!

CHECKPOINT 2–3

List the six major trends that are shaping the world in which you work.

1. _____

2. _____

3. _____

4. _____

5. _____

6. _____

See the end of the chapter for the answers.

NURSING'S RESPONSES TO THE CHANGES

Ruth I. Hansten and Marilynn J. Washburn

Having discussed many of the factors affecting our practice, we now have a clearer understanding of the challenges facing the profession. Many of us will embrace this time as an opportunity for growth, looking forward to changes with excitement and anticipation. Others of us will approach the demands of the future with trepidation and reluctance, longing for "the good old days" of hospital nursing and job security. The sense that "no, Dorothy, we're not in Kansas anymore" can be a cause for celebration or sadness, depending solely on our perspective.

As nurses, we have historically risen to the challenges facing us, from the halls of Scutari filled with wounded soldiers to the streets of New York City lined with homeless, to the ever-increasing population of victims of AIDS. The average nurse of today is 42 years old, possesses at least 15 years of experience, and is certainly able to meet the demands of a changing health care environment (McCarty, 1992). We have implemented many innovative and creative ideas, realizing the importance of our role in shaping the delivery of care to our patients.

CHECKPOINT 2–4

List four changes you have observed that nursing has implemented in response to the dynamic environment of health care.

1. _____
2. _____
3. _____
4. _____

It's important that we get in touch with our successes, keeping a focus on the positive control that we do have with the direction of our practice. Many of us must fight the tendency to succumb to victim behavior, adopting a "poor me" attitude as organizations, physicians, and government regulations vie to regulate and control nursing practice. Joseph Califano, former Secretary of Health, Education and Welfare, reminds us of our control: "But few of us have a greater responsibility or opportunity than the American nurse. Revolutions, like nations, do not drift in a vacuum. They move in a direction. And in the coming years, the opportunity for nurses to help shape the direction of America's health care revolution is enormous" (Califano, 1993). Keeping our focus on the positive, your list above may have included some of the following accomplishments that have been implemented by nursing:

- early discharge planning in acute care settings
- implementation of clinical pathways
- evaluation of technology
- health maintenance education
- increase in home care
- redesign of care delivery systems

Early Discharge Planning

Decreasing lengths of stay have removed the luxury of time that nurses have had in acute care settings in past decades. Gone are the days of lengthy hospitalizations; DRGs and other factors have created a demand for streamlined care. Nurses responded early on by realizing that plans for discharge must begin on the day of admission or sooner, when the preadmission data are obtained. "Discharge planning is a continuum of care rather than episodic. It begins at admission, if not before" (Long, 1993, p. 168). New positions have been created in acute and community-based settings, where it is not uncommon to find at least one "discharge planner" on staff, typically an RN.

Implementation of Clinical Pathways

Clinical pathways, or *critical paths* as they are also called, came into use in the mid-1980s as a modernized version of the nursing care plan. These project management tools are based on multidisciplinary input regarding a particular DRG and are used as road maps or guidelines for effective planning and monitoring of patients' progress. The literature reveals numerous reports of studies that demonstrate the effectiveness of these plans in terms of reducing lengths of stay in acute care settings and achieving desired outcomes in a more cost-effective manner. These benefits are being sought in other settings as well, and the term *extended care pathway*, or ECP, has recently come into use. "There are many other settings besides the hospital in which people can get care, such as rehabilitation centers, nursing homes, and even the patient's own home. We're asking, can you have pathways that cut across all those settings?" (White, 1993, p. 160). Clinical pathways are the backbone of case management, a care delivery design that will be discussed later in this chapter. As nursing moves this planning process outside the walls of acute care and fosters the "seamless approach" to continuous care, we will see clinical pathways adapted in all settings. Examples of two versions of clinical pathways, in written and pictorial pathway form, are shown in Figures 2–1 and 2–2.

Evaluation of Technology

Modernization can be either a blessing or a curse in that we often see new technological breakthroughs result in increased costs and questionable impact on the outcome of patient care. Nurses are positioning themselves on new product committees, evaluating the need for "new and improved" supplies, and participating in the decisions of updating and purchasing equipment. As front line providers, we are continually evaluating the effectiveness of treatment and monitoring the usage of technology with a watchful eye. Utilization review nursing has become a new position for many of us. We have been at the forefront of the ethical and moral dilemmas created by advanced technology as well; often it is a nurse who initiates the discussion regarding the plans for the comatose patient on a respirator or the premature infant with irreversible brain damage.

Health Maintenance Education

Nursing has traditionally focused on the holistic approach of patient care needs, realizing that education for patients is an integral part of their ability to maintain their optimum level of health. As Sister M. Olivia Gowan once wrote, "Nursing in its broadest sense is an art and a science which involves the whole patient—body, mind, and spirit: promotes his spiritual, mental and physical health, *by teaching and by example; stresses health education and health preservation* as well as ministration to the sick" (emphasis added) (Hansten and Washburn, 1990, p. 11). Recent changes in the economy of health care delivery are now supporting this position as insurance groups reimburse for preventive treatment and the system shifts from the traditional episodic, crisis-driven medical model to a continuum of wellness supported by preventive education.

Increase in Home Care

When Lillian Wald began the Henry Street Settlement in 1893, she was organizing the system of delivering nursing care that had been in existence for centuries. Did she realize the distance we would travel in hospital development before returning home? As we complete the circle, we are now seeing an increasing trend in home health and community nursing, settings where nursing has always been the predominant provider. The growth in this area is so significant that "the Bureau of Labor Statistics forecasts that home-health aide will be the fastest growing job category of all, nearly doubling to 550,000 by 2005" (Richman, 1993, p. 53). Home care is truly nursing's arena, and as the trend increases, nurses will continue to identify this as a successful response to the patient's changing needs.

Redesign of Care Delivery Systems

We have repeatedly stated that nursing is responding to the demands of the environment by redesigning or reengineering our delivery systems. Let's take a look at the progression of the more predominant systems to better understand where we are today in terms of the organized structure of nursing. Our discussion will begin with the acute care setting and continue through extended care and the community-based network of the future.

Congestive Heart Failure   5.7 Days   DRG 127

	Day 1	O	C	Day 2	O	C	Day 3	O	C	Day 4	O	C
Consults	Cardiologist if indicated			Cardia Rehab → Nutritional consult → Physical therapy consult (if indicated)			Physical therapy consult if appropriate →			EKG prn		
Tests	EKG → CXR CBC → SMAC Mg-Level U/A PT, PTT (if indicated) Special tests if indicated Cardiac Enzymes/ISOs			Echo → MUGA → Mg level—repeat as needed								
Medications	Review medications prior to admission →			→			Review current meds—give appropriate drug monograph			Review monographs		
Treatment	O₂ (if indicated) → Saline plug Monitor Daily weights (fasting) Strict I&O → VS q 4 hours			→ Daily weights → Vs q 8 hours →			Evaluate monitor as needed					
Nutrition	Diet (as indicated) Fluid restriction as indicated →			→			Reevaluate diet according to D/C plan →			Reinforce D/C diet plan →		
Activity	Bedrest			Bedrest if indicated → Up in chair → Bathroom privileges			Ambulate in room Increased activity if appropriate →					
Teaching	Orient to unit and routine			CHF teaching initiates			Evaluate specific patient needs →					
Discharge Planning	Case Management/Social Services/ Home Health			Assess and implement discharge planning needs			Evaluate discharge needs					
Variance												

Figure 2–1 Clinical Pathway, Written Form. Courtesy of Harbor Hospital Center, Baltimore, Maryland.

	Day 5	O	C	Day 6	O	C	Day 7	O	C
Consults									
Tests	EKG prn ―――――→			――――→					
Medications	Reinforce medication teaching ―→			Re-evaluate discharge medication plans ―→ Appropriate monograph –→ Complete appropriate wallet cards ―→			Review medication plans → →		
Treatment	VS q 8 hours ―――――→ O_2 as indicated ―――→ Daily weight (?) ―――→ D/C monitor (if indicated) →			Evaluate O_2 as needed ―→ → →			→ → →		
Nutrition	Reinforce D/C diet plan ―――→			Evaluate and reinforce discharge diet ―→			→		
Activity	Increased activity ―――――→			→			→		
Teaching	Evaluate specific patient needs			Review all discharge plans			→		
Discharge Planning	Referral to community resources ―→			→			→		
Variance									

EXPECTED OUTCOMES

1. The patient can expect to _____ _____ date
2. The patient can expect to _____ _____ date
3. The patient can expect to _____ _____ date

O = Ordered
C = Completed

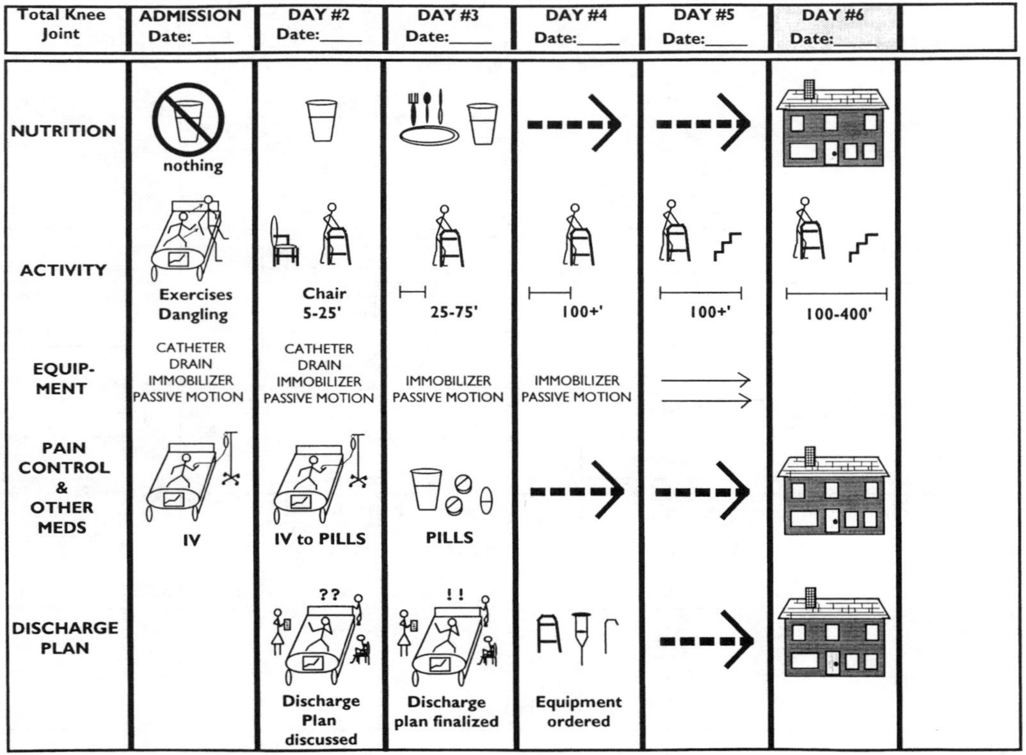

Figure 2–2 Clinical Pathway, Pictorial Form. *Source:* Created by Randall DeJong © 1993, Providence Hospital, Everett, Wa.

Team Nursing

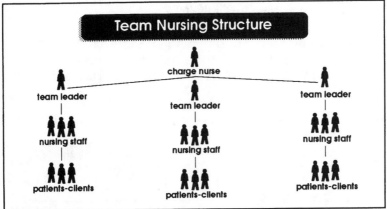

Dennis Burnside

Team nursing began as early as the post-World War II period, when the nursing shortage in hospitals called for the creation of LPNs, nurses' aides, and other auxiliary nurses to meet the increased demand for health care. The attempt to organize these workers into cooperative work groups was the beginning of the "team nursing" concept that was to last throughout the early 1970s. In this model, the RN functioned as the "team leader" and led a group of LPNs and nursing assistants to care for a given group of patients. Tasks were differentiated according to skill level, and the work was divided among the team members based on the assignment made by the RN leader. A series of studies commissioned by the American Nurses Association during the 1950s revealed the following conclusions regarding the differentiation of these tasks among a variety of workers:

> The practical nurse and the nurse aide, often spoken of as temporary, are certainly permanent members of the hospital team. The occupational standard of living, if one may call it that, of the professional nurse has risen so much that she is unlikely to wish to have back *all* her old tasks. Hence, when, if ever, the division of labor in hospital nursing is stabilized, we can be sure it will recognize a variety of ranks of nurse (Hughes, 1958, p. 150).

Clearly, some form of team nursing is here to stay, according to personnel surveys by the American Hospital Association. "Team nursing remains the model caring for the greatest percent of inpatients" (AHA, 1991, p. 9).

CHECKPOINT 2–5

Have you ever practiced nursing in a team model? If so, what were the similarities to the model described above? Can you identify advantages and disadvantages to this system?

See the end of the chapter for the answers.

Functional Nursing

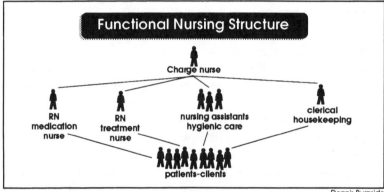

Dennis Burnside

Modifications to the coordinated work groups of team nursing began as adaptations were needed to meet the various needs of the patients. The functional model involves a leader in the form of a charge nurse, with the workload grouped according to the type of tasks to be done. In this system, a medication nurse, a treatment nurse, and nursing assistants provide care according to function for the entire population of patients. The med nurse (either an RN or an LPN) is responsible for the administration of medications to all patients within the setting (unit, floor, or section of the facility). The treatment nurse, similar to the med nurse, provides treatments for the entire patient population. The patients are seen throughout their day by a number of care providers, and the care received is segmented.

This type of system lends itself to areas where patient turnover is less frequent and the patient population is more stable, as in an extended care facility or an oncology, rehab, or AIDS unit. Unfortunately, care *is* segmented, and no one is focusing on the total picture of the patient except the charge nurse, whose workload generally precludes the attention necessary for coordinating individual care.

CHECKPOINT 2–6

1. In what ways is functional nursing different from team nursing?
2. If you have had experience in working in either system, can you recall:
   a) Who was responsible for documentation of care?
   b) Who interfaced with the other disciplines such as physicians, physical therapy, and pharmacy?
   c) How the reporting process occurred and by whom?

See the end of the chapter for the answers.

Total Patient Care

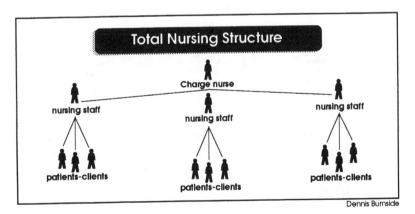

Dennis Burnside

Another modification to the team concept developed in the 1970s when many of us had been accustomed to working in teams and had recognized the benefits of nursing assistants. These nursing assistants (and LPNs) were removed from the staff or at least limited as many hospitals sought a short-lived benchmark of quality, the all-RN staff. With a charge nurse to lead the way, a staff of only RNs was assigned to provide all of the care needed by a given group of assigned patients. Care was no longer segmented, and the advantages to this system were thought to be that the highest level of worker was always available to the patient—a worker who knew the entire spectrum of needs for that particular patient. The argument was made that, "In contrast to team nursing and the assignment of less skilled tasks to cheaper categories of wage labor, primary nursing employs labor power that although more expensive, may also be more productive in that RNs can be assigned to perform a broader range of nursing and nursing-related tasks with little supervision" (Chernomas, 1989, p. 642). This model was (and is) popular in specialty settings such as intensive care units, trauma and emergency care, neonatal care, postanesthesia care, and ambulatory care settings.

Primary Care

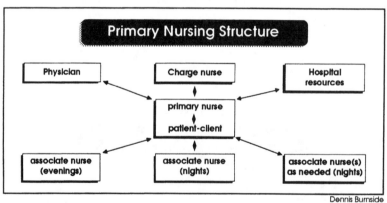

Dennis Burnside

When Marie Manthey introduced her model of care in 1970, she set out to change the organization of nursing's work. Similar to total patient care, and often confused with it, the original concept of primary nursing "simply means one nurse accepting responsibility for managing the care of a small number of patients" (Villaire, 1993, p. 100). As in the total patient care model, the RN is responsible for meeting all of the needs of the patient, but the responsibility extends beyond the limits of a traditional shift since it is expected that the "primary nurse" will coordinate the plan of care for the entire 24-hour period throughout the entire hospitalization. The patient is able to identify one nurse as his or her "own," thereby limiting confusion and providing a sense of continuity. Many variants of primary nursing sprang up all over the country as nursing units embraced the philosophy and the innovative idea of coordinated care.

There are many arguments to support the value of the primary nursing concept, and just as many to refute it. Those of you who have worked in some type of primary care system can well understand both the drawbacks and the advantages. One of the unintentional by-products, we believe, was the unfortunate separation of nursing in yet another arena. The title of *associate nurse* was created to describe the caregivers who were not the patient's primary nurse, and this title led to some feelings of inferiority and separation that are still present today. Also, the model implied that a nurse should be able to meet or at least plan for all the needs of his or her patients. The idea of "being all things to all people" became an unreasonable expectation fostered by nursing curricula and managements and led to reality shock for new graduates and burnout for veteran staffers. Organizational systems, in many instances, could not or would not provide the time and resources needed for this model to work as originally envisioned, and frustration ran high. However, the essence of this model, as described by Manthey, has truly shaped the latest and most responsive care delivery system, case management.

CHECKPOINT 2–7

Describe the major differences between total patient care and primary nursing.

See the end of the chapter for the answers.

Case Management

The concept of case management involves the determination of what care is needed, when, and by what provider so that patient outcomes can be achieved with the most effective use of time and other resources. Using critical pathways as a guide, the case manager coordinates the services of a multidisciplinary team and may or may not provide direct pa-

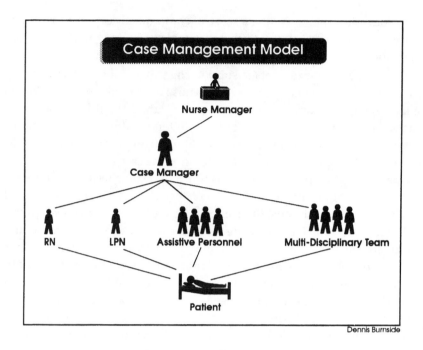

Dennis Burnside

tient care herself. The impact of this model in acute care settings has been significant: literature abounds with survey results demonstrating dramatic decreases in lengths of stay, reduction in utilization of resources, and increased quality of care. "Nursing makes a major contribution to clinical outcomes through powerful interventions based on a diagnostic reasoning process, and by making the system work for the physicians and the patients. Because of nursing's 24-hour access, nursing allocates much of a hospital's resources" (Zander, 1988, p. 28). The model is still evolving as nursing leaders, and other health care providers adapt the process in all settings of health care.

One of the most innovative applications of case management can be found at St. Mary's Hospital in Tucson, Arizona. Implementing their model in 1985, they have demonstrated success by forming an alliance of community case managers and "internal" (hospital-based) case managers to coordinate care across the walls of acute care. "The result is a nursing network with the vision to provide a lifelong continuum of 'care management' with the potential to extend beyond the acute care episode and into new ways of being for our patients and families" (Mahn, 1993, p. 49). Figure 2–3 illustrates the network model of St. Mary's Medical Center.

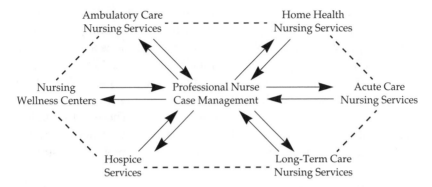

Figure 2–3 Network Model of St. Mary's Medical Center. *Source:* Reprinted from *Patient Care Delivery Models* by G.G. Mayer et al., p. 171, with permission of Aspen Publishers, Inc., © 1990.

CHECKPOINT 2–8

Which of the following are true descriptions of the case manager role?

a) coordinates an interdisciplinary approach
b) may or may not provide direct patient care
c) utilizes clinical pathways to organize care
d) effectively manages resources
e) all of the above

See the end of the chapter for the answers.

Care Delivery Systems in Nonacute Settings

As we struggle for meaningful health care reform, there have been changes in care delivery systems in virtually every organization along the health care continuum. Whereas once acute care providers, such as community hospitals, often seemed to set the pace for changes in the care of the ill, now extended care within the home and community has taken a proactive lead in holistic health care of the public. To be able to care, with fewer dollars, for the ever-growing population with temporary or chronic disability, these organizations have adapted the actual methods of providing care in creative ways.

Long-Term Care. For example, many skilled nursing facilities have used a modified functional nursing structure, with an RN leading in care planning and supervision, an LPN (LVN) giving medications and some treatments, and nursing assistants performing hygienic and ADL (activities of daily living) tasks. With a new emphasis on rehabilitation of their changing client population, they have developed new roles for the nursing assistants. One such role is that of the restorative aide. These individuals receive additional supervision and training related to range of motion, transfers, and other activities, and may work in a team with physical and occupational therapists.

In some states, nursing assistants in long-term care or residential facilities receive additional training to administer oral medications under the supervision of an RN, who evaluates the medication regimen and determines whether the medications should be administered as planned. This function is carefully regulated. Conversations with state board of nursing officials in several states reveal that this practice has been quite effective to date and may reflect a trend (see Chapter 3).

Some extended care facilities who use many nursing assistants have developed the role of "team leader" among the nurse aides. These experienced, skilled assistants have exhibited additional leadership potential and are able to help the RN train, mentor, and evaluate the tasks completed by orientees. Since this group of assistants often exhibits a fair amount of turnover, the creation of this position has also become a means to develop and recognize highly competent, tenured employees.

Working together in pairs or larger groups has been very effective in providing care for patients in these facilities. "Bath teams" are able to turn the debilitated or frail patients with a minimum of potential for employee back injury. The staff who work together enjoy the teamwork and find that time is saved through working together systematically.

Some facilities have developed a care triad: an RN, LPN (LVN), and CNA (certified nursing assistant). This team is assigned a group of patients, and work is divided among them based on their licensure, job descriptions, and their special strengths. In some settings, personnel who were once thought to be "outside" the care team are considered valuable members of the treatment team. Consider an Alzheimer's residential facility and how important it may be for the housekeeper, who often spends a fair amount of time interacting with the patients, to understand current methods of answering questions and directing or helping the residents to their rooms. In other facilities, combining the skills of former environmental services personnel with those of the certified nursing assistant has created a job description for a cross-trained worker who is able to respond to many possible needs. In theory and often in fact, cross-training provides the worker with additional job growth and added potential for individual job mobility, and provides the manager with more productive workers.

RN-led case management has also been used as a very effective method of providing the highest quality care, using all members of the team, within extended care organizations. Just as acute care must focus on discharge planning and effective use of resources, the RN case manager coordinates the care given in the long-term care facility as she or he organizes the discharge plan and aftercare with the interdisciplinary team from the present care site to the community. Many acute care organizations have established linkages with subacute, ambulatory, home care, and extended care facilities so that one RN case manager oversees the care of a particular patient throughout the continuum.

Home Care. Home care enjoyed a rebirth of interest in the 1980s as hospitals dealt with the reimbursement realities of the Prospective Reimbursement System (DRGs, "diagnostic-related groups" or "*Da Revenue's Gone*") and began to discharge patients as quickly as possible. The acuity of patients within the home increased along with the number of elderly and acutely or chronically disabled. This trend fostered the need to intensify the coordination of care that originated in public health programs at the turn of the century. Driven by increasing acuities and diminishing resources, case management has become more sophisticated in the setting where it had its beginnings.

Home health continues to use a multidisciplinary approach to illness care within the home, employing physical, occupational, speech, and respiratory therapists, social service workers, and nutritionists. Psychiatric care has been provided by registered nurses or other mental health therapists. Chores and activities of daily living have been provided by homemakers or home health aides. These assistive personnel also may provide transportation, shopping, and other important living maintenance tasks that do not require licensed health professionals. Supervision of unlicensed health care assistants has been a long-term reality for home health care RNs.

As we reform our system and community-based organizations scramble to adapt to the changing configuration of health care, home health providers continue to use the concepts of case management and multi-skilled, unlicensed assistive workers to provide care.

Ambulatory Care. In ambulatory care arenas, such as physician's offices, outpatient clinics, adult day care centers, short-stay surgeries, and mental health clinics, assistive personnel are employed much as they are employed in acute and long-term care. Positions and job descriptions are created to adapt to the needs of the organization. Surgical technicians, medical assistants, mental health technicians, and rehabilitation aides are trained and perform according to the specific state's practice codes and organizational job descriptions. Experiments with new types of team approaches and combinations of workers to fulfill specific needs are being conducted throughout the country in order to adapt to health care trends and contingencies.

CHECKPOINT 2–9

Long-term care organizations, such as skilled nursing facilities, step-down units, subacute care, swing beds, nursing homes, or adult residential care homes, have responded to health care trends by developing innovative methods of delivering care. Ambulatory and home health care providers have also adapted their systems. What similarities are evident?

See the end of the chapter for the answers.

WHERE DO WE GO FROM HERE?

There is no doubt about it, some form of team process will always be part of the care delivery system of the future. Whether as "practice partners," case managers, or coordinators of patient-focused care, nurses will be part of a group of providers that spans the disciplines. We have heard many nurses respond to the need for clinical delegation skills with the opinion that this is a passing phase and that once reform is implemented, assistive personnel will vanish, leaving RNs to provide all the care once again. We think not. Nor are we returning to the nursing of 30 years ago, to become generalists who assign tasks to other personnel, utilizing the same principles of the work teams of the postwar era. There are distinct differences between the team concept of the past and the current systems we see emerging. We are responding not to a shortage of nurses but rather to a shortage of professional nursing care. Prescott (1989) describes this as occurring when nurses are too busy performing tasks that do not require their knowledge and skill base. Personnel with the minimal base of knowledge to perform tasks will be utilized to perform task assignments, not patient assignments.

Whether you practice in an acute care setting or in the community, you will always be involved in working with other people. Not practicing in a vacuum, you will be called upon to use your skill and expertise to delegate wisely to the multidisciplinary members of the team, maximizing your resources for the most beneficial outcomes for your patient. As Connie Curran sums it up, "We can look at our history and realize that being in nursing is being in the patient care business, and being part of the largest group of care givers in this country. That would produce a redefinition of nursing based on the ethics that underlie the profession, some basic competencies, patient advocacy, clinical outcomes, and coordination of other health care workers in a variety of settings" (Friedman, 1990, p. 3120).

ANSWERS TO CHECKPOINTS

2–1. Increase in the number of elderly; increase in the number of poor.

2–2. Consumer involvement; value orientation of the consumer.

2–3. Influence of the 1980s nursing shortage; health care reform; demographic trends; health care delivery trends; changing nature of work; maturing of the nursing profession.

2–5. Possible advantages to this system include the flexibility in adapting to changing patient needs with varying levels of caregivers, decreased personnel costs with fewer RN salaries than in total RN patient care systems, teamwork divides the burden, more personnel involved with patients so that amenity needs are met. You may have experienced other advantages. Possible disadvantages are that the RN must be able to supervise the care given by others. More personnel may contribute to confusion and communication problems if care is not well organized. If roles are also unclear, conflict may occur and the quality of care may suffer.

2–6.

1. Instead of focusing on patients as a whole, it divides up by function the tasks that must be completed for each client. This system may also use many different categories of caregivers in addition to the RN.
2.
a) Documentation of care is often completed by each person as he or she completes a function.
b) The RN generally interfaces with and coordinates the care with other disciplines, although in many long-term care facilities, LPNs may complete some of this communication.
c) Reporting by all persons involved with the patient must be completed in such a manner that the RN is able to coordinate the total nursing process for the patient.

2–7.

1. The span of accountability for primary nursing is 24 hours around the clock throughout the patient's hospitalization, whereas total patient care is limited to the time on duty.
2. Total patient care implied that one nurse would provide all services; primary nursing coordinates services provided by a number of personnel.

2–8. e

2–9. Use of creative multiskilled job descriptions, case management, varying team configurations, use of all health care workers and disciplines in the delivery of care, linkages throughout the health care continuum, and an ever-present need for the RN to lead, coordinate, and supervise.

REFERENCES

American Hospital Association. 1991. Next steps in Medicaid shortfall data initiative. Letter dated February 6: 7.

Bergman, R. L. (1993). Quantum leaps. *Hospitals & Health Networks* 67 October 5: 28–35.

Blegen, M. A., et al. 1992. Who helps you with your work? *American Journal of Nursing* 92, no. 1: 26–31.

Califano, J. A., Jr. 1993. The nurse as a revolutionary. *Missouri Nurse* 62, no. 2: 10.

Chernomas, R., and W. Chernomas. 1989. Escalation of the nurse-physician conflict. *International Journal of Health Services* 19, no. 4: 641–643.

Donley, R. 1984. Nursing 2000, an essay. *Image: The Journal of Nursing Scholarship* 16, no. 1: 4–6.

Duck, J. D. 1993. Managing change: The art of balancing. *Harvard Business Review* 71, no. 6: 109–118.

Friedman, E. 1990. Nursing: Breaking the bonds? *JAMA* 264, no. 24: 3117–3122.

Hansten, R., and M. Washburn. 1990. *I light the lamp*. Vancouver, Wash.: Applied Therapeutics.

Headlines. 1992. "Team nursing still the top model for hospital care" *American Journal of Nursing* (April): 9.

Hughes, E. C., et al. 1958. *Twenty thousand nurses tell their story: A report on studies of nursing functions sponsored by the American Nurses Association*. Philadelphia: J.B. Lippincott.

Kaufman, N. J. 1993. Selected trends in America: Their impact on health. *Advances* (Newsletter of the Robert Wood Johnson Foundation) Fall: 7.

Kiechel, W. 1993. How we will work in the year 2000. *Fortune* May 17: 38–52.

Long, A. 1993. Discharge planning in critical pathways, lower LOS, better care. *Hospital Case Management* September: 168.

Lumsdon, K. 1993. Patience and partnership. *Hospitals & Health Networks* 67, no. 24: 26–31.

Mahn, V. 1993. Clinical nurse case management: a service line approach. *Nursing Management* 24, no. 9: 48–50.

McCarty, P. 1992. How to keep mature, skilled nurses. *American Nurse* July–August: 9.

McManis, G. L. 1993. Reinventing the system. *Hospitals & Health Networks* October 5: 42–48.

Prescott, P. 1989. Shortage of professional nursing practice: A reframing of the shortage problem. *Heart and Lung* 18, no. 5: 436–443.

Prospective Payment Assessment Commission. 1993. Medicare and the American healthcare system: Report to the Congress. Washington, DC: Prospective Payment Assessment Commission.

The quality march. 1993. *Hospitals & Health Networks* 67, no. 24: 40–42.

Richman, L. S. 1993. Jobs that are growing and slowing. *Fortune* 127, July 12: 53.

Rising health spending makes reform crucial. 1994. *Seattle Times*, January 4, B4.

Rodgers, J. 1981. Toward professional adulthood. *Nursing Outlook* 29, no. 8: 478–481.

Sherer, J.L. 1993. Next steps for nursing. *Hospitals & Health Networks* 67, August 20: 26–28.

Smith, L. 1988. The battle over health insurance. *Fortune* 118, no. 7: 145–150.

U.S. Dept. of Health and Human Services. 1988. *Secretary's Commission on Nursing final report*, p. 1. Washington, DC.

Villaire, M. 1993. Marie Manthey on the evolution of primary nursing. *Critical Care Nurse* December: 100–107.

Wake, M. M. 1990. Nursing care delivery systems: Status and vision. *Journal of Nursing Administration* 20, no. 5: 47–51.

White, M. 1993. Providers tackle care pathways beyond the hospital walls. *Hospital Case Management* 1, September: 160.

Zander, K. 1988. Nursing case management: Strategic management of cost and quality outcomes. *Journal of Nursing Administration* 18, no. 5: 28.

Chapter 3

KNOW YOUR WORLD
- practice
- organization

Know Your Practice:
Is My License on the Line?

Ruth I. Hansten and Marilynn J. Washburn

"I am so tired of those nurses whining about their licenses being on the line! Every time we make any changes around here, someone says something about her license being on the line. I hate that phrase! I don't care what you have to do, but get them some information so they know what the law says about their license status, for goodness sakes!" (hospital administrator contracting our services).

We too, have heard this phrase on numerous occasions, and share some of the same concerns as the administrator quoted above. However, we recognize the plea for what it is, a cry for help and a sincere statement of concern and fear that the licensure status that allows you to practice as a professional nurse is in danger of being jeopardized by some change in the working conditions or whatever new plan administration has created for you. The resolution of this situation lies in Adelaide Nutting's statement, "Knowledge is our only working power" (Hansten and Washburn, 1990, p. 66). Nurses must have a fundamental knowledge of the practice act, both the statute and the rules, that governs the practice of nursing in each state. Armed with that knowledge, nursing can better evaluate new care delivery systems and requests from administrators who are focused on effectiveness and efficiency, and not necessarily the standard of nursing practice.

The statement, "My license is on the line" has been overused by nurses and in many cases is a "fighting phrase" that triggers a very negative response from many members of the management team. If you are justifiably concerned about the legality of the changes in your practice (and you may very well be!), we cannot emphasize enough that you must support that concern with knowledge of the law that governs nursing practice. Unfortunately, most nurses have never received any education about the practice act, and educational reforms are seeing nursing trends classes and professional issues classes deleted from many nursing curricula. If you have not had the opportunity to receive some information regarding the law of nursing, all is not lost. This chapter will focus solely on the topic of the nurse practice act (specifically as it addresses the issue of delegation) and will provide you with many resources that are readily available to you. Read on!

CHECKPOINT 3–1

It is important to know about my nurse practice act because:

a) This information will help me to do a better job clinically.
b) It's not important to me; the board of nursing is paid to tell me when something is not legal, so I don't have to worry about it.
c) This law directs my practice and is the legal foundation for what I do as a professional nurse. An understanding of the law and the rules will help me to evaluate the safety and legality of actions I am requested to take by my employer and any other member of the health care team.
d) As long as I pay my fees and keep my license current, that's all I need to know.

See the end of the chapter for the answers.

THE STATE BOARD OF NURSING

Every state in the nation is replete with governing bodies that overlook various professions, occupations, and pastimes. From the board of pharmacy, to the board of game and fish, we have a significant number of agencies devoted to monitoring our personal and professional behaviors. The board of nursing is one such regulatory agency created by the state government, and is one that most nurses only have contact with on an annual or biannual basis as licenses are renewed and fees are paid. What does the board of nursing do the rest of the year, when they are not collecting fees?

CHECKPOINT 3–2

The *primary purpose* of the board of nursing is to:

a) advocate for nurses accused of unsafe practice
b) approve schools of nursing and grant or revoke licenses
c) regulate the practice of nursing
d) protect the public from unsafe practice of nursing

See the end of the chapter for the answers.

Many nurses are confused about the purpose of the board of nursing, and may find out the hard way that this particular agency is not in existence to advocate for them. The primary responsibility of any regulatory board, whether the board of medicine or the board of cosmetology, is to protect the public safety. Just as the game and fish department writes rules to protect the public from unsafe habits of hunters and other sportsmen, the board of nursing is primarily interested in the safety of the public you serve as a nurse. If you are looking for support and the advancement of nursing practice on a professional level, try one of the professional associations such as the state nurses association. Their role is often confused with the role of the board, when in reality the two are very different.

Let's take a look at each of the answers in the above checkpoint to clarify some common misperceptions.

a) advocate for nurses accused of unsafe practice: If you are ever involved in a board investigation as the result of a complaint made regarding your professional practice, you may find that the approach taken by the board is adversarial and not supportive. Remember, this agency is there to protect the public, not you. If there is reason to believe that you are unsafe to the public, it is their responsibility to take corrective action and to ensure that the public is protected. Thus they often do not come across as being "on your side"—indeed, they may not be! Here again, a working knowledge of how the board functions, particularly their disciplinary process, will give you a better understanding of the legal side of your practice.

b) approve schools of nursing, and grant or revoke licenses: These are certainly duties of any board of nursing, and are methods by which it governs the practice of nursing to ensure public safety. It is important to remember a little history here: nursing as a profession in the United States did not have licensure until 1903. The first licensing law for nurses was actually passed in Cape Colony, South Africa, in 1891 (Donahue, 1985). After many years of struggle, British nurses and American nurses began to make progress, and lawmakers began recognizing the need to protect the public from inconsistent standards and questionable practices. Prior to this time, a "nurse" could receive education through the mail, attend any one of a growing number of nursing schools with a great variety of curricula, or train herself "on the job." Sophia Palmer spoke of poorly qualified schools and nursing imposters in her editorial in the *American Journal of Nursing* in 1903: "How long will nurses permit such conditions to exist when only a strong, concerted action is needed to improve the educational standard, to protect the public and nurses themselves against imposters, and to give trained nursing a place among the honorable professions!" (Donahue, 1985, p. 375). It was shortly after this publication that several states adopted nurse practice acts, providing for the standardization of education and the regulation of practice through licensure.

Today it is the duty of the board of nursing in each state to establish criteria and approve schools of nursing that meet those criteria, thus upholding a standard of education. Through licensure and the disciplinary process for revoking or suspending licenses, the board also supports its prime directive to protect public safety. Such regulation of licensure eliminates the risk of imposters and assures that anyone practicing nursing will have acquired a specific standard of education.

c) regulate the practice of nursing: The process by which each board of nursing regulates nursing practice varies from state to state. Generally, each board is empowered by law to adopt rules or issue advisory opinions concerning the authority of nurses to perform certain acts. Criteria, in the form of standards of conduct, are established by each board and regulated through the investigative process. Powers of regulation extend to schools of nursing and to individual licensees but not generally to institutions or agencies that employ nurses. These groups are generally regulated in other sections of the law. It is not the duty of the board to regulate practice by overseeing what policies an employing agency or institution creates for the employment of a nursing staff. State licensing laws for hospitals and other health care facilities, the Joint Commission on Accreditation (JCAHO), and the Health Care Financing Administration (HCFA) are examples of institution-regulating agencies.

d) protect the public from unsafe practice of nursing: The board of nursing is empowered to implement a disciplinary process that ensures the safety of practice. Although the actual system may vary from state to state, the outcome is the same: nurses found to be practicing in an unsafe manner will be disciplined. Generally there are paid staff members working for the board of nursing who are functioning in the roles of consultants and investigators. In addition to administering the process of licensure, these staff members receive complaints made by the public or by nursing personnel themselves and begin an investigation. The results of their investigations are then presented to the board members for review and action. Hearings may be involved; the individual nurse may have representation by an attorney (the attorney general's office will represent the board), and the case may be presented to the board in this very formal manner. The board members are empowered to rule on the outcome of the hearing or investigation and to take disciplinary action, usually in the form of (1) issuance of a letter of concern, (2) allowance of practice with limitations, (3) suspension, or (4) revocation of the license.

CHECKPOINT 3–3

Powers and duties of the board of nursing include:

a) approving schools of nursing
b) granting or revoking licenses
c) regulating practice of the profession
d) all of the above

See the end of the chapter for the answers.

Composition

Since we have established the significant power of this group of individuals, it is important to know who they are. The composition of the board is defined in statute, with law specifying the numbers of members appointed to serve on the board and the area of expertise that each individual will represent. This ensures that major areas of practice, from management to education, are represented. It is not unusual for the state to require representation from a public member as well, representing the public perspective on nursing practice. Other stipulations regarding geographical location of each member may also be specified, again to ensure broad representation of the profession. In addition to the qualifications of each member, the terms of service are also defined, usually ranging from a two-year to a five-year appointment. Appointment of board members is a political decision, usually from the governor's office, and board members are not paid.

Appointed members, defined by law and serving unpaid terms, make up the board of nursing in each state. The board will employ staff members to fulfill the administrative, clerical, and investigative needs of the board. These individuals are hired by the board and do not participate in the decision-making process of the board regarding licensure, or other matters. The leader of the personnel will most likely be the executive director or executive secretary. This individual oversees the staff and is present at all board meetings for assistance and administrative support. The executive leader and the president of the board represent each state at the National Council of State Boards of Nursing, a source authority to which we will refer often in this book. Collectively this group strives for standardization among the states and issues position papers and advisory opinions, commissioning studies and investigations of current practice trends from a national perspective. (See Appendix A for a complete listing of the boards of nursing, including the National Council.)

Meetings

The board convenes on a regular basis, from as frequently as monthly to as infrequently as quarterly. Meetings are open to the public, and agendas and locations for meetings are easily available by calling your board office. Attending one of these meetings can be very educational and will quickly familiarize you with the process of the functioning of the board. Some boards offer an "open mike" time when nurses may come forward and address specific practice questions for the board's advice and consideration. This is an excellent time to get to know the members of the board and to establish a very important professional relationship.

Resources

Several resources are at your disposal to help you to build your knowledge about the board and the nurse practice act.

The Nurse Practice Act

If you do not have a copy of your state's practice act, we highly recommend that you call the board office and request a copy. Make certain that there is one where you work, as well as one for your own personal reference. Be certain to request the statute and the administrative code so that you have all of the legal documents regarding your practice.

Board Consultants

Members of the staff may be called consultants or investigators or advisers, and have specific areas of expertise. There may be individuals on staff who advise regarding scope-of-practice issues, impaired nurse programs, nursing school criteria, and so on. These individuals are excellent resources for questions you may have regarding the safety of your working environment and the use of assistive personnel, and may be of valuable assistance in answering that question that led you to believe your license might be on the line. Consultants or other staff members, including the executive director, often make themselves available to visit schools of nursing, professional association meetings, or health care facilities. They are usually very willing to provide an overview of the law and the duties of the board, and to advise on specific questions. They may not issue black-and-white answers, but they will be able to direct you in the process of evaluating your particular situation.

Advisory Opinions

Often the law is written in very generic terms and requires some interpretation. It is usually not possible or practical to write law that speaks to every unique situation that a nurse may encounter. In this case, the board may issue an advisory opinion that further clarifies the law and addresses practice in a more specific manner. In recent years, as the use of assistive personnel has increased, several state boards have issued advisory opinions to offer assistance to the practicing nurse in interpreting the expectations of the law. Since that time, many state practice acts have been changed, and the requirements of the delegating nurse have been more clearly delineated. You may request a copy of any advisory opinion written by the board and are encouraged to do so if you are uncertain about any practice issue. Subjects of advisory opinions may include abandonment, mandatory reporting, acceptance of assignments, and delegating to unlicensed personnel.

Committee Involvement

Within the working structure of any board of nursing is the creation of committees for the overseeing of specific areas of practice. These committees are chaired by a board member and staffed by one of the investigators or consultants employed by the board. Committee members are professional nurses who have an interest in the work of the committee and have expertise in that area. For example, a board may appoint a committee to look at scope-of-practice issues for the advanced practitioner or may create a committee to look into the legal and legislative interests of nurses in the state. These committees may review a particular part of the rules that is confusing or controversial, and may draft an advisory opinion (see above) that is then presented to the board for approval. Prior to legislation (a lengthy process), *many* advisory opinions were issued on the subject of delegation.

Committee meetings are open to the public and are another source of information regarding what is happening on a state level in terms of nursing practice. Your membership on one of these committees may be an opportunity for you to share your expertise and to develop your leadership and professional skills.

THE NURSE PRACTICE ACT

We have made numerous references to this document, and believe that it warrants a word or two of explanation. The nurse practice act is the general term applied to the law, or statutes, written in each state to regulate the practice of nursing. In fact, it has different names in different states: Wisconsin Statutes Relating to the Practice of Nursing, the Law Relating to Registered Nurses, the RCW (Revised Code of Washington), the Texas Administrative Code, and so forth. Whatever the title, this document is the legal framework of practice. It is written through the legislative process, meaning that any changes in the language must be initiated in the form of a bill passed by both the house and the senate and signed

CHECKPOINT 3–4

Check the following statements that apply to you:

❑ I have a copy of the nurse practice act for my state.
❑ I know who the members of the board of nursing are.
❑ I have attended at least one board meeting.
❑ I have served on a committee for the board.
❑ I have spoken with one of the staff or members of the board regarding a question I had.

If you checked two or more: Congratulations! You are well on your way to having a solid foundation of knowledge about your practice. If you checked fewer than two: Oops! Call your board of nursing now, and start getting informed!

into law by the governor of the state. For this reason, the statute relating to nursing is typically very general in terms, allowing for broad interpretation and application over an extended period of time. Changes in law may require several years to enact, depending on the nature of the change and the amount of support or controversy it engenders.

Basic components of the practice act will include:

- the creation of a board of nursing, defining membership and qualifications
- the listing of the powers and duties of the board, including meetings
- the licensure process, including qualifications, fees, renewal, permits, reciprocity
- definition of nursing
- approval process for nursing schools
- authority to adopt rules and regulations

RULES AND REGULATIONS

Because of the durability of the law, specific areas such as staffing ratios, acceptability of assignments, complete listings of the procedures allowable for nurses to perform, detailed definitions of such concepts as supervision and delegation, and so forth are not usually addressed in law. However, the statute enables the board to adopt rules and regulations that serve to clarify and amplify the intent of the law. If you are confused, consider the following anatomical analogy: the law is like a skeleton, providing the framework for the muscle and flesh of the rules. Rules can only be written that have support by statute, but can be much more specific in nature.

Members of the board of nursing may write rules and will often use committee input to create them. Once written, rules undergo a similar, yet simpler process of promulgation to become official. Many issues that are cause for the concern about whether your license is on the line are addressed in the more detailed rules and regulations. For example, the increased usage of assistive personnel has caused most states to clarify the reporting relationship of these individuals and to be more specific in the definition of *supervision* as it pertains to the process of delegation. This topic will be explored in great detail in the rest of this chapter.

CHECKPOINT 3–5

The following is one of the major differences between a rule and the law:

a) There are no differences since nurses are disciplined according to the law and the rules.
b) Law is more specific in nature since it must go through the legislative process for approval.
c) Rules are more detailed in nature than the law and must be based on and supported by law.
d) Rules can be written by anyone, and laws must be written by legislators.

See the end of the chapter for the answers.

THE TEST

We have now spent considerable time building your foundation of knowledge about the state board of nursing and the nurse practice act.

It's time to put that information to the test and ask you some key questions that will be major determinants of whether your practice with assistive personnel puts you at risk. Please answer the questions given in Exhibit 3–1 as true or false, according to the practice act in your state. Ready?

How did you do? Using statements of the National Council of State Boards of Nursing (NCSBN) and a representative sampling of state practice acts, let's review the answers.

Exhibit 3–1   Test on the Nurse Practice Act

Please answer the following questions as true or false:

____1. Once I delegate a task to an unlicensed health care worker, I am no longer accountable for what happens.

____2. My state's nurse practice act specifically allows me to delegate nursing care activities.

____3. My state's nurse practice act specifies that I must know the competencies and abilities of the person to whom I delegate.

____4. My state's nurse practice act states that I may be in violation of the standards of conduct if I delegate tasks to those I have reason to know lack the ability to perform the function or responsibility.

____5. If I fail to supervise those to whom nursing tasks have been delegated, I may be disciplined by the state board.

____6. If a nursing assistant makes a mistake during a task I have delegated, it would mean I could lose my license.

____7. Employer policies or directives can relieve me of my responsibility for making judgments about the delegation of nursing activities.

Source: Reprinted with permission from Loretta O'Neill, Ruth Hansten, and Marilynn Washburn, and the Washington Organization of Nurse Executives, © 1990.

Question 1: FALSE

This brings us to the definition of delegation, a fundamental that will be emphasized many times since it forms the basis of the legal expectations of your role. Dictionary definitions of the term *delegation* include "to assign, entrust or transfer." The NCSBN (1987, p. 227) has issued the following definition as it specifically applies to nursing:

> Delegation: "nurses entrusting the performance of selected nursing tasks to competent unlicensed persons in selected situations. The nurse retains the accountability for the total nursing care of the individuals."

Note the general nature of this definition. Those individuals who are looking for a black-and-white list of what may and may not be delegated will be a little concerned at the apparent ambiguity of this defined process. Take heart! The definition, as with statute, is intentionally generalized to allow *you*, as the registered nurse, to practice the art of nursing. No authority can begin to cover every unique and specific practice issue that may arise. This definition considers your expertise and knowledge to be guiding factors in your decision of which selected tasks and in which selected situations you deem it appropriate to delegate care. Your primary legal obligation is to ensure the competency of the individual you are working with, and we will explore that issue in detail.

To answer the first question, when you delegate a task to an unlicensed assistant, you remain accountable for the total nursing care of the individual, according to the definition above. What causes concern for many is the concept of accountability and the feeling that "if I am accountable, why delegate in the first place?" The term *accountability* has been applied to the nursing profession liberally and with minimal clarification of the meaning of the term. It is often linked with responsibility, authority, and autonomy, other broadly defined terms that translate to being the one who shoulders the blame if something goes wrong. This is not necessarily the case. Being accountable means being answerable for what one has done (in this case the decision to delegate the task) and standing behind that decision and/or action. For example, the nursing assistant to whom you delegated the task of obtaining vital signs made an error in the procedure of taking the blood pressure. The nursing assistant is *responsible* for his or her performance, and you are *accountable* to the patient for the decision you made to delegate the task and for taking action and correcting the error. As we continue through the remaining test questions, it will become clear just what you are accountable for in terms of patient care.

Question 2: TRUE

Within the statutes or rules of all nurse practice acts is the definition of nursing. Many of these definitions clearly address the function of delegation; others imply the process, as in the following examples. According to Chapter 18.88 of the Revised Code of Washington (1993), "The practice of nursing means the performance of acts requiring substantial specialized knowledge, judgment and skill. . .in. . .(3) the administration, supervision, *delegation* and evaluation of nursing practice." And according to Chapter 378, Section 20-87a of the Connecticut Nurse Practice Act (1991), "The practice of nursing by an RN is. . .the process of diagnosing human responses to actual or potential health problems, providing supportive and restorative care, health counseling and teaching. . .*collaborating in the implementation of the total health care regimen.*" A survey completed by the Montana State Board of Nursing in 1992 revealed that of the 41 respondents (there are 62 jurisdictions of the National Council), 28 have specific language regarding delegation; all the others imply the process within the definition of nursing.

Question 3: TRUE

Many state practice acts have adopted language from the NCSBN and specifically address the legal requirement that nurses know the competencies of the delegate. In their *Concept Paper on Delegation* (1990, p. 1), the NCSBN stated: "Boards of nursing must develop clear rules on determination of competence of persons to perform delegated nursing tasks or procedures, the level of supervision necessary, and which acts may be delegated." We anticipate that all states are in the process of promulgating rules that specifically address this area. Here are two examples from states that have already done so. Chapter N 6 of the Wisconsin Statutes and Administrative Code Relating to the Practice of Nursing (1993) states under "(3) Supervision and direction of delegated nursing acts" that "in the supervision and direction of delegated nursing acts an RN shall: (a) delegate tasks commensurate with *educational preparation and demonstrated abilities* of the person supervised." Section 610-X-6-.02 of the nurse practice act of Alabama (1989) states, "Delegation, Management and Supervision: (2) The registered nurse shall delegate selected nursing functions to others in accordance with the education and *demonstrated competence* of the person."

Question 4: TRUE

Knowing that the delegate is not competent or prepared educationally and proceeding to delegate the task anyway will certainly be a violation of the standard of practice in any state. All nurse practice acts list specific acts that are in violation of the standard; indeed, this is where you will find the highest degree of clarity! It's quite easy to identify what will get you in trouble. According to Section 1443.5 of the Standards of Competent Performance (California, 1992), the RN "(4) Delegates tasks to subordinates based on the legal scopes of practice of the subordinates and on *the preparation and capability needed* in the tasks to be delegated, and effectively supervises nursing care given by subordinates."

For example, as an RN in a rehab center, you assign a rehab aide the task of feeding a resident who has dysphagia. You know the aide has had difficulty in the past and in fact can recall one instance when the aide almost caused the resident to aspirate part of a tomato. But you are extremely short-staffed today, and it's in the aide's job description, so you guess he'll just have to learn with practice. WRONG! Don't put your license in jeopardy by making this kind of decision. You will be responsible for the correctness of this delegation, and in this case, the task should not be delegated to this individual. Your choices may include working with the aide, assigning another aide (whom you know to be competent) to feed the patient, or doing it yourself.

Question 5: TRUE

Among the terms commonly defined in every practice act is *supervision*. The NCSBN (1990, p. 2) defines the term as follows:

"Supervision is the provision of guidance by a qualified nurse for the accomplishment of a nursing task or activity with *initial direction* of the task or activity and *periodic inspection* of the actual act of accomplishing the task or activity."

Note that the italics identify the two important components of supervision:

1. *Initial direction*—the instructions you provide when first delegating the task: for example, "Please check the blood pressure on Mrs. Jones and report it to me immediately" or "Bathe Mr. Hawley three times this week, on Monday, Wednesday, and Friday during your visit. Use the bath oil Mrs. Hawley has gotten from the doctor. I'll be in on Friday to assess his skin and see how you are doing."
2. *Periodic inspection*—the decision you make regarding the frequency of checking back with the delegate is based on your judgment of the current situation. It is a defined expectation that you will provide supervision in the form of follow-up with the delegate. In the example above, the home health nurse is "periodically inspecting" the home health aide on Friday. He or she may be doing this weekly, or as infrequently as monthly, depending on the circumstances.

Failure to provide either the initial direction or periodic inspection will be interpreted as a failure to adequately supervise the delegate and will be the basis for disciplinary action of the RN, as Section R4-19-403 of the Arizona nurse practice act illustrates: "Unprofessional conduct, unfitness to practice nursing. 9. *Failure to supervise persons* to whom nursing functions have been delegated or assigning unqualified persons to perform functions of licensed persons."

Supervision may be direct and on-site, with the RN immediately available, as in the acute care setting. It may also be indirect, with the RN still accountable for the supervision of the individual but not physically present at the site of care. Home health practice, community settings, and some long-term care facilities are areas where the supervision by the RN is indirect. "The nurse who delegates an act to another assumes responsibility for the supervision of the act, whether the nurse is physically present or not" (NCSBN, 1990, p. 2).

Just as supervision may be direct or indirect, there are varying levels of supervision on which you will base your decision regarding the frequency of periodic inspection:

1. *Never delegated:* certain acts, including the assessment, evaluation, and nursing judgment, are never delegated. In addition, some states specify certain procedures that are never to be delegated but can be

performed only by the RN. Detailed discussion on this will follow later in the chapter.

2. *Unsupervised:* when an RN is working with another RN in a collegial relationship, he or she is not in the position of supervising the other RN unless the delivery model identifies the relationship through a charge nurse or other designated capacity. For example, when three RNs are working on one unit, they are not supervising each other and are not accountable for the fundamentals of supervision unless one of the three is working in the capacity of a charge nurse, resource nurse, or team leader, as defined by the facility.

3. *Initial direction/periodic inspection:* supervision of an individual, either licensed or unlicensed, whom the RN knows in terms of competency and has developed a working relationship with over time. An RN working in a dialysis center with a dialysis technician may be comfortable in giving initial report and direction and then following up two or three times during the shift. A home health nurse in the field may have worked with a home health aide for the past year and be confident in meeting with the aide on a biweekly basis for evaluation of the assigned cases.

4. *Continuous supervision:* when the working relationship is new or the RN has reason to believe that the delegate will need very frequent to continual support and assistance, the highest level of supervision is required. A new graduate nurse being oriented on the skilled care unit will need to have someone assigned as a preceptor to provide continuous supervision until he or she has demonstrated a level of expertise that the supervising RN is comfortable with. A new graduate should *not* be placed on the night shift of an extended care unit, where the supervision by another RN is indirect, through the director of nursing at home! A nursing assistant who has just completed the nurses' aide training course will need continual supervision throughout orientation until the RN is satisfied with the new assistant's demonstrated level of skill.

It is important to remember that the RN, in assessing the appropriateness of delegation, also assures that the level of supervision needed to assure safe practice is indeed available. "The decision to delegate should be based on . . . consideration of the level of supervision available and a determination of the level and method of supervision required to assure safe performance" (NCSBN, 1990, p. 3).

CHECKPOINT 3–6

Determine the level of supervision that is appropriate in each of the following situations:

1. A student nurse who is assigned to your orthopedic unit to care for two patients. Her instructor is in the facility but also has eight other students assigned to her.
2. A fellow RN who is working with you and Marge, the charge nurse.
3. A school health aide who has been assigned to work with you at the junior high—this is her first day.
4. A mental health assistant who offers to give the IM medications because he "was a medic in the Army."

See the end of the chapter for the answers.

Question 6: TRUE, but only if you delegate inappropriately

This is the question that often stumps many of the nurses we work with and is often the basis for their concern about professional responsibility and "their licenses being on the line." In the eyes of the law, you will be evaluated according to the manner in which you delegate a task and the supervision you provide to the delegate. Delegates are responsible for their individual performance of the task they are trained to perform. You cannot assume (and are not expected to assume) responsibility for the personal performance of all individuals on the health care team. Again, we reference the NCSBN (1990, p. 3): "The delegate is accountable for accepting the delegation and for his/her own actions in carrying out the act. . . . The delegator would be expected to provide supervisory follow-up such as intervention on the behalf of the client and corrective action." The state of Washington has further clarified (in WAC 246-839-010) what is expected of the delegator within its definition of supervision: "Supervision of licensed and unlicensed personnel means the provision of guidance and evaluation by a qualified RN for the accomplishment of a nursing task . . . and *the authority to require corrective action.*"

Due to the controversy and concern voiced by nurses across the country, states are responding to adopt rules that more clearly state the nurse's responsibility in working with other personnel. One of the barriers to effective delegation is the fear that the delegating nurse has regarding his or her accountability for the results of a task performed by another individual. Being clear on where that line of responsibility is drawn will help to remove that barrier and allow the nurse to function at the level of his or her professional education, providing the optimum of care to the individual.

Exhibit 3–2   A Delegation Case Study

An RN on a med/surg unit in City Hospital is working with a nursing assistant whom she has known and worked with for the past six months. Today she delegates the task of taking vital signs on all patients on the unit, giving particular instruction about Mrs. Avery, a fresh post-op with a new AV fistula in her right arm. Mary, the NA, is instructed to take Mrs. Avery's blood pressure on the left arm, as noted in the kardex and on a sign above the patient's bed. Mary nods in understanding and begins her assignment. Making rounds later, the RN finds Mrs. Avery in bed, the blood pressure cuff firmly in place over the new AV fistula in her right arm! The cuff is inflated and Mary is nowhere to be found!

What is the RN accountable for in this example?

Did she delegate correctly?

Is her "license on the line" for working with an incompetent aide?

What is Mary (the NA) responsible for?

Let's discuss the case presented in Exhibit 3–2. What is the RN accountable for in this situation? According to our discussion of the legalities of nursing practice, we know the RN is accountable for assessing the situation and the decision to delegate. She is also accountable for supervising the delegate by providing initial direction and periodic inspection. According to the scenario described, all of these things were done by the RN.

Did the RN delegate properly? Recalling the regulatory requirements of delegation, you know that the RN delegated properly if she knew the competencies of the NA. Knowing they had worked together for several months, one assumes that she had opportunity to assess job performance and knew that this NA could competently take vital signs.

Is her license in jeopardy? Not at this time. The RN assessed the situation, made a reasonable assignment, and provided initial direction. In the performance of periodic inspection, she has discovered a potentially harmful circumstance. The action she takes now will determine whether she completes the legal expectation of a delegator, that of taking corrective action. The RN must assess the patient's condition, checking the patency of the new fistula, notifying the physician if necessary, *and* following up with Mary to make certain this does not happen again. (For more on the feedback process, see Chapter 10.)

What is Mary responsible for? According to our legal guidelines, the delegate is responsible for accepting the delegation and for her own actions in carrying out the act. If the patient has been harmed as a result of the improperly placed cuff, *Mary* is responsible for the damage.

Working with other individuals always poses some risk, but no one individual can provide all of the care that a patient needs. The RN who must rely on the LPN to pass the medications correctly knows that the LPN is responsible for the accuracy of the medication administration and is personally responsible for any error that may be made in performing that act. The physician (the primary delegator on the health care team!) who delegates the administration of the chemotherapy to the oncology nurse knows that the oncology nurse is responsible for performing that act correctly. Understanding our legal boundaries helps us to minimize risks and to function at the highest level of our scope of practice.

Question 7: FALSE

The NCSBN (1990, p. 3) clearly states its position: "While employers and administrators may suggest which nursing acts should be delegated and to whom the delegation may be made, it is the nurse who ultimately decides and who is accountable for deciding whether the delegation occurs....In fact, if the nurse decides that the delegation may not appropriately or safely take place, but nevertheless delegates, he/she may be disciplined by the board of nursing."

Employee policies cannot override the law and rules of nursing and will not protect the nurse who is following policy but acting outside of the practice act. Be careful about this false sense of security; the practice act is the ultimate authority by which your performance will be judged. Conflict with an employer may be difficult and unwanted, but as a practicing professional, you will find that it is in your best interests to discuss the differences with the employer. No health care facility can stay in business long by breaking the law or asking its employees to do so. (Refer to Chapter 4 for further discussion of the employer relationship.)

An example of employer policy differences involves the recent case of the University of Chicago Clinical Research Center (Illinois Nurse, 1993). The employer in this instance had developed a policy allowing unlicensed assistive personnel (UAP) to be delegated the task of drawing blood. Nurses felt this was an unsafe delegation, citing the following concerns: (1) drawing blood involved the administration of Heparin; (2) the procedure is a complex nursing task requiring professional judgment, particularly in the CRC, where there are frequent blood extractions and the use of long-term indwelling lines; and (3) the RNs were not involved with the UAPs or knowledgeable about their skills, training, and qualifications. This conflict posed several risks to the RNs; they could face charges of abandonment for refusing to follow the policy, or they could be disciplined by the board of nursing for supervising an UAP in an undelegatable task. Fortunately, the RNs were willing to be involved in the resolution, and, using the assistance of the Illinois Board of Nursing, they were able to successfully change the employer policy. UAPs at this medical center are now delegated "technical" tasks, and nursing is involved in the decision-making process.

THE LPN ROLE

Very little has been said up to this point regarding the role of the LPN. Rules and statutes that have been cited speak to unlicensed personnel in some instances and to both licensed and unlicensed personnel in other instances. During recent years, the role of the licensed practical (or vocational) nurse has been altered a great deal in response to closer scrutiny and further clarification of the various roles of nursing. It is not unusual for us to see the LPN role diminished in many areas as functions previously allowed through employer policy have been eliminated or restricted. We have received letters of concern from LPNs who are struggling to understand the "new" restrictions placed upon them, and we feel it is essential for the RN to understand the legal scope of this delegate as well as that of the unlicensed person.

The role of the LPN was created in response to the increased demands for nursing personnel during World War II. Because all of the needs could not be filled with RNs, a new level of caregiver was created that required less education and could be trained faster. Due to the limitations of training, the role of the LPN was defined as being under the supervision of either an RN or a licensed physician, with the understanding that this individual would not have autonomy of practice. During the nursing shortage of the 1970s and then again in the 1980s, there were many instances in which employers expanded the role of the LPN, allowing LPNs to perform functions not clearly outlined within their scope of practice. Assessments, IV medications, tracheal suctioning, and insertion of naso-gastric tubes are examples of the procedures that were not previously within the LPN scope of practice. Roles became blurred as the employers responded to shortages, and it was not unusual to find an LPN taking the same assignment on a hospital unit as the RN. Little attention was paid to the differentiation of the roles, and indeed, many RNs have difficulty articulating the differences!

An LPN is still limited in scope of practice, and whether the practice act and the governing board are separate or combined with the RN boards, the limit is still the same. LPN practice is "recognizing and meeting the basic needs of the client, gives nursing care *under the direction and supervision of the registered nurse or licensed physician* to clients in routine nursing situations" (WAC 308-117-020, Washington).

In several states (for example Colorado, Washington, and Texas) the LPN is prohibited by law from delegating nursing tasks, and this function is allowed only by the RN. The definition of supervision as described earlier is applicable to RNs working with LPNs, and the need for initial direction and periodic inspection of these members of the team must be demonstrated. The difference in the roles of the RN and the LPN should be reflected in policies, job descriptions, methods of assigning, and documentation, no matter what the setting.

CHECKPOINT 3–7

1. In my state, the LPN (may/may not) delegate selected nursing tasks.
2. At the facility where I work, there (is/is not) a difference in the role of the RN and the role of the LPN according to policy.
3. I (know/do not know) what the limitations of the LPN are in this state.

See the end of the chapter for the answers.

DELEGATION AND THE NURSING PROCESS

Although the operational definition of delegation is purposefully general, there are some guidelines for the RN to use when evaluating the decision of whether to delegate. In fact, as some of you will be delighted to know, there are some very specific statements regarding what may *not* be delegated under any circumstance. For example, according to the NCSBN (1990, p. 1), "9. While tasks and procedures may be delegated, the functions of assessment, evaluation, and nursing judgment should not be delegated."

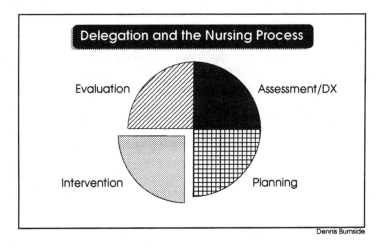

The part of the nursing process most readily delegated involves the component of intervention. Tasks, procedures, technical duties, and so forth all fall into this category and are part of the patient's care that may be readily performed by another individual besides the RN. However, as a reminder, the decision is yours to make, and one we hope that you base on each specific situation, considering carefully the patient's response and the outcome you desire. In one setting, you may choose to delegate the task of a clean dressing change to the nursing assistant, knowing that the wound is healing and that the patient has been taught what to observe in the process. In another setting, you may elect to do the dressing change yourself, wanting to assess the skin and teach a family member to look for signs of infection.

Specific limits to interventions that may not be delegated to unlicensed personnel are outlined in each state and vary according to their law. The more common restrictions include:

- medication administration
- any procedure that requires piercing of the skin (as in drawing blood or giving injections)
- surgical asepsis
- tube feeding
- suctioning

Many states strictly prohibit the delegation of the administration of medication, but several states are recognizing that this is appropriate in some settings. Group homes for the developmentally or mentally disabled, community settings for the physically handicapped, group homes for the elderly, and long-term care facilities are all examples of areas where assistive personnel may be allowed to administer medication. Currently at least 20 states allow medication administration by medication aides in carefully described circumstances (Montana, 1992). These carefully described circumstances include the involvement of the RN in the training and supervising of the assistive personnel. Oregon has developed a very specific training course, as have other states, in order to meet the needs of very particular populations.

Although our diagram of the nursing process appears limiting, we want to make certain that you understand that parts of the process of assessment, planning, and evaluation may also be delegated. When a new patient is admitted to any health care setting, it is common for the initial data assessment of vital signs, height, and weight, as well as chief complaint, to be obtained by someone other than the RN. The LPN may perform additional interviewing and gathering of data in order for the RN to complete the assessment. The question of whether an LPN may perform a complete patient assessment remains an area of controversy. Arguments range from the opinion that the education of the LPN does not provide sufficient theoretical base for assessment to the opinion that an LPN can be taught "basic assessment skills" as long as the data are interpreted by an RN. Once again, the accountability of the assessment rests with the RN, and it is the RN who is best prepared through education and experience to assess the patient.

Planning is another area of the nursing process that may invite participation from the other members of the team. Nursing assistants may have the opportunity to spend additional direct time with the patient and may learn information that would assist the RN in best planning the care for the patient during hospitalization or while under the care of the agency.

A home health aide who visits the home on a more frequent basis than the RN will certainly have valuable input for the RN who is making the monthly visit.

Evaluation involves the interpretation of data to make judgments regarding the effectiveness of the interventions, and rests primarily with the RN. Again, the other members of the team may have observations and other information that will assist the RN in the evaluation, but the responsibility for the judgment belongs to the RN. It is his or her critical analysis that will be necessary to determine if the nursing diagnosis is correct, if the outcomes targeted are reasonable, and if the patient is responding to the interventions that have been performed. This systematic process involves the coordination of all members of the team and requires the organized skill of the registered nurse.

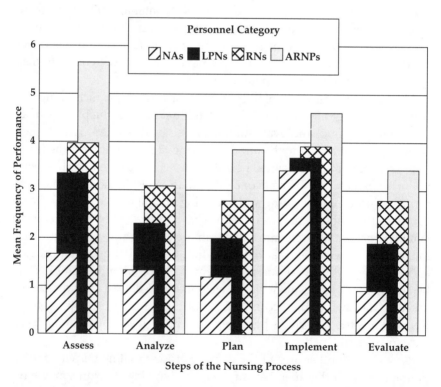

Figure 3–1 Average Mean Frequency of Performance Values for Nursing Process Activity Statements, by Personnel Category. *Source:* Reprinted with permission of the National Council of State Boards of Nursing, Chicago, Illinois.

The bar graph in Figure 3–1 illustrates the overlap of the performance of the various components of the nursing process by the four levels of nursing personnel. This study involved the survey of over 15,000 providers, randomly selected from all states, by the Research Services Division of the NCSBN (1994). The purpose of the study was to obtain data to delineate the roles of the four levels of personnel and to facilitate the delegation of nursing activities to unlicensed personnel. A complete report of this study will be distributed at the Delegate Assembly in August 1994.

The survey demonstrated a specific pattern regarding the performance of the activities of the nursing process. The frequency of each component is ranked as follows:

NAs and LPNs: implementation, assessment, analysis, planning, evaluation.

RNs: assessment, implementation, analysis, evaluation, planning

Nurse Practitioners: assessment, implementation, analysis, planning, evaluation

From this study it is apparent that nursing assistants and LPNs report spending more time implementing care, whereas RNs and nurse practitioners spend more time in assessing the need and type of care to be given.

CHECKPOINT 3–8

Check the following statements that apply to you:

❑ I know what I may not delegate to unlicensed assistive personnel according to my state's practice act.
❑ I know which parts of the nursing process I may safely delegate.

SUMMARY

In this chapter we have discussed the fundamental knowledge of the nurse practice act that is essential to being able to determine if the delegation you are considering will truly "put your license on the line." Understanding the limitations of your practice act, as well as the purpose and the powers of the board of nursing, are key factors in dispelling the fear of responsibility for the actions of those with whom you work. No single individual can provide all things to all people, and the risks involved in relying on others can be minimized with the knowledge of legal definitions and expectations.

You are encouraged to seek the resources available to you: obtain a copy of the nurse practice act in your state, request any advisory opinions that have been issued on the subject of delegation, and contact your board of nursing to learn more about the process of ensuring the safety of the public through the regulation of nursing practice. It's your license—protect it!

ANSWERS TO CHECKPOINTS

3–1. c

3–2. d

3–3. d

3–5. c

3–6.
   1. initial direction/periodic inspection
   2. unsupervised
   3. continuous supervision
   4. never delegated

3–7.
   1. The LPN may or may not be allowed to delegate nursing tasks. Check your state's nurse practice act for the correct answer in your state.
   2. There *is* a difference (there should be!). This difference should be apparent in the job description, the system of care delivery, and the reporting and documentation expectations of the LPN.
   3. I *do* know the limitations of the LPN in this state. (If you do not, do you feel safe in delegating to an LPN?)

REFERENCES

Donahue, M. P. 1985. *Nursing, the finest art*. St. Louis: C. V. Mosby Company.

Hansten, R., and M. Washburn. 1990. *I light the lamp.* Vancouver, Wash.: Applied Therapeutics.

Illinois Nurse. 1993. University of California RNs stop inappropriate UAP activity. *Chart* November–December: 16.

Montana State Board of Nursing. 1992. State survey delegation of nursing tasks [letter]. January.

National Council of State Boards of Nursing. 1987. Statement of the nursing activities of unlicensed persons. Book of Reports, Ninth Annual Convention, August 25–29, pp. 221–229.

National Council of State Boards of Nursing. 1990. *Concept paper on delegation.* Chicago.

National Council of State Boards of Nursing. 1994. *Preliminary report: Role delineation study of nurse aides, licensed practical/vocational nurses, registered nurses and advanced registered nurse practitioners.*

Chapter 4

KNOW YOUR WORLD
• practice
• organization

Know Your Organization: What about Where I Work?

HISTORICAL DEVELOPMENT— OR HOW DID WE GET HERE?

Ruth I. Hansten and Marilynn J. Washburn

"My manager is always talking about the mission and values of this organization. Big deal. All that seems to really mean is how much work can they get out of us without paying us any more. They keep changing things and talking about this wonderful quality program at the same time they're taking our jobs and giving them to assistive personnel."

In the previous chapters we have begun to create a foundation of knowledge regarding the legal support you have as a practicing professional. At the same time we have discussed some of the primary reasons for the constant state of change that many organizations are experiencing, with the intention of offering you some basis for understanding what you as an employee might be experiencing. We must now take our assessment one further step and take a clear look at the environment in which you work so that you may not feel the way the individual does in our example above.

Those of you who are groaning at the idea of a little history, please stay with us on this one as we explore a quick review of organizational development in order to better appreciate the framework of the health care sys-

71

tem as it has evolved today. It is unusual for many of us to question why things are the way they are. For most, if the environment in which we are working is challenging, unfulfilling, or supportive, we don't question the rationale but seek instead to make changes or to be grateful for what we have in terms of a job and make the best of it. But why are you in a top-down, chain-of-command system? Or if you are in a more progressive style of participative management, complete with administrative support for multidisciplinary team building, why is your organization making this change? If you are a student, thinking about future career options, what work setting would fit you best?

CHECKPOINT 4–1

Are the following statements true or false?

____ 1. There is only one style of organization, and the administrator always controls the decisions.
____ 2. There has been little change in the way health care professionals are treated as employees.
____ 3. Most health care organizations have a mission statement and have always had one.
____ 4. Unions are involved in all health care facilities and have been since hospitals first opened.
____ 5. Employer policies are more important than the nurse practice act.

See the end of the chapter for the answers.

How did you do with the checkpoint above? As we continue our discussion, keep these questions in mind. We will be reviewing the role of unions, mission statements, and policies in the evolution of the health care system from its humble beginnings to the challenges of today. Most important of all will be the process of delegation as part of your changing work environment, and the role the organization plays in the process.

IN THE BEGINNING

If we were to go back before Nightingale's day, we would discover that health care was not an organized system. There were few hospitals, and the general expectation was that the women of the family would provide the majority of ministering to the sick. There were few effective medicinal resources, and society as a whole had not fully organized its system of work.

The industrial revolution, the progression of medicine, and the advancement of technology brought significant changes to the newly forming hospital system. Almshouses and military and public hospitals offered the only early options for health care outside of the home. With the advent of anesthetics and septic technique, the demand for hospitals increased since it was no longer desirable for doctors to perform surgery at home on the kitchen table, where many had demanded surgery be done, and where people had felt safer than they would risking their lives to the high level of infection at the hospital.

The world continued to change rapidly as transportation made it easier for families to be mobile and industry became more organized in its structure. Salaried management emerged in all industries, and administrators and professors joined the ranks of universities. In hospitals, however, the decision-making power was shifting to the physicians, who were more and more in control of the admissions to a hospital. Boards of trustees were being replaced by medical boards, who held controlling authority over the administration of the hospital. It was not unusual for physicians to own small, private hospitals and to employ a management team to enact their decisions. As the hospital setting grew and physicians were able to belong to several hospitals, their needs for administrative services increased as well. Administrators were empowered with increasing authority to oversee the employees, ensuring that the hospital ran smoothly internally so that the physicians could perform their services. Hospital management then followed the mainstream of scientific management principles, and a top-down, controlling approach was embraced.

In the meantime, nursing was advancing quickly, organizing nursing schools, setting minimum standards for licensure, and responding to the needs of the people in the community in addition to the institution. Lillian Wald was an exemplary leader in the late 1800s, developing the Henry Street Settlement and advancing the system of public health. Under her direction, the first system for nurses in public schools was created, and nursing services for insurance policyholders were initiated (Christy, 1984). Nursing was defining its role in many arenas outside the hospital, but it was the hospital that remained the benchmark for the health care system.

Hospital development was rapid throughout the twentieth century, responding to many diverse sociocultural events. World Wars, the Great Depression, and the changing face of disease from polio epidemics to demands for organ transplants kept the hospital system in constant turmoil. The treatment of employees, including nurses, became more controlling, as hospital managements adopted policies and systems to strengthen their control over an internal environment in response to increasing public and federal involvement. Unions found their place in health care after World War II, representing nurses and health care workers alike who fought for employee protection and the insurance of individual rights.

THE UNIONIZED ORGANIZATION AND DELEGATION

Karen McGrath

What could unions possibly have to do with clinical delegation? Whether you are considering or already working in a facility where nurses are represented by a union, it is important to understand the role of the union in ensuring a fair and reasonable work environment.

Since before the turn of the century in this country, workers have struggled to assert some measure of control over working conditions. Leaders came from the ranks of employees in a number of trades or industries; they included miners, garment workers, auto workers, and longshoremen. They understood the workplace and what was needed to prevent abuse and exploitation of employees. They worked to educate and unite workers, to establish equitable wage standards, and to generally improve the quality of work life.

Health care employees are relative newcomers to the union movement. Federal laws, the Railway Labor Act of 1926 and the National Labor Relations Act (or Wagner Act) of 1935, were enacted to protect workers' "right to self-organization, to form, join, or assist labor organizations, to bargain collectively through representatives of their own choosing, and to engage in concerted activities, for the purpose of collective bargaining or other mutual aid or protection" (National Labor Relations Act, Section 7). Until 1974, however, private, not-for-profit health care institutions were exempt from coverage. Individual states passed laws governing collective bargaining rights for public sector employees.

Other laws advancing unionization included the Taft-Hartley Act (or the Labor-Management Relations Act) of 1947, which further defined the rights and duties of both labor and management, and the Landrum-Griffin Act (or the Labor-Management Reporting and Disclosure Act) of 1959, which spelled out the rights of union members. These measures went a long way to eliminate abuses and corruption that had come to light.

The American Nurses Association (ANA) and its constituent state nurses associations (SNAs) had since their inception in 1896 been addressing employment standards for nurses, and until the mid-1940s had achieved only limited success. The approach had focused on educating nurses and consumers about matters affecting the recruitment of qualified nurses. In 1946, the ANA House of Delegates took a bold step by approving a plan for a national economic and security program. A key piece of the program called upon the state nurses associations to act as collective bargaining representatives for nurses. Many of the SNAs began to build their own programs with trained staff to meet this challenge. Today, 26 of 53 SNAs have full Economic and General Welfare (or Labor Relations) programs that are responsible for representing nurses in a variety of work settings.

In addition to the SNAs, many other unions represent health care employees, including nurses. During the 1970s and 1980s, the economy in the United States began to shift away from the manufacturing sector to a growing service sector. Health care, as a large part of the service industry, became fertile ground for organizing, and unions looked to bolster shrinking membership numbers by shifting their attention to this arena.

No matter which union a group has selected as its representative, knowing some basic principles will maximize your union experience (if you work in a facility where the employees are represented by a union) and make it work for you and your patients. Remember those key phrases from the Wagner Act: collective bargaining, mutual aid and protection, and concerted activity? They assume people working together toward a common goal. It begins with a secret ballot election in which an identified employee group decides if, and by which union, it wants to be represented. The group becomes a bargaining unit and proceeds to elect local leaders from within its own membership. The new leaders' task is to seek out and represent the needs and desires of the membership. The union provides experts in labor relations and industry trends and standards to guide and advise the leaders as they negotiate a collective bargaining agreement (a contract) with the employer.

In order for all of this to be successful, the membership has certain rights and responsibilities as well. The union has the legal responsibility to represent all members fairly, and the members are expected to join and support the union they have selected. This is one of those instances where the old axiom about the house divided truly applies. The union *is* the membership and functions democratically. The members give direction to leaders by participating in meetings and voting on matters of concern. In order to be an effective member, you must be informed and involved. Your degree of involvement will depend on your own desires as well as other personal and professional demands on your time. Attending meetings, reading the literature, volunteering for committees, and becoming a unit representative are degrees of involvement open to you as a union member.

When dealing with management, the most successful bargaining units are able to demonstrate unity and credibility. An adversarial relationship is not necessary and is often counterproductive to reaching mutually acceptable solutions to problems. Management representatives who recognize and respect the collective bargaining relationship are also most often successful in maintaining a measure of what is known as labor peace. The process lends itself to the popular thinking of participative management: total quality management (TQM) and continuous quality improvement (CQI). The difference in the unionized setting is the balance of power. The assistance of the union in dealing with the management structure is intended to level the playing field.

But what does all of this have to do with clinical delegation?

An employment contract typically covers such topics as wages, premium pay for unusual or extra shifts, holidays, vacations, insurance benefits, seniority, work schedules, and a grievance procedure for dispute resolution. In addition, contracts covering nurses very often speak to staffing and patient safety concerns and establish joint labor-management committees designed to open communications. One of the committees that is very important for nurses is the Nursing Practice Committee.

This committee is composed of nurses elected by members of the bargaining unit who meet from time to time with representatives of nursing administration to discuss issues of concern with policies and procedures affecting patient care delivery. The issues may be raised by either the nurses or managers, are thoroughly researched, and require a written response from administration detailing what is to be done to resolve the issue. In most cases a joint solution can be found.

Now, let us see how the system works in three practice settings.

Setting 1: Sunshine Community Hospital

Sunshine Community Hospital has announced to the staff in its Friday newsletter that nursing will be changing in a very innovative way. It is the wave of the future and will free the nurses from such mundane tasks as bathing and feeding patients, walking patients, changing dressings, and administering medications. A two-week training program has been developed, and the first trainees will begin on Monday. For the past 15 years, nurses have functioned in a primary care delivery model, with a few LPNs on some of the units to help with the heavier patients.

Mary Ann has worked at the hospital for five years and never felt the need to join the union. She is not alone here; less than half of the nurses belong. Her nurse manager tells her not to worry: they have researched these new delivery models and know what they are doing. "Just trust us."

The local leaders contact the union office to find out what to do. The staff representative advises that they need to request a meeting with management to ask questions and gets a letter out immediately. Management reluctantly agrees to meet but firmly states that the plan is already in place and moving along. The Nursing Practice Committee has not met for some time because the leaders could not find nurses interested or willing to invest the time. The first meeting to discuss the change in staff mix is difficult because not everyone knows everyone else. The nurses are angry, and management is defensive of its plan. At the second meeting, the nurses are able to articulate their concerns about the new plan and begin to ask questions about such things as the new care partners, the training program, and the acuity of the patients in relation to the new staff model. The third meeting yields an agreement to conduct a study of the effect of the new plan on patient satisfaction.

This process has taken three months. In the meantime nurses have begun to work with the new care partners and have found it difficult to relinquish many of the bedside activities that have been so much so a part of their daily routines. They complain to leaders that this new model has doubled their patient load while not giving them much more help, and they demand to know what the union is doing to stop this. Mary Ann is among several nurses who resign rather than practice this way.

Setting 2: Northern Visiting Nurse Service

Northern Visiting Nurse Service has been experiencing a growth spurt. Referrals are up as patients are discharged sooner, often needing nursing follow-up. Maureen finds herself going home later and more tired, even though she loves home care and still feels professionally challenged. She has been a state nurses association member since graduation but has never really paid much attention to the contract. The raises have been nice, and she enjoys a fairly good relationship with Jean, her supervisor.

A memo from the Director of Patient Care Services warning about the excessive use of overtime results in increased grumbling in the office, and Maureen is worried. Jean's response is that the directive is from upstairs and there is nothing she can do. Posted on the bulletin board, next to the overtime memo, is the list of bargaining unit officers. The same day, she locates the chairperson and asks if the union can do anything about the mounting pressure. She expresses her frustration with an administration that appears to have lost touch with the facts of direct care. John is very understanding and reports that nurses have been calling him all day.

As they talk, it becomes apparent that the problems are sicker patients requiring more time, more paperwork, and orienting new nurses without an adjustment of workload. John invites Maureen to a meeting of the bargaining unit to discuss the issues. She is able to repeat her concerns, and John leads a discussion of possible solutions to be presented to administration. At the next labor/management meeting, John presents the issue along with a time study done by several of the nurses. Administration's initial response is that the nurses just have to dig in and bear with it until the new nurses are able to make visits independently. John continues to discuss the solutions developed by the group, concentrating on the enormous amount of paperwork required. As he describes the different forms and their purposes, it becomes clear that some are redundant information and simple enough that clerical employees could transcribe the information from reports that the nurses complete. The nurses have calculated that approximately one hour per day is spent by nurses on an activity that could be done by current clericals, saving the agency a significant amount in overtime costs or lost visits. The director is impressed and commits to examining the issue further, looking at the paperwork to determine if a report is really needed and, if so, who could fill it out. John reports that

Maureen will head a bargaining unit task force to examine the agency's preceptor program with a goal of maximizing the orientation experience while being sensitive to the workload of the preceptors. The director states that she is eager to see the results.

Setting 3: Toowell Memorial

Across town, at Toowell Memorial, the Nursing Practice Committee is meeting at its usual time this month, and the nurses see a new item on the agenda. The director of nursing describes a new staff mix model they have been interested in trying. She shares material from professional journals on trends in nursing management that point to a delivery model incorporating nonlicensed nurse extenders to free nurses to be more involved in the care management of patients. Sharon is the local unit's chairperson. She is able to report on concerns expressed by staff nurses at a recent symposium sponsored by the union. It is agreed that supervisors and the union's leaders will conduct meetings with staff nurses in the next two weeks to detail the proposed plan and listen to the nurses' concerns and suggestions.

At the conclusion of these meetings, the committee reconvenes to try to work on the nurses' concerns, and several changes are made to the plan in response. At Sharon's suggestion, the committee agrees that the plan will be better received if it is examined again by the staff nurses. A pilot program is planned for a volunteer unit, with criteria established for measurement. The nurses will be provided training in delegation skills, an expert from the state nurses association is invited to discuss the practice act implications of the new care partners, and the training program for care partners is jointly developed. The experiment goes well, with only a few modifications to the plan needed. Regular progress reports are published in the union's newsletter to the nurses.

Three months later, Sharon and her local unit colleagues on the Nurse Practice Committee assist staff nurses from the pilot unit to present the results to the local unit's members. Ninety percent of the hospital's staff nurses are members and attend the meetings to vote. The plan is overwhelmingly approved, and the nurses leave the meeting looking forward to having the new staff mix plan introduced on their unit.

As you can see, the presence of a union is not a guarantee that employment is secure and that no changes in your practice will ever be made. Selecting a union can be important, but it is not enough. As with any process, you have to make it work. It is a little like buying a car. Without one, you may take a bit longer to get around, but it does not do any good just left to sit in the garage. For managers, having a union is not a sign of failure. It can provide a vehicle for discussion and change. A contract provides structure that everyone can understand and work with to resolve problems.

CHECKPOINT 4–2

1. Union representation
   a) is available in all states
   b) is required in all hospitals
   c) has always been available for health care employees
   d) relies on membership participation to be effective

2. Being a member of a union
   a) means that I will always have a job
   b) is required by my licensure
   c) provides me with an additional opportunity to join with fellow employees in an organized fashion to discuss working conditions with management
   d) is prohibited by my nurse practice act

3. I can be involved in changes in care delivery that result in my need to delegate nursing care by
   a) being an active union member and attending Nurse Practice Committee meetings
   b) by participating in the management of my (non-union) work setting by attending staff meetings and serving on committees and task forces that plan changes in care delivery and staffing
   c) keeping myself informed and updated on trends in nursing practice
   d) all of the above

See the end of the chapter for the answers.

ASSESSING THE HEALTH CARE ORGANIZATION

Ruth I. Hansten and Marilynn J. Washburn

THE NONUNION ENVIRONMENT

If you aren't in a union environment, never fear! In many states or locales, nurses are not represented by a union, nor do they feel a need for one. When management practices in a participative fashion, with true empowerment of all staff, such as in shared governance or self-directed work teams, staff nurses concerns are equally important and valued. Wise administrators develop staff through education and encourage autonomy in decision making regarding patient care. Wise staff become involved in committees or task forces (whether union or not) that develop policies and procedures and plan for innovative practice that will ensure quality and cost-effective care. "Organizations are realizing that they are in partnership with their workers in delivering health care" (O'Grady, 1992, p. 178). And it is your responsibility as a professional nurse to uphold that partnership.

Whether the facility you work for has union representation for its employees or not is only one part of the picture. Several factors must be assessed as we continue our knowledge of the organization.

THE MISSION STATEMENT

Today's contemporary health care facility carries with it the history of intensifying social demands and the increasing involvement of federal policy. The focus of any health care organization must shift from a singular perspective to a systems approach or global perspective on patient and client needs. Traditional roles and traditional management techniques will no longer be effective in the reformed system. Organizational systems are emerging in which the employees are truly valued members of the team and in which it is believed that the employee is responsible to think and achieve. With this major shift in premise is the need to begin at the root of the organization—the mission statement.

Having received a wake-up call from a public that has loudly voiced its dissatisfaction with the health care system, organizations are reexamining their values and mission statements to make certain they are guiding the shift from a product emphasis to a service approach. Mission statements of the early hospitals in the mid-1800s focused on primarily religious and moralistic objectives. It was not unusual for a hospital to identify its mission as one of providing homes for the orphans or the poor and creating a Christian environment. The advent of surgery and the relief of acute illness caused many hospitals to redefine their mission in terms of medical objectives, and the emphasis shifted from a moral stance to an approach that clearly identified the purpose as the treatment of disease and injury (Starr, 1982, p. 158).

The health care organization of today has broadened its perspective, integrating the social, moral, and medical objectives in a more holistic expression of the mission of the institution. For example:

> St. Mary Medical Center is a community of people working together to provide a broad spectrum of high quality health care services to residents throughout Southeast Washington and Northeast Oregon. Faithful to the tradition of the Sisters of Providence since 1879, the mission of St. Mary Medical Center is to continue its leadership role in offering these services in a Christian atmosphere, respectful of the dignity and worth of each individual, with special concern for the poor and oppressed (St. Mary Medical Center, 1993).

The components of quality, cost effectiveness, and accessibility are common to most mission statements today. Most will also include a component relating to the employee, and the statement may look something like this: "To promote the continuous professional growth of each employee within a supportive environment."

The mission statement may also be supported by a list of "values," those fundamental beliefs that form the framework of the culture of the organization. Diann Uustal has done extensive work in the area of values, specifically as they relate to nursing. She states that "values provide a frame of reference through which we integrate, explain and appraise new ideas, events and personal relationships" (1985, p. 105).

One example of supportive values that we particularly appreciate is found in the mission statement of Community Home Health Care:

> We value: . . .
>
> Clear, honest and timely communication among staff.
>
> Involving staff in decisions and changes that affect them.

Communications that nurture information-sharing and staff support.

Staff that understand and support our charitable mission (Community Home Health Care, 1993).

In meeting the demands of the changing times, we are encouraged by mission and values statements that address the involvement of the employee. As Toffler (1990) points out, in this time of turbulence, organizations depend more on their workers for success than on any other single factor. Support through the mission, the values, and the culture of the organization will be essential for you in understanding and safely implementing the process of delegation. This foundation is critical in making certain that nursing continues to be actively involved in decisions and changes that directly affect the patient, particularly in the redesign and addition of personnel for the delivery of care.

CHECKPOINT 4-3

Knowledge of the mission and values of my employing facility is important in delegation because:

a) They are not important because no one follows them anyway.

b) I'm not sure because I have never seen the mission statement.

c) They clarify the basic premise of the agency and will enable me to assess what value the organization places on employee involvement, particularly in redesigning the care delivery system.

d) The mission will tell me if I'm in the right place or not and if I need to join a union to improve the working conditions.

See the end of the chapter for the answers.

Congratulations! You've made it this far, and we promise you that the following discussion will be firmly focused on contemporary issues (except for a brief reminder of history!).

By now you know that we are emphasizing the importance of the nursing process and continually applying it to our discussion of delegation. A clearer understanding of your organization, or the one in which you will work, requires the assessment of several factors that directly affect you in working with, delegating to, and supervising other health care workers.

Knowing the answers to the questions in the four major areas of assessment outline in the assessment tool in Exhibit 4–1 will help you to be able to practice professionally and safely, to the fullest potential of your license. A brief discussion of each area should be helpful in completing your knowledge base.

THE ORGANIZATIONAL STRUCTURE

Whether the setting in which you work is an acute care hospital or any one of a number of alternative health care facilities, there will typically be an organizational chart that describes the reporting relationships of personnel. Although traditional frameworks are continually changing, we have not yet found a substitute for the "snapshot" provided by a chart showing the titles of positions and/or departments/units and their relationship to everyone else in the agency. This chart serves only as a road map of the facility: it may identify landmarks but will not describe everything about each location. Unlike earlier organizational charts that demonstrated the traditional top-down hierarchy, today's chart may resemble the one in Figure 4–1 or Figure 4–2. These two charts clearly demonstrate the evolution of one organization in the past ten years.

Although the chart may provide the framework for the agency, it leaves several questions unanswered. You will need to further assess the degree of RN participation supported on committees, particularly collaborative practice and interdisciplinary committees, which may not be represented on any chart. These informal groups may be very instrumental and powerful in planning changes in personnel and care delivery.

As we discussed in great detail in Chapter 3, and will review in subsequent chapters, when an RN delegates, he or she is responsible for supervising the delegate and taking any corrective measures that may be necessary as a result of the delegate's performance. Clearly defined reporting mechanisms and systems that facilitate the fulfillment of this responsibility of the RN are necessary ingredients for the organization that expects the RN to delegate nursing tasks.

Exhibit 4–1 An Assessment of a Health Care Organization for Support of the Delegation Process

Yes No

Organizational Structure

____ ___ 1. Is there an organizational chart?

____ ___ 2. Are there clearly defined reporting systems for RNs supervising delegates?

____ ___ 3. Is there sufficient communication among the various units?

____ ___ 4. Is the mission visible to everyone and is it followed?

____ ___ 5. Are there interdisciplinary committees in which RNs participate?

Quality

____ ___ 1. Is a quality program currently in place?

____ ___ 2. Does the model focus on outcomes?

____ ___ 3. Is it supported by management *and* staff?

____ ___ 4. Are nurses actively involved in the process?

____ ___ 5. Do RNs participate in determining the criteria for measuring quality?

Safety in Practice

____ ___ 1. Are there policies addressing standards for appropriate staffing?

____ ___ 2. Is there a nurse advisory committee involved in addressing problems related to staffing?

____ ___ 3. Are the policies directly affecting nursing evaluated for their consistency with state regulations?

____ ___ 4. Do RNs have responsibility and autonomy for continually appraising the care delivery system and implementing changes as needed?

____ ___ 5. Are assistive personnel roles created or enlarged without the input and evaluation of nursing?

Educational Resources

____ ___ 1. Are unlicensed assistive personnel adequately trained and oriented (using validated competencies and measurable outcomes)?

____ ___ 2. Is there a system for providing additional skill development for assistive personnel when the need is identified by an RN supervising an employee?

____ ___ 3. Are RNs offered frequent educational opportunities to develop supervisory skills?

____ ___ 4. Is there a documentation process for establishing competency in all skills required by the job description?

____ ___ 5. Is there a mentorship or preceptorship program for all new licensed personnel?

____ ___ 6. Is information regarding new changes in health care and health care regulations, including the nurse practice act, readily available?

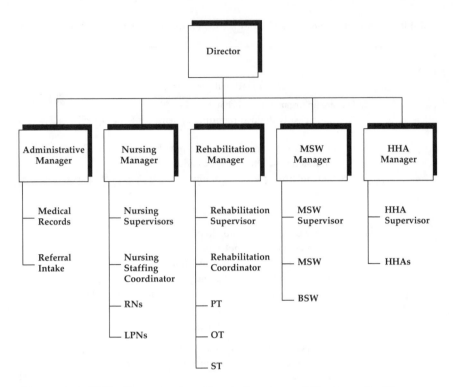

Figure 4–1 1980s Organization Chart. Courtesy of Community Home Health Care, Seattle, Washington.

CHECKPOINT 4–4

Knowing the organizational chart of the employing agency can tell me

a) everything I need to know about the chain of command
b) nothing, because my facility does not have a chart
c) the framework of the reporting relationships of units/departments/or supervisors
d) the committee I should join to discuss delegation

See the end of the chapter for the answers.

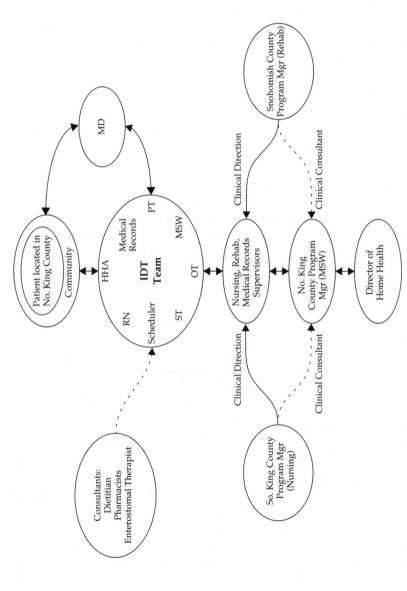

Figure 4–2 1990s Organization Chart. Courtesy of Community Home Health Care, Seattle, Washington.

THE QUALITY PROGRAM

When 56 percent of the hospitals surveyed in 1989 by the Joint Commission on Accreditation of Healthcare Organizations received contingencies for quality assurance activities, Continuous Quality Improvement (CQI) and Total Quality Management (TQM) programs were implemented with great zest (Curtin, 1992). Responding to market changes and increased competition for the patient, more health care agencies shifted their focus to emphasize a service approach. The race was on to improve systems and to streamline the delivery of care in any way possible.

Unfortunately, many nurses report that they have not been included in the loop when it comes to quality improvement programs. They remain ignorant in many cases, not fully understanding and certainly not participating in the new programs that have resulted in many of the changes that directly affect nurses.

Let's briefly review the change in quality focus and see where it has taken us so far. When the JCAHO created their Agenda for Change in the late 1980s, one of their major guiding concepts served to foster the rapid growth in a new idea of quality. Driven by increasing consumer demands to demonstrate results and value for the dollar, the JCAHO stated that "continual improvement in the quality of care should be a priority goal for a health care organization" (1990, p. 2). The opinion was expressed that the assurance of quality was an unrealistic expectation and that a continuing effort to improve quality was more achievable. Greater emphasis was and will continue to be placed on outcomes rather than on the structure or process for attaining those outcomes.

We can all remember the somewhat punitive flavor of the quality assurance program, which seemed to be little more than a search for who was doing something wrong. This search-and-punish approach made staff unwilling to participate in quality programs because they felt they had more than ample opportunity to serve as targets for blame. Replacing this traditional approach with the more positive program of analysis of an entire event, and looking for ways in which to improve the outcome of that event rather than pointing the blame, invites the participation of nurses concerned for the improvement of patient care.

Although all this rationale for the shift in emphasis to results, or outcomes, makes a lot of sense, the point must be made that success for any health care improvement plan will require the involvement and support of all employees, as well as commitment from management. Involvement is a major issue, and nurses will need to seek out that involvement if it is not readily offered. Decisions made that affect the delivery of patient care in an attempt to improve the quality of the outcome must include the nurse executive, stipulates the JCAHO standard. Through this standard, nursing leaders have received the support for integration into health care facilities' administration and now have an opportunity to involve staff nurses in all clinical improvement efforts, including the creation and use of assistive personnel.

CHECKPOINT 4–5

Are the following statements true or false?

____ 1. The emphasis on quality is now on structure and process.

____ 2. CQI stands for continuous quality improvement, a tool used to facilitate the monitoring of outcomes and look for ways to improve them.

____ 3. JCAHO does not support the involvement of nursing in quality improvement efforts.

See the end of the chapter for the answers.

SAFETY IN PRACTICE

We now come to the very significant issue of staffing. In our collective years of nursing experience, we heard more times than we can remember that staffing was "unsafe" or "insufficient" and that the quality of care, not to mention the safety of the patients, was being seriously jeopardized. It is a problem that has plagued nursing since the beginning, when Florence Nightingale realized that one night nurse could take care of four times as many patients if they were all in one room. Nurses have studied, quantified, computerized, centralized, and decentralized the process in an effort to ensure that the staffing levels in any health care setting are safe and adequate. Through nursing shortages and abundance, always driven by the constraints of the budget, we have strived to create workable solutions to the ever-present dilemma.

Solutions to the issue of adequate and safe coverage of nursing personnel include the development of policies that describe the procedure and, in many instances, quantify different levels of care dependent on staff available. In acute care and extended care settings, we have noted policies in place that determine the actions to take for providing Optimum Care, Good Care, and Essential Care. This prioritization of levels of care is one method by which the nursing division plans for variances in staffing and clearly outlines the expectations of performance in a given situation.

Many nursing committees have developed tracking mechanisms, similar to the tools used in a CQI program, to monitor patient acuities and staffing levels, and their relationship to the achievement to various desired outcomes. Nurses may complete "assignment despite objection" forms that record and alert management to staffing concerns.

Because of the high degree of variability of patient needs, minimum standards of staffing from a regulatory standpoint are often difficult to make. California has attempted to revise the regulations of Title 22, which currently sets the minimum standard of one licensed nursing staff member for every two patients in critical care areas. A proposal causing much controversy has been the request for an additional minimum standard in other acute care areas to provide a ratio of one RN for every eight patients ("Response to Staffing," 1992). Such minimum standards take away the flexibility of both the employer and the nurse, argue many administrators, and the controversy continues.

In addition to the fundamental issue of how many staff, there is the very real question of what *kind* of staff should be utilized to provide the best care. For many of the reasons we have discussed elsewhere, new assistive personnel are being added to the team at a rapid rate. "As of March, 1993, the ANA had compiled a listing of approximately 23 health care titles for persons who provide care and are not licensed. . . . Additionally, there are approximately 49 new titles of persons recognized, but not licensed under state statutes" (Carson and Moss, 1993, p. 2).

The list is extensive, including assistants many of us have never heard of but may at some time be delegating care to in the future. Med technicians, hospice aides, orthopedic physician assistants, psychiatric technicians, geriatric assistants, personal care aides, and many more have joined the ranks of assistive personnel. As these new positions are created and utilized in the work setting, it is imperative that RNs be involved in determining how they are trained and supervised. The employer who would take the RN out of this loop of the decision process is not following regulations that provide the RN with the ultimate decision regarding the appropriateness of delegation.

CHECKPOINT 4–6

1. Standards of staffing:
   a) are difficult to establish due to the variability of patient needs
   b) may limit the flexibility of the employer and the health care provider
   c) have been set in California to address the critical care areas
   d) all of the above

2. New positions for health care assistants:
   a) have increased significantly during recent years
   b) are decreasing as employers recognize that an all-RN staff is the best
   c) must be delegated to by the RN if the employer says so
   d) none of the above

See the end of the chapter for the answers.

EDUCATIONAL RESOURCES

We have repeatedly noted that the RN is accountable for ensuring the competency of the individual to whom he or she delegates any nursing task. In order to fulfill that responsibility, certain factors must be in place. Employers who do not provide for the adequate screening and orientation of employees are placing themselves and their patients at risk. RNs need to assess the facility for such tools as skills checklists, performance-based job descriptions, periodic update and renewal of specific skills, and provision of continuing education. Accrediting agencies (JCAHO, the American Osteopathic Association, etc.) and regulatory bodies (the state department of health) have various requirements for the provision of the assurance of competency of employees.

Once hired, personnel need to be oriented, with a plan for evaluating their performance and skill levels at periodic intervals. The RN must make certain this process is in place in order to be able to provide the supervision that is required of the delegate. What department is responsible for overseeing the orientation process? Are nurses involved in precepting or mentoring? This is a time-consuming responsibility, and not one that nurses have traditionally been trained in, so the availability of preceptorship training is valuable and demonstrates the importance the agency places on the program. New employees who are expected to perform on the day of hire and are not partnered with anyone are placing everyone at risk.

SUMMARY

We have taken a detailed look at how to assess the organization in which you work in terms of its "delegation-friendliness." Certain factors, such as policies that define reporting relationships and staffing levels, and measures taken to validate the competency of the employee, are critical to the success of the RN in practicing delegation. Also critical to the success of the delegator is his or her level of involvement in the organization. Participation on committees, task forces, and so forth, whether union or not, is an important component of professional control over changes in patient care.

Simply understanding why the organization is managed the way it is and why decisions are made is not enough. The RN has a real opportunity to shape practice in the working environment by being actively involved in assessing, planning, and evaluating the decisions made regarding the delivery of patient care. Support for this involvement comes from the regulating and accrediting bodies, as well as from the progressive movement of quality improvement programs. Missions and values are the driving forces of the assessment, and congruency with the professional values of the practicing RN will assist in the attainment of a satisfying partnership from which the patient benefits.

ANSWERS TO CHECKPOINTS

4–1.
   1. false
   2. false
   3. true

4. false
5. false

4–2.
1. d
2. c
3. d

4–3. c

4–4. c

4–5.
1. false
2. true
3. false

4–6.
1. d
2. a

REFERENCES

Carson, W., and R. Moss. 1993. The Oklahoma Board of Nursing v. St. John Medical Center. The American Nurses Association, memo, July 30, p. 2.

Christy, T. 1984. Portrait of a leader: Lillian Wald. Pages from nursing history. *American Journal of Nursing:* 84–88.

Community Home Health Care mission statement. 1993. Seattle, Washington.

Curtin, L. 1992. Of commissions, omissions, and just plain missions. *Nursing Management* 23: 7–8.

Joint Commission on Accreditation of Healthcare Organizations. 1990. The Joint Commission's agenda for change. Oakbrook Terrace, Ill.: JCAHO, p. 2.

O'Grady, T. 1992. Of rabbits and turtles: A time of change for unions. *Nursing Economics* 10, no. 3: 177–182.

Response to staffing. 1992. *California Nurse* (October): 4, 12.

Starr, P. 1982. *The social transformation of American medicine.* New York: Basic Books.

St. Mary Medical Center mission statement. 1993. Walla Walla, Washington.

Toffler. A. 1990. *Powershift.* New York: Bantam Books.

Uustal, D. 1985. *Values and ethics in nursing: From theory to practice.* Greenwich, R.I.: Educational Resources in Nursing and Holistic Health.

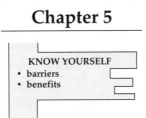

Chapter 5

KNOW YOURSELF
* barriers
* benefits

Know Yourself: What Personal Barriers Must I Overcome To Realize the Benefits of Effective Delegation?

Ruth I. Hansten and Marilynn J. Washburn

"Do I dare ask June to take care of that complaining patient when she has so much seniority here? Besides, if I don't do the care myself, I'm sure I'll forget how to be technically proficient! How can I remain a *real nurse* and still supervise some of the care?"

Delegation in a clinical setting is essentially a complex interaction of very personal relationships. Your personal relationship and communication with your supervisor, your coworkers, and those you supervise are absolutely fundamental to provide safe and effective care for those you serve. But your relationship with yourself is the cornerstone of the process. Your own thought processes and the words you say to yourself, your "self-talk," determine your ability to perform the delegation process. The thoughts expressed above show that this supervisor or charge nurse will certainly not feel confident to assign June part of the care of that patient or client.

Hundreds of nurses throughout the United States have expressed their concerns about the delegation process and their ability to supervise other personnel. Their anxieties are a product of several realities: the remarkable interpersonal nature of and risks inherent in the delegation process, unique personal barriers known to each individual, and lack of experience or education regarding delegation in the clinical arena.

Often compounding the personal barriers surrounding the delegation process is the fact that many nurses first recognize the need to delegate in response to comprehensive changes in their organization. They may first discover that they need to learn to delegate when they are told that they will be working in new care delivery systems, often with unlicensed assistive personnel. The whole idea of delegation then becomes tainted with the anger and fear surrounding the changes they are experiencing.

CHECKPOINT 5–1

We've now established that knowing oneself more intimately, understanding and acknowledging one's barriers and strengths in the delegation process, will help each nurse work more effectively with assistive personnel. The bonus for each nurse? A better work life! Safe care for patients! Feeling more "in control."

1. What's in it for me? Why do I care about how I feel about the delegation process?
   a) I need to understand myself to be able to interact appropriately with those I supervise.
   b) Dwelling on my negative emotions and feelings is a great way to avoid learning about this topic altogether.
   c) If I can work more effectively with others, I'll feel better about work and about myself, and care for my clients will be improved.
   d) I don't care: all this assistive personnel junk is a plot to get rid of nurses and give terrible care.

See the end of the chapter for the answers.

EXPLORING BARRIERS

It's not uncommon for us to teach delegation skills to nurses throughout the country and find at the end of the workshop that several people have not absorbed a word of what was said. We've discovered that these folks are so caught up in their negative feelings about the changes occurring in their organization that they've been unable to listen. We recommend that readers who are feeling negative about the whole issue or are being *required* against their will to read this book spend some time considering their personal barriers to delegation in some detail.

When you think of delegating to other health care workers, what feelings/thoughts enter your mind? Write them down now as you reflect.

_____

_____

_____

_____

_____

_____

Here are a few that have been shared with us:

- fear
- anger
- loss of trust in management
- loss of control
- loss of achievement
- concern about quality
- burnout
- stress
- feeling overwhelmed
- lack of enjoyment in work
- decreased job satisfaction
- confusion
- feeling betrayed
- feeling abandoned
- excitement
- ambivalence
- apathy
- loss of security

If you've been delegating to unlicensed health care workers for some time and this is not a new experience for you, recall your first emotions and concerns when you first began to try to tell someone else what to do and actually supervised their work. Do any of the above feelings and thoughts apply to you at that stage?

The same emotions are repeated throughout the United States and internationally, as we travel and discuss delegation with nurses. We've determined that many of these feelings are related to a nurse's individual responses to the changes in his or her work life and the method by which the change took place. In organizations where changes in care delivery systems and use of assistive personnel were implemented with a larger proportion of employee involvement and participation, and in which staff were educated and understood the rationale for the change, the intensity of negative emotions was apparent to a lesser degree. In organizations in which economics demanded immediate action, or in which the culture did not support a measured and educational approach, so that staff participation in developing the roles of the assistive personnel was discouraged, anger, fear, and distrust were expressed vehemently. In multiple organizations, the addition of new, unlicensed workers was accompanied by layoffs of nursing personnel. When this occurred, the rage and pain were often nearly debilitating. Whether the change in your facility was planned well or not, and whether you are furious or merely uncomfortable, the fact remains that you must find a method of dealing with your emotions to be able to move on and provide effective patient care. (For those of you still contemplating a change in care delivery systems with the addition of new supervisory roles for RNs, please see our discussion of the process in *The Nurse Manager's Answer Book,* Chapter 13.)

Whether you have experienced a change in your work life or system of care delivery, or whether you've always delegated to other health care workers, the negative emotions can be a huge stumbling block to effective supervision. Whether anger or apathy, these emotions may override your best intentions to communicate clearly when giving an assignment to the patient care associate who just replaced your best friend who was part of the first round of layoffs.

Nurses often discuss the grief process in their daily work. In home health, acute care hospitals, or long-term care, the stages of the grief process being experienced by clients or their families provide a model to use in our interventions. Just as we may recognize Mr. Brown's anger as a part of the grief process as he watches his wife die, rather than personalizing the anger that was directed at the nursing staff, we must step back and superimpose the grief process model on our personal or unit care plan for knowing ourselves and our emotional barriers.

Our first step to overcoming our emotional barriers is complete: that of naming our emotions. Identifying our emotions allows us to use the only completely replenishable resource, our brains, to harness our emotional energy. Let's go through the steps of the grief process and determine how we can use our energy in a productive manner for our own self-care.

Denial

The first step of the grief process itself is denial.

Denial is a great emotion. It allows us some time to garner our internal fortitude and get ready to deal with the onslaught that's just around the corner. We haven't fully realized the impact yet, but soon we'll be ready. The negative, destructive side of denial is acted out by people who refuse to pull their heads out of the sand. Having one's vision blinded will not allow one to react appropriately, learn the necessary skills, and adapt to the changes.

This stage of the grief process is often exemplified by seminar participants who write on their evaluations, "I refuse to delegate. I'm finding a job where I don't have to delegate." Amusingly enough, it seems that these nurses have been unable to hear that they were already delegating in their present roles. As professional nurses, they were supervising a secretary, new personnel, perhaps students. The only place we could determine would be an appropriate setting for someone who refuses to delegate would be private nursing practice in a sand dune in the Sahara Desert—a perfect place for placing one's head in the sand, so this would be a fitting alternative work assignment!

For those who remain in the denial stage, it may be helpful for coworkers to point out the studies that show positive outcomes for nurses delegating some of the care. (See the end of this chapter.) It may also be appropriate to note that the nurse practice acts, the National Council of State Boards, and even the Code for Nurses discuss delegation as a part of nursing practice.

For example, the American Nursing Association Code for Nurses states,

> The nurse exercises informed judgment and uses individual competence and qualifications as criteria in seeking consultation, accepting responsibilities, and delegating nursing activities to others. . . . The nurse must assess individual competency in assigning selected components of nursing care to other nursing service personnel. The nurse should not delegate to any member of the nursing team a function for which that person is not prepared or qualified (American Nurses Association, [1976], 1985, p. 1).

Since this code was established in 1976 and reaffirmed in 1985, apparently a few nurses have been using this code to guide them in delegating for the last several decades!

Nurse practice statutes and rules, as noted in Chapter 3, often specify that delegation is a part of nursing practice. The Massachusetts Board of Registration in Nursing states that the functions of an RN include delegating:

> A registered nurse, within the parameters of her/his generic and continuing education and experience, may delegate nursing activities to other registered nurses and/or health care personnel, provided that the delegating registered nurse shall bear full and ultimate responsibility for: 1) making an appropriate assignment 2) properly and adequately teaching, directing and supervising the delegate and 3) the outcomes of that delegation (244CMR: 3.02, in Massachusetts Nurses Association, 1992, p. 7–8).

Oregon Administrative Rules (1990, Chapter 678, Section 851-45-011) list specific standards for registered nurse teaching and delegation to unlicensed persons. Many states, such as Washington, include delegation as a part of the definition of nursing: "The practice of nursing means. . . 1) observation, assessment, diagnosis, care or counsel, and health teaching of the ill, injured or infirm, or in the maintenance of health or prevention of illness of others. . . 3) The administration, supervision, delegation, and evaluation of nursing practice" (Revised Code of Washington, 1993, Chapter 18.88.030). It's hard for even the most recalcitrant person in denial to avoid the fact that delegation is a part of nursing practice by law!

As we further explore the stages of the grief process, we may also consider the individual's usual response to change. In the Pacific Northwest, the coming of the winter is often heralded by the first storm from the Pacific Ocean. Some people enjoy the hallmark event of visiting these rocky beaches when the storm is far off. One nurse may see the storm clouds approaching and leave. Others may decide to stay on the beach, but no matter how hard the winds and waves roar and crash, they are determined to dig in their heels and stay in their accustomed spot. When the first waves pound the shore, these nurses are flung onto the barnacle-encrusted boulders, and emerge between waves, bruised and bleeding. Others, seeing the storm clouds and waves on the horizon, may gauge the waves' rhythm and the wind's velocity and dive right in! These nurses body surf to the shore, gently gliding to the ground at the ebb of the wave. Consider yourself: Are you the nurse in denial who is continually bruised and broken by changes, the nurse who tries to dig in and keep your heels in one place while sands shift around you? Or are you one of the nurses who sees the turbulence coming, judges the best method of adjusting, and survives the storm? You may never be able to love or to welcome change, but do realize it is a fact of life. *Change can't be controlled, but your response to it can be.*

Anger

Anger is a great emotion. It is a very powerful, normal part of the grief process. It is *not* wrong to be angry, but it is maladaptive and downright destructive for us to use our anger against each other or ourselves. Some of us move into anger early on in the process of care delivery changes and remain in this stage for lengthy periods of time. Nurses aren't used to dealing with their anger effectively. Instead we often try to deny it because we don't believe it's *nice* to be angry. We say instead that we are "upset" or "burned out" or "worried about patient care."

One of the operational definitions of anger is "unmet expectations." If you or someone you know is angry, which expectation has been left unmet?

Were you told that the *only* way to be a "real nurse" was to do *all the care* yourself? Was it your school of nursing's expectation that their graduates would always be nurses doing "total patient care"? Those expectations caused a fair amount of frustration and job dissatisfaction with new graduates who worked in long-term care, rural hospitals, and home health, where supervising others has always been a standard piece of the job description.

Were you expecting that your type of practice wouldn't be altered? Although you've known health care reform was needed for years, did you hope you wouldn't be affected? We often meet nurses who have avoided (denial again?) any current literature as they focused only on their clinical area and improving their expertise. Sound advice for producing expert clinicians, but unfortunate as a set-up for feeling anger when hit with changes in work life. Were you hoping that your administrative people would have asked for more input before implementing a new care delivery system? Would you like to have been involved? Valid expectations, certainly, but often the people in the administrative posts are reacting to rapid change while trying to preserve their own jobs. Perhaps they didn't have time, or didn't know how, or didn't think staff wanted to be involved.

Did you think there was a nurse shortage when you went to school, and did you think you'd chosen a profession that would always afford you the job security you'd wanted? This is another valid reason to be angry, but when one realizes that 2,389 people per day were laid off in other areas of the nation's business in 1993 (Richman, 1993), one begins to think more about how to continue to be marketable in one's skills.

If you've been angry or even depressed, which expectations seem to be the foundation of your anger? Determine the expectations and write them down now.

_____

_____

_____

Think about it: Are my expectations still reasonable? Where did these expectations come from?

_____

_____

_____

All of the above are commonly expressed "unmet expectations." Remember, anger is normal. All of that great energy must not be wasted, though. Be angry, express it, and then use it to make things work out better for yourselves and your patients.

Be aware of where your anger is percolating! Is the energy going home with you and being discharged at your family? Are you finding yourself on a "short fuse" with your coworkers? (Be aware particularly of negative emotions coming forward to those who replaced your friends, if you've had that experience. They did not ask to replace your friend; they came looking for a job to support themselves also.) Or have you noticed that you find less joy in the things you used to like about your job? This may be the burnout that occurs when people turn their anger inward. Serious depression may ensue. Remember, express the anger and then get on with it! How can you best adjust, learn, cope? How can you make certain the care that is given works the best for the patients and other consumers? Use your energy to be involved in creating the best methods of supervising the added personnel.

Bargaining

"Today I don't have time to teach Helen to do the I and O's. I'll do it myself. But tomorrow, I'm sure I can find the time to assign it properly."

Bargaining, like denial, buys some time for the individual to adjust. We may bargain with ourselves, with other staff, with management. However, after the first few bargains, nurses may find themselves back into the maladaptive sides of denial and anger. Usually, our bargains don't work so well for our own adjustment. We often hear of nurses who stay at work overtime repeatedly because they are in the bargaining stage of the grief process. They don't ever find the time to do the supervision part of their jobs properly.

Another common bargaining statement goes something like this: "Well, I'll see how this delegation and care partners idea works out in the next month. And if I don't see major improvements in quality of patient care, I'll find another place to work." This nurse is slipping into the "denial" stage once again.

Bargaining, like all other stages, is normal. It allows for adjustment and adaptation as nurses begin to try out their new skills. But if it continues, it will strangle the bargainer's ability to delegate safely and effectively.

As we return to our first example above, the bargainer avoids teaching the assistive person how to do a routine task because it will take too much time, but may be on overtime doing the I and O's herself. She may have the added satisfaction of seeing every drop of urine herself, thus meeting her own (and perhaps her nursing instructor's) expectations. However, the delegate (Helen) does not fulfill her own expectations of her role. There will be anger from Helen at some point, as well as anger from the exhausted RN. The maxim applies here that if you give a person a fish, you feed him for a day, but if you teach a person to fish, you feed him for a lifetime. Encouraging personal growth is one of the foundations for personal empowerment.

So bargain if you must. But force yourself to continue to expand into your role as a supervisor. Both you and your delegates have the opportunity to become empowered.

Depression

Here's where anger rears its flaming head again. That anger that wasn't expressed, that energy that wasn't channeled to help you and those you serve, is revisiting itself on your life. Depression is anger turned inward. When you are depressed, all problems that would normally be a part of your day now seem insurmountable mountains. You don't even go to the beach to see the waves; you are at home trying to get yourself out of bed and off to work.

We are convinced, as we work with nurses everywhere, that burnout as experienced within our profession is a by-product of the difficulty we have experienced collectively in dealing with anger. It's okay to be angry. It's normal. But determine which expectation you had that wasn't met. Decide whether that expectation is still operational and realistic. If you decide that it is not, your anger won't be as acute. If it is, then use the energy to quit whining and be involved in sculpting what you want out of the future.

We aren't psychologists. If you find yourself to be clinically depressed and unable to function normally, or if you know someone who is, urge him or her to contact a psychology professional for help. But if you have a mild depression related to work issues, we are certain you'll feel better if you take just one step to *do* something to adjust to the changes. We think reading this book and working out the exercises may be one of those action items that will help. Follow up with committee work or a discussion with your boss or your coworkers about what things are bugging you and what you think can be done about it. *But whatever you do, GET INVOLVED!* It's a sure cure, and far less expensive than antidepressant medication.

Acceptance

The last stage of the grief process is acceptance. This term needs to be clarified a bit since often people believe that accepting the whole idea of change within their organization or accepting the role of supervisor within their jobs means a real leap of faith. Some may shout, "Yes, Yes, Alleluia, I have seen the light! Let me work alone with a hospital full of patients and be the only licensed person on duty! Let me be the only public health RN in our town! Let me be the only RN in our long-term care facility!"

This idea of "life-altering" acceptance is not realistic. However, it is possible for nurses to overcome their barriers to delegation and to actually enjoy working with a group of people to achieve their goals. Many tell us they find more job satisfaction and many other benefits. But for now, recognize that acceptance is a gradual process. One nurse may first accept that yes, change is needed. Some nurses go back and forth through the stages of the grief process, as is normal in other grief situations. One nurse may then accept that it probably *is* more cost-effective to deliver care with assistive personnel. Others may first accept that they may be able to master the process and feel safer and more "in control." All of these incremental steps in acceptance will lead the nurse to effective delegation.

For those readers who are still having difficulty with the idea of this process and who are still in a former stage of the grief process, the most basic acceptance is this:

It is possible to learn to delegate effectively and deliver safe, effective nursing care.

We've considered the emotions that are often present when nurses first begin to delegate. Although some of these emotions depend on the manner in which care delivery systems changes are introduced, there is a great similarity of emotions expressed across the country, ranging from excitement to anger to apathy. Using the grief process and the concept of change as a model, we've asked you to identify your own emotions and the stage of the grief process. We've explored the positive and negative sequelae of the stages and the emotions and encouraged you to:

1. Use your brain power to harness and identify your own emotions.
2. Determine the stage you or your coworkers are experiencing.
3. If you feel angry, decide which expectation you've had that hasn't been met.
4. Consider whether your expectation is still realistic.
5. Use your emotional energy for *action:* by reading this book, by using the skills, by being a part of task forces or discussion groups.

CHECKPOINT 5–2

Which stage of the grief process is being experienced by the following nurses?

1. Nurse Powell sits reading the paper with her back turned from the manager as the manager tries to discuss the rationale for the changes in the care delivery system.

2. John, the charge nurse, decides to take on a larger patient assignment today because he doesn't think the other nurses have the time to supervise the nursing assistants.

3. Pat has agreed to be on the task force for clarifying the expectations of each of the new roles. Pat has seen other roles being used in various ways in other health departments in other cities where she's been employed.

4. Sharon, a new graduate, has been calling in ill frequently the last two months. She says she's having trouble getting out of bed at 10 PM and feels overwhelmed by the supervisory role she must play with the assistive personnel at the Rehab Center.

5. Tom turned in his resignation today. He said he wanted to find a job where nurses were allowed to practice "professional nursing."

See the end of the chapter for the answers.

OTHER BARRIERS

Personal feelings about implementing a new system of care or about the changes in health care themselves are often barriers to effective clinical delegation. But many other personal barriers may be present within each nurse. Some of these may be related to past experiences, whether from undergraduate education, past experiences or training, or clinical realities nurses have faced during their career. Let's examine these and determine which may be operational in your own life.

Take the self-assessment quiz in Exhibit 5–1 to determine how much these barriers challenge you in implementing the clinical delegation process.

Exhibit 5–1   Delegation Self-Assessment

Answer the following with Strongly Agree, Agree, Unsure, Disagree, or Strongly Disagree.

____ 1. I hate risk: I don't think risk of any kind should be present in health care delivery.

____ 2. It's very difficult for me to trust the people I work with. How can I be sure they'll do what I want them to?

____ 3. Letting go of the tasks I like to do is impossible for me. I get all my positive feedback from doing my clinical tasks exceptionally well.

____ 4. There's so little I can control about my daily work that I find it very difficult to lose the control I have by doing it all myself. How can I control others enough to be certain everything is done my way?

____ 5. I'm finding that overcoming my old habits of "doing it all myself" is more difficult than giving up (choose one) cigarettes, or chocolate, or fine wine. Giving up things that are comfortable for me and are a part of my daily life is not my cup of tea.

____ 6. I feel very little achievement when someone else does the nuts and bolts of the care. I want to do that myself so I can feel the satisfaction of crossing tasks off my list.

____ 7. If everyone else does the tasks on the care plan, I'm confused about what's left for me to do.

____ 8. When people tell me they have time to help me, it's difficult for me to tell them what they could do to help. I could use some help with organizing my work.

____ 9. I do all the work in my area better than most people. I am an expert clinician and I would hate for the clients to receive an "inferior" product if I am not the person actually performing that care.

____ 10. I really hate to make people mad when I assign them work. I'd rather do it myself than give out a bad assignment.

____ 11. There are few people that work as hard as I do. I often find myself with the most challenging assignments. I rarely ask for help. Often, I'm behind doing my charting after the shift is over while the "slackers" go out for pizza.

____ 12. I am uncertain about what can be delegated to the personnel in our department. The roles are unclear and I'm not comfortable with the state regulations and rules.

____ 13. I hate to even think about delegating care to anyone else!

____ 14. If I don't do the tasks I'm used to doing, I wonder if I will still be a *real nurse*? I've worked too hard to become a clinical "has-been."

____ 15. I've never seen or worked with anyone who is a good delegator. I wouldn't know what it's like.

Now look at the items with which you agreed or strongly agreed. These will most likely be your highest barriers. Those that are marked "unsure" may also crop up as problems for you in learning and implementing clinical delegation skills.

Let's dissect each of these in more detail.

Barrier 1: Risk Aversion

We certainly aren't advocating that you take risks with your patients' lives! However, when we delegate to others, there is always some risk. You cannot absolutely guarantee that the delegate will not err (just as you may err yourself) or that all will be completed exactly the same way you'd prefer. Following the delegation process correctly will minimize the negative aspects of the inherent risk. Think about the risk involved in *not* having assistive personnel available to help you do the work. There's some risk there as well.

Barrier 2: Being Able To Trust Others

We aren't encouraging you in any way to trust implicitly all the people with whom you work or even those within your personal life. It doesn't make sense, and this kind of blind, trusting approach is the same that allows charlatans and con artists to take advantage of the elderly, for example. However, in delegating aspects of care to others, some degree of trust must develop. Delegates must trust that you'll be there to help with problems. You must be able to trust delegates to do what they say they will, and to communicate changes in patient condition.

How does trust develop? In all relationships, trust develops from risking enough to establish the relationship and then by experiencing the objective results of your relationship. If your expectations are fulfilled, you begin to develop an image of that person as one who can be trusted. When one problem occurs in which that trust is violated, it's difficult to regain the same ease of communication and positive relationship. For example, Pat, an LPN (LVN) had been working with Jo, an RN, for several weeks, and during that time, Jo had always telephoned physicians promptly for changes in orders. This time Pat thought that Mrs. Smith's condition was worsening quickly and told Jo. Jo, however, did not come to check on the patient promptly and did not call the physician promptly to discuss the changes in condition. Even though Jo may not have considered the changes important enough, the message given to Pat was loud and clear: she didn't think that Pat's input was important. It will take a long time for Jo to regain Pat's trust.

Barrier 3: Letting Go of Some of the Amenities or Technical Tasks

Letting go of those tasks that have been important to you in the past is difficult but necessary for growth to occur. Is it reasonable to expect that our nation is willing to pay, for example, $20 per hour for you, as an RN, to empty foley catheters and trash cans when someone else can be paid $10 per hour to do the same work? In an era of limited resources, yours must be used to the fullest extent. If you aren't doing the professional role of the RN, who is? Occasionally when leading a seminar, a nurse will remark: "But I *like* to do the baths and bed changes! That's why I went into nursing!" If that is true for you, it's time to think about *why* you are in this profession. Is there anything within the *professional* role of the RN that would also give you some satisfaction? For example, if you became an RN because you wanted to help people, or to make a difference in people's lives, then you can certainly do a better job using *all* your skills, beyond the merely technical to the intellectual. (For more information, review Chapter 6, regarding the PTA model.)

Barrier 4: Fear of Loss of Control

Nurses would like to be able to control a lot more about their work. We can't control what kind and acuity of patients are admitted through our emergency departments. We can't control our caseload in home health or the number of Alzheimer patients that become residents at our long-term care facility. At the beginning of our shift, it's difficult to know how our best-laid plans may be upset by the inevitable human factors we may encounter. So we try to control everything we can.

When we delegate care to others, we can't control their every move. No one expects that we will be able to control our coworkers like robots. However, as we now understand the process of delegation more fully, we know that we *can* control how we delegate: how we assess ourselves and our barriers; how we appraise the strengths, weaknesses, motivation, and preferences of our delegates; how we match the task to the delegate; how

we communicate; and how we evaluate and give feedback to those we supervise. There is more control than we expected!

Barrier 5: Overcoming Old Habits

As we've already discussed, the rate of change is increasing at a dizzy-
ing speed. It's probably more difficult to change the way we work than to
change some of our personal habits. We often spend more time at work
than with our families! "Doing it all myself" sometimes seems like the
best way to make certain it is done correctly. But when there isn't enough
of you to go around, when it's impossible for you to "do it all," give yourself a break. Try to use the delegation process. Just as some nurses find it
is easier to give up that piece of cheesecake after lunch little by little, some
nurses find that overcoming the old habits engendered by former care delivery systems may be done in stages. If you decide to "go cold turkey,"
remember to be kind and supportive to yourself and those with whom
you work.

Barrier 6: Needing To Cross Tasks off a List

Some nurses are so task oriented that they rush through their "morning
work" and get all their "work" done by noon. Their work, they announce,
is the bed/bath/assessment ritual on their unit. Changing your to-do list
to include such things as discharge planning and coordinating care for
each patient is less concrete and, to some, less satisfying. If you see this as
one of your barriers, begin new "lists" that focus on processes or outcomes rather than tasks. Include such items as "getting report and giving
feedback to each delegate." Nurses have stated that this strategy has
helped them overcome the nebulous feeling of having achieved very little
each shift. And when clients or patients achieve a goal with your help,
celebrate it! The *outcome* for the patient or family is the most important
achievement of the entire team!

Barrier 7: If I Don't Do What I'm Used To Doing, What's Left for Me To Do?

This barrier is closely related to Barriers 3, 5, and 6. If you've delegated
tasks and can't see the implications of your professional role, we recommend that you read the discussion of the PTA model in Chapter 6. Also,

think about those things that you've wanted to complete but have been unable to because you've had to deal with so many details of care before. (Patient education? Emotional support? Coordination of all health care disciplines? Family conferences? Discharge planning? Communication with other professionals?)

Barrier 8: Needing Help with Organization of Work

We know you recognize the phenomenon: a nurse who is excellent at performing discrete tasks or processes, but has difficulty seeing the forest for the trees. He or she may be unable to break down the overall work to be done into manageable pieces. Learning to be more "organized" is difficult; however, we've seen some successes. If this is a barrier for you, talk to the nurses you find to be the most organized. Ask them to show you how they divide up their work. Sometimes one worksheet or method of organizing will work better for one nurse than another. Keep asking until you find one that makes sense to you. Often a visit with your manager or clinical instructor will be useful. He or she may even authorize some time to shadow or work with someone who is efficient in delivering care.

Barrier 9: The Supernurse Syndrome

It's great to know you are out there caring for us and our families! Being an expert in your area and being extremely conscientious about your work are certainly positive qualities. However, it is tough for a Supernurse to let others grow in their skills. After all, those served may not receive the highest quality of care while others are developing their skills. Unfortunately, Supernurses cannot be everywhere at all times, particularly in this environment of cost containment. Supernurses who find themselves unable to delegate will also become overwhelmed and burned out as they try to "do it all." If you are a Supernurse, find some examples of care given by others that is satisfactory, maybe even good. Keep looking for those examples so that you will feel less guilty about the care you weren't able to deliver alone.

Barrier 10: Wanting To Be Liked

Who will be happy to take the assignment of the abusive patient who is throwing stool and is having diarrhea and needs constant pericare?

Which nurse wants to manage the case of the patient with multiple personalities who likes to talk about child abuse exploits? If you are the person in charge of making those types of assignments, you wonder what will happen if you assign your best friend to care for these challenging patients. What will he or she slip into your coffee at the next coffee break? Will anyone ever ask you to go out for social time after work?

One of the most difficult aspects of being in a supervisory position is the struggle over the question: Is it more important to be liked or to be respected? You, through your nurse practice act and by virtue of your job description, must take a leadership role. Would you rather "like" your supervisors and leaders or *respect* their decisions and leadership abilities? Think about how others earn your respect. Respect is generally earned through performing supervisory duties faithfully. You have been entrusted to ensure that patient/client/resident care is the highest quality possible. Making the best assignment for the "difficult" patient should not be based on who will be the most angry and vengeful. It should be based on the best match of assignment and delegate.

Barrier 11: The Supermartyr Syndrome

We've started a new group, Supermartyr Nurses Anonymous. It's a 12-step program, and the first step is to announce, "Hi, my name is Mary, and I'm a Supermartyr nurse!" Identifying the problem yourself is the first step. However, ask any of your coworkers; they already know who the Supermartyrs are. (Some of them may have used your need to be needed and indispensable by giving you some extra work!) Ask your coworkers to help you limit yourself to doing what is reasonable and what is performed by others with your job description. You must take care of yourself so that you can take care of others. (For additional information, see *The Nurse Manager's Answer Book*, Chapter 16, on codependency.)

Barrier 12: Uncertain about Rules, Regulations

Nurses who don't want to delegate may be those who are still unsure about what is included in their roles and job descriptions. They may also worry about "putting my license on the line!" when working with unlicensed caregivers. There are two main strategies for dealing with this barrier.

First, get some education. After you've read the information in this book, call your state board and get a copy of your nurse practice act. Ask questions of the board staff. Ask your facility to have a speaker from the state come and discuss your concerns.

Second, clarify roles within your organization. Ask to have a staff meeting to clarify who is supposed to be doing what. Find out what the assistive personnel may expect of you as well. What do they think their roles are? Where are you all in agreement? Where is there confusion? This is one of the most essential points for overcoming barriers to delegation. *Clarify expectations.* This discussion often goes beyond who should do what task and ends up discussing such things as being called by name, being asked with a please and a thank you, and who really should answer the phone or call lights or talk with physicians or other professionals.

As you clarify roles, you may also find you need to develop a skills or evaluation checklist for each role. We've seen many of these used to assist in overcoming the barrier of confusion about roles.

Barrier 13: Denial

Some of you may not even want to think about delegation! If this is the case for you, or for some of your coworkers, it will be pretty difficult for you to learn how to supervise effectively. We suggest that you are remaining in the denial stage of the grief process. Review the information earlier in this chapter and continue to read on as we evaluate the potential benefits you may reap as you learn how to delegate effectively.

Barrier 14: Am I Still a Real Nurse when I Delegate?

Many nurses continue to harbor this fear even as they continue to do an expert job of delegation and supervising others. Since we have experienced this fear ourselves as we entered supervisory, management, and executive roles, we have struggled with the uncertainty and concerns about remaining "clinically expert."

The first step in overcoming this barrier is to consider why you went into nursing at all. When we ask this question, we get a wide range of answers. Think now about why you decided to be a nurse.

My reason for becoming a nurse was _____

_____

Is this still your reason for being a nurse? Why do you do your job?

_____

Now define for yourself what nursing is _____

_____

Can you still fulfill your definition of nursing, and the reason you went into nursing, if you ask someone else to do some of the tasks?

For example, if you went into nursing to make a difference in other people's lives, and to you nursing is a profession that uses the nursing process (assessment, nursing diagnosis, planning, intervening, and evaluating) in a holistic manner with patients, families, and social systems to aid the individual and his or her significant others to move toward their own definitions of health or wellness, then certainly you can use the help of others in performing your duties. We as nurses have done that since the days of Florence Nightingale.

If you still think nursing is only doing the tasks, it's time to think about what else may satisfy you within your new or emerging role. If you must still perform all the care to feel fulfilled, consider *why* you are doing your job. You won't feel fulfilled from the tasks that you do but from *why* you perform your professional role.

Barrier 15: No Role Models

As we ask groups of nurses how many of them have had excellent role models in the delegation or supervisory process, very few have acknowledged delegation mentors. Perhaps this is because nurses weren't looking for this skill in others when it seemed less important. Perhaps this is because nurses determined that other nurses were highly organized, or efficient and effective, or just that things always went well, but didn't connect clinical delegation skills with the end-product: better patient care.

If you don't have a role model, never fear! You will have all the information you'll need to be successful.

CHECKPOINT 5-3: ASSESSING STRENGTHS

We've discussed most of the potential obstructions to delegation and have focused on personal barriers. Look at Exhibit 5-2 and determine your most sterling qualities. These strengths will give you the needed boost to expanding your delegation skills and bridging your barriers.

DETERMINING THE POTENTIAL BENEFITS

Each nurse may have a barrier or two to conquer, and all have multiple strengths they can use to overcome those barriers. Think about how we evaluate the problems or needs of our clients and families. We identify their strengths for coping and use them in our plan of care. Often the plan of care includes education and practicing new skills. That's our plan for you as you learn (or refresh your memory) about the process of clinical delegation.

In order to mobilize the energy to leap over these barriers, nurses need to visualize what's waiting on the other side of the wall. What outcomes can be expected?

Exhibit 5-2 Assessing Strengths

___ I understand my job description as well as the roles of those who assist me.
___ I have studied the state nurse practice act and feel certain about its regulations.
___ I am highly organized in doing my work.
___ I am ready to overcome some old habits and learn some new ways of working.
___ I look at nursing with a broader perspective than "tasks."
___ I am willing to take some careful, calculated risks and slowly gain trust by supervising the assistive personnel.
___ I am cognizant of my own strengths and weaknesses, and I am asking for feedback from my coworkers about my "Supernurse" or "Supermartyr" tendencies.
___ I have delegated before, and it has been a great learning experience for me.
___ I am focusing more on being worthy of my coworkers' respect than on being liked by everyone.
___ I have learned from some excellent role models, or I can be a role model myself because I am already expert at this skill.
___ I am willing to learn!

If you are able to overcome your barriers or at least prevent them from being a stumbling block on a daily basis, and if you become an expert at delegating and supervising others, what will the potential benefits be?

_____

_____

_____

As we began to educate nurses about delegation, we completed informal qualitative research with nurses from all areas of care delivery who had been delegating to assistive personnel for some time. We asked them what benefits had been realized from learning to delegate well. They told us the following had occurred:

- More time for myself (breaks, lunches)
- Personal growth
- Empowerment and growth of the assistive personnel
- Making better use of my brain power and assessment skills
- More time for professional nursing (educating patients, emotional support, coordination of care, planning, communication with other professionals and family, discharge planning)
- Less stressed out with "doing it all"
- More sense of team and support of each other
- Collegiality
- Someone to help gather data, answer lights
- Better job satisfaction

Since nurse researchers have increased their emphasis on emerging care delivery systems, some data are now available. For example, Blegen et al. (1992) at the University of Iowa began a study through the *American Journal of Nursing* in April 1991, asking nurses, "Who Helps You With Your Work?" The study indicated that "nurses who reported delegating the routine aspects of patient care and those who planned by delegating most of the care were more satisfied with their jobs. . . than those who did all the care themselves" (Blegen et al., 1992, p. 28).

Another study published in the *Journal of Nursing Administration* in March 1993 showed an improvement in patient satisfaction after assistive personnel were introduced (Neidlinger et al., 1993). In the same journal, Lengacher and Mabe (1993) reviewed several models of nurse extender use and found differences in each. In a model in which RNs supervised nursing assistants, the following outcomes were discovered: "increased staff satisfaction, patient satisfaction, and unit pride, a visible improvement in the work environment, increased nurse-patient contact, reduced waste of supplies, and increased documentation in the patient record. Staff members believed that they were more efficient and worked less overtime, and patients and physicians were more satisfied" (Lengacher and Mabe, 1993, p. 17).

We have personally worked with organizations who have implemented new care delivery systems or have merely improved the delegation skills of their RNs, and they have found the following benefits:

- Patients are happier when they don't have to "bother" the RN for minor requests and when they know that someone is available to answer their call lights (acute and long-term care), resulting in improved patient satisfaction surveys.
- Families are beginning to recognize the impact of professional nursing practice on their family member who is a resident in long-term care (or any area).
- Organizations remain solvent financially from fiscally responsible staffing.
- Physician and staff satisfaction improves as nurses are able to multiply their effectiveness and improve their communications with each other, and are helped with tasks, as evidenced by positive responses on nurse and physician satisfaction surveys.
- Nurses with physical disabilities are able to continue to be clinically involved in a supervisory capacity.
- Nurses are beginning to understand the full scope of their professional responsibilities and implementing their role, resulting in more frequent, in-depth planning of care, evaluation of interventions, and practical, appropriate care pathways/plans (all areas).
- Better discharge planning (acute, long-term, and community health care) occurs, resulting in decreased lengths of stay, fewer readmissions, and more effective and efficient use of resources.
- There is better communication between health care disciplines (since RNs have time to coordinate care), and care planning is individualized and meaningful since all members of the team gather and share data, resulting in appropriate use of other disciplines' talents, streamlined institutionalized and home care, and fewer errors.

- Charting reflects the patient status at more frequent intervals since more people are involved.
- Better patient outcomes are accomplished: achievement of the individualized outcomes the patient and team have agreed upon as goals at the beginning of their relationship.

Whether the potential bonuses materialize in your work area will be determined, in large degree, by the energy you put into delegating effectively and making the system work the best for you and your patients.

CHECKPOINT 5–4

This section has allowed nurses to evaluate themselves as an integral part of the delegation process. You have determined:

1. emotional barriers related to a change in care delivery system
2. other barriers to delegation
3. your strengths related to your ability to delegate effectively
4. potential benefits to overcoming the barriers

Have you determined how to deal with your emotional barriers and those of your coworkers? Have you chosen strategies to overcome your barriers to delegation, using your strengths to overcome the obstacles? Keep visualizing the potential benefits for you and for your patients. After all, the *real* bottom line is delivering quality care for those we serve, achieving the *outcomes* we've planned together.

ANSWERS TO CHECKPOINTS

5–1. a and c

5–2.
1. anger, depression, or denial
2. bargaining

3. acceptance
4. depression, anger
5. denial, bargaining, or anger

REFERENCES

American Nurses Association. [1976], 1985. *Code for nurses with interpretive statements.* Kansas City, Mo.

Blegen, M., et al. 1992. Who helps you with your work? *American Journal of Nursing* 92: 28.

Lengacher, C., and P. Mabe. 1993. Nurse extenders. *Journal of Nursing Administration* 23: 17.

Massachusetts Nurses Association. 1992. *Do you know your responsibilities as a nurse?* Canton, Mass.

Neidlinger, S., et al. 1993. Incorporating nursing assistive personnel into a nursing professional practice model. *Journal of Nursing Administration* 23:33–34.

Richman, L. 1993. When will the layoffs end? *Fortune,* September 20, 54.

RECOMMENDED READING

Hansten, R., and M. Washburn. 1993. *The nurse manager's answer book.* Gaithersburg, Md.: Aspen Publishers, Inc.

Chapter 6

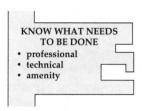

KNOW WHAT NEEDS
TO BE DONE
- professional
- technical
- amenity

Know What Needs To Be Done: If I Delegate All My Tasks, What's Left for Me To Do?

Ruth I. Hansten and Marilynn J. Washburn

"Hi! I'm your supervisor for this evening's shift, and I'm making rounds to see how everyone is doing. Do you need anything, or is everything going okay?"

"I don't know—things are a little crazy. We've got admissions coming, a transfer from the unit, and two late discharges. Mary's upset because Dr. Jones just yelled at her in front of a patient, and we haven't seen Steve for quite awhile. I wish he'd show up so we could get some work done. It looks like everyone will be working overtime just to get their charting done. I don't know how *you* could help."

The process of working with other people successfully requires a knowledge of the total picture, knowing what needs to be done in terms that are clearly defined. In the example above, the nurse responding to the supervisor has a general idea of the work waiting to be done but has not done an organized assessment or prioritized what's really happening on the unit. Without a plan, she can only react to the issues that are happening at the moment, and she is unable to accept or direct help when it is offered from the supervisor. The result can be a feeling of chaos and frustration for everyone involved that can be sensed by anyone walking into that kind of environment. The patients will certainly sense this as well, seeing the frenzied staff running in and out of the room and apologizing for not having enough time to spend with them right now.

Not everyone is organized by nature, and certainly we are not all equally endowed with the ability to see the whole picture. Fortunately, there are steps to take that will assist us in developing these skills so that

121

situations like the one presented above can be avoided. In this chapter we are going to discuss those steps by first exploring a model that delineates three major aspects of the nursing role. We will then discuss planning objectives for optimal conditions and the process of prioritizing those objectives when conditions and resources are limited in some way.

Despite all of our attempts and the multitude of systems created to date, nursing has not been carefully contained within a list of items that are to be done. In fact, as Marie Manthey challenges, "Good nursing care. It's so simple, we all know it. The picture is brilliantly clear. But what are its boundaries? When can any nurse say, 'This patient has had enough nursing care.' The question seems almost sacrilegious. The answer seems to be, 'Never!' There is always one more thing a good nurse can think of to do for someone who is ill" (Manthey, 1991, p. 27). Yet, resources *are* often limited, and boundaries must be set. Not having the ability to be all things to all people all the time, we must begin to define what needs to be done by first defining the role of professional nursing.

CHECKPOINT 6–1

As we've discussed so far, working successfully with others involves an understanding of what needs to be done in terms of the total picture and planning how that can be accomplished by delegating to the members on the health care team.

I can begin to do this by:

a) defining and clarifying *my* role as a professional nurse
b) relying on the supervisor to assist when things get tough
c) doing all things myself, meeting all of the patients' needs as they occur
d) letting members on the team do all of the work so that they can advance

See the end of the chapter for the answers.

DEFINING THE ROLE

Looking at the brief hundred-year history of our profession, we can cite countless examples of nursing's amoeba-like progression. Many of us have heard the comment, "Get a nurse to do it if no one else will!" Throughout the course of history, nursing has willingly taken on work that no one else was willing to do. From mopping floors to sterilizing instruments, from cleaning contaminated wounds to caring for the highly infectious, nursing has been there to meet the need. As a result, we lack clear definition of *what* we do. Further, we are now training others and delegating to them tasks that have been a part of our scope of practice. Without a finite definition of our role, the idea of delegating any part of it invokes fear in many as they ask the question, "If I delegate all of these interventions, what's left for me to do?"

Studies have been done that assist us in finding some delineation to our role. One such study by the health care consulting firm of E. J. Murphy of Buffalo reported that "the average RN in a hospital does 93 different jobs within the course of a week, making the job eight times as complex as that of a manufacturing worker" (E. J. Murphy, Ltd., 1992, p. 9). And one of the most promising studies to date has resulted in the Nursing Interventions Classification. The result of five years of research under the Iowa Intervention Project, the taxonomy is a listing of 336 nursing interventions, with standardized descriptions of each (McCloskey and Bulechek, 1992). With this type of standardized listing, nursing could begin to be itemized in the patient billing process, gaining visibility and a clearer definition of our involvement in health care delivery.

THE PTA MODEL

Consider looking at the nursing role as made up of three areas of practice in what we will call the "PTA model." In this model, nursing provides Professional, Technical, and Amenity care to a given group of patients or clients. Whether the setting is acute, long-term, or community care, the nurse can be described as functioning in one of these three areas. Let's look at this more closely to see what is meant.

Amenity

During the past decade, this area of our role has received heightened attention as health care as a business became the issue and executives sought an element that would give them a "leading edge" over the health care facility down the street. The "service mentality" was developed and promoted, and we educated our "consumers" to expect hotel-style treatment. Those who could afford to redesigned their interiors, making them more "home-like" and friendly, and hired marketing personnel to assist them in "going the extra mile." Patient questionnaires were designed to help us to measure performance in terms of how hot and fast the meal was delivered, how "friendly" the nursing staff was, and how clean the rooms were. (Check your facility survey to see what questions are currently being asked.) Massages, wine with dinner, guest trays, and a vase for the flowers became important factors in "quality nursing care." The quality of our amenity service is highly visible to management and marketing, in terms of patient surveys, letters to the administrator expressing thanks or dismay, and the gifts of boxes of chocolates for the nurses. These were signs we had done our job well. The subtle education to the patient and family to expect the "amenities" of care was complete. This expectation extends to all areas of health care, from the homey, friendly labor/delivery rooms with the champagne dinners to the extended care center with the ice cream shop in the courtyard. (We think these amenities are nice touches and very important when you are ill, or aging, or experiencing a significant event in your life—but a note of caution should be made that this is not the *primary* function of the registered nurse.)

Technical

This is an obvious area of the nursing role, and one we take pride in and fight to maintain. Examples of our technical expertise include cannulating a vein, catheterizing a child, irrigating the Blakemore tube, balancing the hemodynamic monitor, and giving a painless injection. These technical tasks are highly visible and their outcomes easily measured, making their performance obviously important. Quality improvement monitors, incident reports, medication error analyses, and patient complaints tell us how well we are performing in this area of our role. Physicians see the outcomes of these technical interventions and measure our effectiveness by the number of incidents they must deal with and the number of complaints from family members when the orders to change their loved one's dressing three times daily have not been carried out.

The two areas of "amenity" and "technical" contain many tasks that are readily delegated to other personnel. It does not take a registered nurse to pass meal trays, deliver flowers, walk the dog in a long-term care center, or clean the room. And the increasing numbers of health care technicians offer many willing hands to be trained to perform the majority of our technical duties. LPNs (LVNs) pass meds, change dressings, and start IVs in some states, and patient care assistants are also passing some medications, completing glucose tests, drawing blood samples, and providing all of the hygienic care required. With so much of our role clearly being done by others, what is left for the registered nurse?

Professional

This part of our model presents the greatest degree of difficulty for many nurses. Answers to this question range from comments regarding attitude, image, and the number of years of education the nurse has completed. Yet we are not seeking to describe how we attain or present this part of our role, but rather *what* comprises the very heart of RN practice. What can you do, and do well, that *cannot* be delegated? What ensures a high-value experience for the patient that is both efficient and effective? We hope you are saying to yourself that it is the implementation of the nursing process! For it is through your educational foundation, your ability to make assessments and plan the care, that you can effectively coordinate the efforts of the health care team and evaluate their effect. This collaborative coordination is *essential* to the successful functioning of any health care delivery system and cannot be eliminated or replaced. Tasks may be performed by anyone trained to do them; it is *your* ability to critically identify the need and evaluate the outcome that remains when all else is delegated. According to the National Council of State Boards of Nursing (NCSBN), delegation means "entrusting the performance of selected nursing tasks to competent persons in selected situations. The nurse retains the accountability for the total nursing care of the individual" (NCSBN, 1990, p. 1). Retaining that accountability through the implementation of the nursing process as we coordinate the entire picture of our patient's needs is the very core of our professional role.

Why do we find it difficult to articulate the professional component of our role? Realize that we tend to measure what we value. The inverse is also true in that we value what we measure. Notice that in the above description of the professional area of practice we have not described any tools of measurement or discussed the visibility of performing the nursing process. As nurses, this is an area where we need to place more emphasis, and not continue to allow others to dictate our practice in terms of measurement and value. Clinical errors and patient surveys have been our standard measurement tools in the past, keeping us at a task-oriented technical and amenity level of practice. However, beginning efforts are being noted as more nurses are tracking the impact of their case management and translating outcomes into terms that are highly visible to physicians, patients, the general public, and administrators alike. We must continue to shift our focus from those easily identified and measured parts of our role and understand that "there is a growing gap between the organization's need for nursing to assume an enlarged role in the redefined care delivery system and the traditional task-oriented role decreed by influential elements of the medical profession" (Hanrahan, 1991, p. 35).

Implementing the nursing process is relatively easy to describe on paper and to other nursing personnel. However, it is not visible in the same manner as giving a bath, changing a dressing, or starting an IV. It is visible only when connected to outcomes, when the whole picture of the patient's care is evaluated in terms of whether the plan of care was achieved in a timely fashion and no untoward results occurred. It is visible only when we make the connection, when we call attention to the fact that the length of stay for a specific critical pathway has decreased by one day due to consistent nursing planning and coordination of the care. It is visible only when we note that inappropriate readmissions to an acute care facility (less than 24 hours post discharge for the same diagnosis) have been eliminated due to the discharge instructions, education, and follow-up provided by the nursing staff. It is visible only when we research the connection between our continuous teaching of diabetic foot care and the decrease of lower limb amputations among diabetics. Our professional visibility does not come from checking a task off a "to do" list but from our continuous education of our publics regarding the *outcomes* of our interventions.

Yes, there is much to be done after you have delegated tasks to the other members of the team. What remains clearly defines you as a registered nurse, and is the "heartland" of our profession. As Adelaide Nutting challenged us so many years ago, "Perhaps, too, we need to remember that growth in our work must be preceded by ideas, and that any conditions which suppress thought, must retard growth. Surely we will not be satisfied in perpetuating methods and traditions. Surely we will wish to be more and more occupied with creating them" (Donahue, 1985, p. 366).

CHECKPOINT 6–2

Complete examples 2 through 4 of Table 6–1, providing your own examples of professional, technical, and amenity care, noting who it is visible to and how it is measured.

See the end of the chapter for the answers.

Table 6–1 Examples of Professional, Technical, and Amenity Care

The PTA Model	Professional "the whole picture"	Technical "expert skill level"	Amenity "the caring touch"
Example 1	discharge planning	passing medications	changing linen
Visible to	colleagues	physicians/patient	patient/family
How Measured	length of stay	medication errors	patient surveys/letters
Example 2	diabetic teaching in the home setting	giving insulin injection	fixing a snack for the patient's family
Visible to			
How Measured			
Example 3	medication instructions	changing a dressing	changing ice water
Visible to			
How Measured			
Example 4			
Visible to			
How Measured			

GETTING THE JOB DONE

Whether we are providing professional, technical, or amenity care, we must first establish *what* needs to be done. In our example at the beginning of this chapter, the head nurse of an acute care unit noted several issues that needed attention but was not certain how or by whom these issues would be resolved. What needs to be done in this example, and in every situation you face, is no different than the nursing process. (There seems to be no substitute for the nursing process—what a wonderful tool!) Let's take a look at how it applies here.

I. Assess

In any situation, whether in an outpatient clinic, a dialysis center, a home health agency, or wherever you practice, the first step in getting the job done is to assess the situation. Get a global picture of the outcomes you and your team would like to achieve during this shift. Once again, focus on outcomes, on the results of your actions, not the actions themselves. Set your optimal goals by looking at what your ideal outcomes would be if you had no limitations: all patients/clients receive safe care, all medications and treatments are given on time and discussed with each patient to increase their knowledge and understanding of their care, all documentation is completed accurately, everyone is off duty on time (no overtime!), and so on. These are very general outcomes; you should have specific outcomes related to the patient population and setting in which you are working.

Consider the following example of what can (and does!) happen when the staff is not focused on outcomes but is focused solely on tasks. This story is told by Dianna Mason, in *The Politics of Patient Care* (Mason and Talbott, 1985).

Mrs. Smith was a 90-year-old woman who had been admitted to the hospital from a nursing home for treatment of congestive heart failure. Her medical condition and the change in the environment exacerbated a problem with confusion accompanied by a loss of interest in eating. She was on a 40-bed medical unit that had a nurse-patient ratio of 1:8 to 1:12. The nurses were "too busy" to spend much time trying to feed her, particularly since she ate only small, frequent meals. They had sicker patients who demanded their time and attention, including a comatose patient on a respirator. As the patient continued to lose weight, she became obviously malnourished and more confused. The physicians ordered that she be fed by nasogastric tube. When she tried to pull out the NG tube, wrist restraints were ordered. The bolus tube feedings, for which the nurses now made time, gave the patient diarrhea, which quickly led to decubiti, since the restraints prevented her from turning her buttocks away from the incontinent stool. As the diarrhea continued, she became more malnourished and finally died after suffering great humiliation and classic iatrogenic "unhealth" care.

Although many factors affect the nurse's decision as to how time is spent, none of these factors is as significant as the primary need to make all decisions based on clearly defined outcomes. If the staff had taken the time to plan the outcome for Mrs. Smith, would there have been more emphasis placed on feeding her? Can this task be delegated if the nurses are "too busy"? Keep this example in mind as we continue our discussion of the process of what needs to be done.

CHECKPOINT 6–3

Identify three optimum outcomes you might focus on at the beginning of your shift.

II. Plan

Often we are so anxious to begin the shift that we do not recognize the value of planning. Remember that old adage Mom taught you (or was it an old nursing professor?), *"Fail to plan, plan to fail."* When you are tempted to skip this step and just jump right into the tasks at hand, be aware of the price you will pay in terms of feeling disorganized, moving from one job to another, and reaching the end of the shift with no clear sense of achievement. Your team members will no doubt share a sense of mounting frustration, since they are not certain what to do next and will spend considerable time waiting for you to delegate or being overwhelmed at the confusion. As little as 15 minutes at the beginning of any shift reviewing the outcomes, and determining what can be reasonably done and by whom will be much more effective than getting a quick report and going for it! (Further discussion of the communication process in delegation will be covered in Chapter 8.)

This planning step applies to all settings where you may be employed, from extended care centers where the emphasis is on long-term planning, to the ambulatory surgery center where you must consider the list of scheduled cases for the day and plan for who will react the patient, to the home health setting where there is much planning to be done to maximize the amount of time spent in each visit. Once you have agreed to set aside the time to plan, a word or two must be said about the process. (Are you surprised? You didn't think we would just leave you to plan on your own, did you?) Planning requires not only determining outcomes but realizing that some prioritization must occur if resources are not unlimited. We propose the following steps.

1. *Get the global picture:* don't limit yourself to just your assignment, but have an understanding of what fellow team members are also expecting to accomplish during this shift. For instance, if you are working in ambulatory surgery, be aware of all of the scheduled surgeries for the day, not just the ones assigned to your area. If you are in a home health agency, do you know what cases the other nurses on your team are carrying? On a skilled care unit in a long-term care facility, be aware of the assignments of the other team members on the floor, not just your assigned rooms. Expanding your awareness of the expectations of the other workers in your area will help you to offer assistance when you have time or to know who might be called upon to help you, and to foster a sense of teamwork instead of isolation. The worst words we can ever hear (or speak!) are *"It's not my patient."* Establishing a global picture implies that we have an awareness of what's happening around us, not just with the patients immediately assigned to us.

Often the perception or the mood of the unit or work setting is colored by the events of the previous shift or day. If the night shift in a corrective facility had a difficult time with an inmate who had to be "taken down," an undertone of anxiety may be communicated and carried over to the next shift. An awareness of the events of the previous 24 hours will lend a better understanding to what the "whole picture" of the time ahead will be. Perhaps things are not really as difficult as reported, and the team can move ahead, planning for outcomes with the understanding that the events of the previous shift have ended and that feelings carried over are now affecting the information shared. The weekend call coverage for a visiting nurse may leave a very lengthy message regarding the noncompliant attitude of the patient and his refusal to complete the medication regimen, but your phone call on Monday morning reveals a much calmer patient who is willing to talk about his IV therapy and consider completing the treatment plan. Beware of self-fulfilling prophecies—get the whole picture and make your own assessment so that you can effectively plan your care.

2. *Set optimal goals:* decide what you really want to achieve during this time in your work setting, given the best possible conditions. (No one is late to work, staffing is adequate, everyone is ready to work together, and so on.) As in our discussion above, focus on outcomes, not on creating a laundry list of tasks to be done. What do you want to be the results of your professional efforts today? Remember, every action you take is a subtle form of education to your public (whether it's the physicians you work with, your fellow team members, the patients, or their families and visitors). What is the best impression you can make and the clearest message you can send regarding your professional ability?

3. *What is reasonable to expect:* part of planning involves being able to anticipate events and determine potential responses. What happens if a patient "crashes," or one of the team members becomes ill, or you receive three unexpected transfers? Given limited and changing resources, what is reasonable to expect will be accomplished today? How do we let go of the ideal and optimum outcomes and be "okay" with less than the best? Can we give ourselves permission to do less than the optimum, and under what conditions is this acceptable? (See Chapter 3 for a discussion on policies and procedures in working with limited staff.)

4. *Set priorities:* given limits to the resources we work with in terms of supplies, staff, and time, we must be able to determine those outcomes that are essential to achieve, and prioritize our work. We can do this effectively by evaluating each desired outcome according to the following criteria:

- *Life threatening or potentially*—has the patient proven to be a risk to him- or herself and others, therefore requiring continual restraint and supervision? Has the patient demonstrated a labile response to medication, thereby requiring constant monitoring?
- *Essential to safety*—was the code cart checked and restocked after the last code? Have you received the latest training regarding universal precautions, and do you take the time to practice them to protect your safety as well as that of your patient? Does the patient weigh

200 pounds and require two people to assist in moving? Does the resident require 24-hour observation because of a recent fall while unattended?

- *Essential to the medical/nursing plan*—do the vital signs need to be monitored every two hours when there has been no significant change for the past 24? Is the monitoring of intake and output essential to the outcomes we have established for this patient? Does the lab work that has been ordered on a daily basis reflect the best therapeutic evaluation for this client? Does the 10-year-old really need to be awakened for a neuro check every hour when he's been stable for the last 24?

Often by asking these types of questions we can further assess the work to be done and prioritize according to the reasonable goals we have set. Failing to take the time to ask these questions continually keeps us in the task-oriented, technical- and amenity-based roles of our position and does not allow us (or the patient!) to benefit from what we do best. We can continue to keep ourselves very busy, getting tasks done, not delegating appropriately, and therefore depriving the patient and our employer of the skills we are most needed to provide. It may seem far easier to cross "beds and baths" off a list, pass all of the medications, and complete the treatments than to *assess* the need for these interventions, *plan* who will do them, *supervise* the interventions, and *evaluate* their effect. However, because we are the professional nurse accountable for the total patient care for a given group of individuals, the implementation of the nursing process while delegating tasks to others is our primary responsibility.

III. Intervene

For many years, our focus has been on systems and processes, supported by criteria of the Joint Commission on Accreditation for Healthcare Organizations (JCAHO) and state regulations. Beginning in the late 1980s, JCAHO developed their Agenda for Change, noting there would be a shift in emphasis from systems and processes (tasks and how they are completed) to an emphasis on the outcomes of the service provided. Further support came from quality management programs: Total Quality Management (TQM) and Continuous Quality Improvement (CQI) replaced the traditional Quality Assurance (QA) monitoring departments found in most organizations. This change has intensified our need to be

CHECKPOINT 6–4

Prioritize the following tasks based on the desired outcome of providing safe and effective care for Mr. Bailey, a 68-year-old total hip replacement who is two days post op, alert and oriented, stable, and planning on being discharged in two days. Use the criteria (L) life threatening, (S) safety, (E) essential to medical/nursing plan, and (N) nice to do, but not a priority.

___ 1. administer medications as ordered for arrhythmia
___ 2. instruct patient regarding postdischarge care
___ 3. monitor vital signs every four hours
___ 4. order meal for patient's wife
___ 5. assist patient with ambulation after discussion with PT
___ 6. place side rails up when patient has been medicated for pain

See the end of the chapter for the answers.

continuously aware of the cause-and-effect relationship our interventions have on the patients for whom we provide care. Successful practice requires that we as nurses change our focus too, always looking at the process outlined above: setting goals, realizing limits, prioritizing, and then implementing the plan, always with the patient's desired outcomes as our guide.

Job Analysis

With outcomes at the top of our list, having completed the above steps to the process, we are ready to put the plan into action. Armed with priorities, we must determine who can best carry out the interventions necessary. This can be done by completing a quick "job analysis." (A note of caution here, so that we don't lose you entirely in a wave of disbelief—we *know* how busy you are on the job and realize that you will not have the luxury of spending precious time completing a job analysis when there is work to be done *now*. However, as you are reading this book, there *is* time to learn and understand the technique so that you can quickly apply the principles in your work setting, making the most out of the resources you have by delegating appropriately.) Supervisors often tell us that this is one of the most difficult skills to master and that if there were some way to help nurses to organize their work and base the completion of that work on the resources available by getting the right person to do the job, they would be amazed. So although a job analysis sounds like something out of a personnel manual, we encourage you to read on to learn perhaps a new method for mastering that skill.

Giving a bath is only a task, and can be done by anyone if the focus is only on the task. What is the outcome desired by giving the bath? Is it to make the patient feel more comfortable? Is it to assess the condition of the skin and to provide an opportunity to more completely assess the patient? Is it an opportunity to teach a family member how to complete range of motion exercises while also giving a bath? Knowing the desired outcome of the job to be done will have a significant effect on the selection of *who* should perform the task.

Current analysis of the work done by an RN has revealed that significant time is spent in performing tasks that could be performed by someone else who does not have the knowledge and skill of the RN. Redesigns in care delivery are therefore focusing on isolating those functions that only an RN can perform and grouping the remaining tasks to be done by assistive personnel with minimal training. In many instances, the assistive person is then given a task assignment and not a patient assignment. This is a major difference from the team process of previous years.

A job analysis involves the following basic steps:

1. *Break the job or jobs into parts:* for example, if the job to be done is to start an IV, are there any parts to the process? Assembling the supplies, obtaining the proper IV solution, starting the IV, and monitoring the administration and documenting the procedure are all parts of the job.
2. *Evaluate the job in the following terms:*
   a) Knowledge: what kind of knowledge is necessary to do this job? In the example of starting the IV, one needs to know the type of equipment required, how to use it, basic anatomy and physiology to select a site, the policy of the facility regarding the procedure, the potential effects of the fluid to be administered, and the physician's orders regarding rate and method of administration.
   b) Skills: what skills are required to perform this task? Starting an IV requires the ability to be organized (having all supplies on hand before starting the insertion makes the process smoother!) and

psychomotor ability to insert the cannula into the vein and attach the tubing.

c) Personal traits: what personal traits (personality characteristics) would be helpful? The ability to remain calm, appear confident, explain the procedure to the patient, and be reassuring is certainly helpful in starting an IV on anyone.

3. *Match the job and the delegate:* given the analysis of the required knowledge, skills, and personal traits, who is the best person on the team to perform this job? In the case of starting an IV, the RN would be best qualified. However, the answer may change if the setting changes— consider a renal dialysis center where technicians have been trained to access a dialysis cannula, or a radiology department where the radiology technician starts an IV for the administration of contrast media. In these instances, the technicians are performing a task with a specific, predetermined outcome and have been taught the skill of IV insertion and the potential complications of their specific application. The RN, however, will be more knowledgeable regarding the continual administration and monitoring of IV medications and fluids for therapeutic interventions. Once again, consideration of the outcome desired is essential in making the decision of who performs the task.

CHECKPOINT 6–5

Perform a job analysis of the following:

1. Assessment of AM vital signs of 12 patients on a med-surg unit in a local hospital:
   a) knowledge?
   b) skills?
   c) traits?
   d) who would do this job?
2. Teaching insulin administration to an insulin-dependent 60-year-old diabetic who lives alone:
   a) knowledge?
   b) skills?
   c) traits?
   d) who would do this job?

See the end of the chapter for the answers.

The core of health care reform involves this very basic process of job analysis. As Virginia Trotter Betts, President of the American Nurses Association (1993, p. 3) states, "Whether it is in primary healthcare services—which can be safely and appropriately delivered by qualified nurses—or acute and critical services which require the experienced judgment of a registered nurse, the success of health care reform will depend in part on *matching the right provider to the need.*" Indeed, recent studies have shown that as much as 70 percent of the care provided by physicians can be provided by nurse specialists and practitioners, making this a costly mismatch of the job to the delegate (American Nurses Association, 1993). Studies also demonstrate that the RN spends as much as 65 percent of his or her time performing non-nursing tasks that could be easily delegated to assistive personnel (Brider, 1992).

CHECKPOINT 6–6

Would you delegate these tasks to an unlicensed care-giver?

1. Helping a stable patient walk
2. Evaluating patient response to pain medication (in an acute care setting)
3. Collecting intake and output data on ten patients
4. Making rounds with physician
5. Assisting in ADLs with a homebound 70-year-old
6. Feeding a two-year-old recovering from a spica cast application

See the end of the chapter for the answers.

Let's see how the whole process can be applied to the example given in Exhibit 6–1.

Making Assignments

Another important part of implementation of your plan involves the making of assignments to the members on your team. If your work setting is a facility that provides care for patients on a continuous basis, whether it is a psychiatric treatment center, a long-term care or extended

Exhibit 6–1 The Adult Day Care Center

You are the only RN working in an adult day care center. A rehab aide from a local staffing agency will be working with you today, and 17 clients are scheduled to visit, arriving at various times and staying until 4 PM, when the center closes.

I. Assess What Needs To Be Done

Supervising and providing for the physical needs of the clients, while maintaining a safe and recreational environment. Diets will need to be monitored, medications given, and follow-up done with two of the families regarding their concerns.

II. Plan

a) The global picture—17 clients will be visiting, spending various lengths of time. All 17 have been here before, and the report from yesterday's nurse states there have been no problems for the past three days. Mr. Darcy's family tends to want to stay and talk about how hard it is to care for Mr. Darcy at home. Perhaps he needs to be placed in a long-term care facility? Mrs. Morris complains about the food, saying it's not hot enough and there's not enough of it to make sure her bowels move. Her family is worried about her taking so many laxatives.

b) Optimal goals—to provide safe care in a fun environment, setting aside time to talk with Mr. Darcy and Mrs. Morris about their concerns, and to spend at least 10–15 minutes with every client to do a quick assessment.

c) Reasonable to expect—there may be at least one "walk-in," and there may be numerous phone calls about the program. One of the clients may be difficult (it seems like someone always has an "off" day!). The rehab aide has never been here before, so will need some time for orientation.

d) Set priorities—orient rehab aide, pass medications, provide physical assistance to all clients, meet with clients as time allows (first with Mr. Darcy and Mrs. Morris).

III. Intervene

a) Break the job into parts—(1) physical care for the clients: assist to the bathroom, personal hygiene as needed, helping with snacks and meal set-up at lunch, assisting with ambulation for exercise in the afternoon; (2) assess patients' current physical status, take blood pressures, weight, skin condition; (3) pass medications, review orders and supply of medications, assess clients throughout visit for any prn needs.

b) Consider knowledge, skills, and personal traits of available staff (a job analysis)— interview rehab aide, determining background and experience in assisting with ambulation, hygienic care, blood pressures, and weights, and assessing his personal traits for consideration in leading exercise group, card games, or other entertainment. (He says he has passed the medication administration course for nursing assistants and is allowed to do this at group homes—will you let him?)

c) Match the job to the delegate—RN will orient aide, pass meds, interview and assess each client, take phone calls to market the facility, follow up with Mr. Darcy and Mrs. Morris (could the aide follow up with Mrs. Morris at lunch, making certain her meal was sufficient and hot?). Rehab aide will assist with physical needs, ambulation, feeding, taking blood pressures, and talking to the clients, sharing information with the RN in order to complete the assessment of each client.

continues

Exhibit 6-1 *continued*

IV. Evaluate

Throughout the day, check with the aide as well as the clients to make certain all needs are being met, that the aide does not feel overwhelmed or bored (is there more that he could be doing as he gets more comfortable with the setting, or is he confused if he has never worked with geriatric clients before?), and that you are satisfied with your abilities to achieve the goals outlined for the day. If three new clients came in unannounced and Mrs. Morris had a reaction to the stool softener she was taking, were you able to reprioritize and "let go" of some of your expectations (perhaps rescheduling some of the assessments for later in the week)?

---

care facility, an ambulatory care unit, or an acute care facility, you face the task of dividing up the workload and maximizing the resources available. In plain terms, this means making assignments, a skill that generally is not taught, but rather is learned "on the job." (Your charge nurse calls in sick, and you are asked to take her place, never having done so before. The supervisor says, "It's not so hard—all you have to do is make the assignments." Sound familiar?)

Institutional policies and JCAHO criteria provide the starting place for making assignments. Each work environment will vary, depending on the uniqueness of the patient population, but certain standards will apply in all settings. According to the 1994 JCAHO *Accreditation Manual for Hospitals* (pp. 12–13):

NC.2.1.2 Assigning responsibility to nursing staff members for providing nursing care to patients is based on consideration of the following seven elements:

1. *Complexity* of the patient's care: how involved is the care that is required—is this a multi-system failure or a primipara post delivery?
2. *Dynamics* of the patient's status: how often is the patient's condition changing? Is this a brittle diabetic with blood sugars all over the map, or a stable post appendectomy waiting for discharge instructions?
3. *Complexity of assessment:* what is required to completely assess the patient's condition—can the assessment be performed quickly, involving a stable patient, or is this an emergency admission involving a motor vehicle accident that resulted in numerous injuries?

4. *Technology* involved: is this patient being monitored for cardiac dysrhythmias, on a PCA pump, with two infusion pumps, and renal dialysis daily? Or is the patient on a psych unit, stable physically but severely depressed, not requiring any technological intervention?

5. *Degree of supervision:* what level of supervision is required by the nursing personnel based on their skill and competence? Are the members of the staff experienced and able to work together without difficulty, or is there a new team member who has never provided care for this type of patient before?

6. *Availability of supervision:* is the appropriate nursing supervision available to provide the degree of supervision determined in #5? Is there someone on the unit who is responsible for overseeing the actions of the team and assisting and evaluating when necessary—or is this the night shift in a long term care facility and the director of nursing is available by phone?

7. *Infection control and safety precautions:* to what degree are universal precautions enforced? Are all staff trained in safety issues, CPR, etc., or is someone being assigned to provide care who has not yet received this type of instruction?

Note: these criteria speak only to the acute care settings; JCAHO does not make specific reference to the process in other settings such as home care or long-term care. However, we feel that these basic guidelines are important to keep in mind when making assignments in any setting.

CHECKPOINT 6–7

What other factors do you consider when making assignments?

Hopefully, you included some of the following factors in your list:

- *Location:* no one likes to be running from one end of the hall to the other if it can be avoided. This has traditionally been one of the major criteria for making assignments, and it still used today since some units have wings, pods, or blocks of rooms that make up their assigned area. Likewise, in a community setting, no one wants to be driving from one end of town to the other, so most nurses are assigned to specific regions or districts.

- *Continuity of care:* as rapidly as patients are moved through any system, it is essential that some degree of sameness be provided. If you had the patient yesterday, it would be nice to care for him or her again today. This is more than a nicety; familiarity with the patient assists in planning and evaluating his or her progress.

- *Personal preference:* it is nice if we can all have the opportunity to do what we prefer, and hopefully you have matched your preference with your job setting. If surgery is your thing, you probably are more skilled in this area and would be best on a surgical unit or in an OR suite. Beyond this, we all have certain types of patients we prefer (see Chapter 7, "Know Your Delegate"), and considering this when making an assignment is beneficial to the patient and the employee.

- *Acuity system:* many facilities employ a system for determining the acuity levels of all patients so that the work may be distributed more equably among the team. Past systems have ranged in sophistication from the most detailed computer process to the basic 1 through 4 categorizing of needs. We have yet to find a perfect system, and continually emphasize that this is a dynamic and not a static environment, with continual changes in patient needs that must be consistently met. Be wary of the importance that is placed on this system; it can be a very divisive tool as members of the team argue about how many "acuity points" they were assigned. It can also be a very useful tool for monitoring staffing needs and the changing demands of the patient population.

- *Care delivery system:* whether your work setting uses a case management system, primary care, team nursing, or any one of a number of new systems being currently created, this will influence how assignments are made.

Keeping all of these factors in mind, refer to the assignment exercise in Exhibit 6–2 and see what you can do.

We hope that you took the time to try your hand at making this assignment. Even if you do not currently work in an acute care setting and never have the opportunity to make assignments, it is a good method for "getting the global picture" and understanding what your fellow colleagues experience. It is also an excellent tool for prioritizing and per-

Exhibit 6–2 The Assignment

The following patients are on your unit during the day shift:

101: 65 yo total hip, day 2, has hyperal, is confused, family problem, very unhappy with care.

102: 35 yo bowel resection, day 3, very happy that cancerous bowel was removed, ready to begin to learn home care.

103: 82 yo choleycystitis, day 1, patient admitted by daughter because she wanted to go on vacation. Physician furious that ER physician admitted him. Patient is very stable and fun to take care of. Requires little care, will probably be sent home, or to another place if tests ok. Doubt pain is cardiac.

104: 35 yo total hysterectomy, day 2, very stable, requires little care, ready to go home in AM.

105: 29 yo motor vehicle accident day 3, multiple lacerations, bruises, dressings and wound care with saline/peroxide flush, takes about one hour to do wound care.

106: 19 yo motor vehicle accident day 3, girlfriend of patient in 105. R/O fx pelvis, R/O possible pregnancy. Family upset, patient screams with pain, pain meds being held due to ? pregnancy, some arguments with doctor and family. R/O drug dependence.

107: 81 yo TURP day 2, patient from group home for disabled, ready to return tomorrow. Alert, friendly, understands instructions.

108: 74 yo TIA day 1, CVA now evident, extending, family discussing code decision with doctor, very unstable vital signs, on q 15″ neuro checks.

109: 71 yo with abd pain, new admit, probable diverticulosis, has had hx in the past, stable. Language problem, speaks only Vietnamese.

110: 42 yo pneumonia, day 4, on 2 IV antibiotics q 4–6 hours.

Plan your assignment with the following staff:
Yourself (RN Charge Nurse):
LPN (LVN):
Nursing Assistant:

Source: reprinted with permission from Ruth Hansten, Marilynn Washburn, Loretta O'Neill and Washington Organization of Nurse Executives, © 1990.

forming a job analysis so that you become more skilled at matching the job to the delegate.

Often, when we use this exercise in our workshops, many individuals will look at us expectantly, waiting for the "right answer." There is none. Those of you who are responsible for making assignments know that to be true. If you were to use this exercise in a small group of your coworkers or at a staff meeting, you would quickly find that everyone has a little different idea regarding how the work should be assigned. What *is* important here is the ability to define outcomes, organize the work flow, and justify the choices you have made.

Let's discuss some of the more typical responses to this exercise, since we have noted that although individual approaches vary, there is a pattern of assignments based on the criteria we have discussed earlier in the chapter. The primary factor for consideration seems to be the type of care delivery system the charge nurse is most experienced with and is therefore likely to implement in this exercise. Other factors of room location, personal preference, continuity of care, and the acuity system are not fully applied because that information is not provided in the information given in the exercise. However, the criteria of JCAHO, particularly the complexity of the patient and the availability of supervision, should be considered.

Keeping these criteria in mind, we often see an assignment that gives the charge nurse the most "difficult patients," while the LPN is asked to do the treatments and meds on all patients and the NA is expected to do the typical "beds, baths, and answer the call lights." That assignment would look like this:

RN: 101, 106, 108, 109, all IVs, discharge planning for 103, 104 and 107

LPN: all treatments, all meds except IVs, 102, 103, 104, 105, 107, 110

NA: beds, baths, vital signs on all patients, answer call lights, assist where needed

This pattern reflects the idea of "equity," where the charge nurse feels she or he must carry at least as many patients as the LPN, and often more, to justify the position of charge nurse and to make certain everyone knows she is not just "working the desk." Does this reflect the best utilization of resources to meet the desired outcomes? Have we even thought about outcomes, or are we merely performing a task-oriented function? What outcomes would you determine are reasonable *before* you make the assignment? (Remember our process as described earlier in the chapter, and refer to Exhibit 6–3 for a list of potential outcomes.)

What is different about what the RN may do with the patients she has assigned herself as compared to those who are not directly assigned to her? If the RN is assigned "patients," how many is she really responsible for?" Can the LPN be solely responsible for a patient assignment? What plans, if any, are made for an emergency—are there any other tasks that can be delegated?

Exhibit 6–3   Potential Outcomes for Patients 101–110

101: Short-term outcome: to determine the source of the confusion and take steps to correct the underlying problem; by the end of the 24 hours, a reoriented patient who is ready to undertake the long-term outcome of going home and has the ability to ambulate with a one-person stand-by assist.

102: Short-term outcome: patient will learn first steps of procedures for home care, with discharge planned for next day.

103: Short-term outcome: review of lab tests will rule out pain from other sources. Dietary/medication home regimen will be completed. Patient's disposition will be to home with home health assistance or respite care.

104: Outcome for today: patient will have bowel movement, ambulate, and verbalize home care of incision and bowels, medications such as hormonal replacement. Will probably go home today with family to assist since no one is allowed to wait for the AM for discharge unless fever or other variances occur.

105: Outcome for today: plan for home care will be discussed, wound will show evidence of beginning granulation. Home assistant will begin to learn wound care procedure. Referral to VNS completed.

106: Outcome for today: determine pregnancy status with blood test, family/MD/patient/hospital care team will set up conference for devising longer term plan, discuss question of drug dependence and rehabilitation. Patient will be pain-free.

107: RN or assistant from group home will receive instructions for discharge care, patient will verbalize home care plan.

108: Code status will be discussed and a decision made as quickly as possible. Depending on decision, the most likely outcome is that patient will receive terminal care, family will receive grief counseling.

109: Patient's history and assessment will be completed through use of interpreter. Origin of pain will be determined and treated so that patient will be pain-free. Discharge plan will be initiated depending on information obtained about normal health and ADL support if needed.

110: Origin of pneumonia will be discovered and treated. (Is patient getting better on current regimen? Have cultures and sensitivities been done if he not? If treatment is working, how long will it be necessary?) Discharge plan will begin based on prognosis and current respiratory status. (Is this patient a candidate for home IV antibiotic therapy?)

Another assignment we often see reflects the practice of "care partners," where the care delivery system involves the pairing of a licensed and unlicensed caregiver to provide for the needs of a given group of patients. This assignment would look something like this:

RN: 108 (to discuss transfer to another unit), 109 (to obtain transla-
       tor from family member or staff roster), all IV medications

LPN: 101, 102, 103, 104, 105, 106, 107, 110

NA: 101, 102, 103, 104, 105, 106, 107, 110 (working with LPN)

This same rationale may be used to make the following assignment, pairing the NA with the RN and leaving the LPN to function as a provider of total patient care. In this case, the RN must assess the patients assigned to the LPN:

RN: 101, 105, 106, 108, 110

NA: 101, 105, 106, 108, 110 (NA may be trained in doing clean
       wound care for room 105, may assist with frequent monitor-
       ing of 108)

LPN: 102, 103, 104, 107, 109

A functional care delivery system would result in the following assignment and might provide the best opportunity for each individual to do what he or she knows best:

RN: all initial assessments, all IVs, discharge planning on 102
       (with teaching of home care) and 104, rounds with physicians,
       family and physician conference re: code status of 108, resolu-
       tion of complaints of 101, placement of 103, and discussion
       with family and physician of 106. Would also plan for all
       transfers and admits.

LPN: all medications (except IVs), all treatments, post-op teaching
       of 104

NA: hygienic care on all patients; vital sign monitoring; assist with
       transfers, admits, and discharges; provide total care for 103
       and 104

All staff share the answering of call lights

A word about call lights: in many instances we have seen this to be a major stumbling block to the work flow on any unit. As in any personal relationship, it is often the little things that make the difference, affecting whether the relationship will be successful and positive or doomed to difficulty because of assumptions regarding who is or is not doing his or her share of the work. If this sounds familiar to you, a frank discussion at a staff meeting or with the members on your shift will be necessary to clear the air. Is it reasonable to expect the nursing assistants to answer all of the call lights? (We are making no judgments here; the answer will depend on your particular environment.) What is the perception of everyone on the team regarding this expectation? Do the nursing assistants see the nurses sitting at the desk or having friendly conversations with visitors and physicians while call lights are ringing off the wall? If you are transitioning from an all-RN staff and adding unlicensed personnel, make certain that these seemingly benign issues are discussed at the beginning of your working relationships (see Chapter 7 for a complete discussion of role clarification). Taking time for this kind of discussion will make the task of making assignments easier and result in a smoother working relationship for everyone.

IV. Evaluate

Okay, so you've taken the time to assess the needs, plan and prioritize the outcomes, and implement your plan through careful job analysis and matching of the job to the delegate, and making the assignment based on specific criteria. Wow! What's next? The final step of the nursing process as we know it involves the evaluation of what we've done. Considerable discussion will be provided on this topic (see Chapter 11) as it relates to the process of delegation. What needs to be covered here relates specifically to the evaluation of whether we did the right things (effectiveness) and did them correctly (efficiency).

Once again, the true measure of our success goes back to the outcomes we determined to be our goals in the first step of our assessment. Did we achieve what we set out to do? (You would be amazed at how many nurses do not ever ask the question!) We wonder—if you never stop to evaluate your outcomes, how do you ever know if you have achieved them? How do you measure success? Or, to put it one more way, we took the time to determine where we were going; shouldn't we take the time to determine if we got there?

The use of two criteria, effectiveness and efficiency, makes our evaluation process simple. Let's look at efficiency first (since we know this to be one of those terms met with disdain by many nurses). Every nurse realizes the importance of doing things correctly. Few professions carry as serious consequences of an incorrect procedure or intervention as health care does. Unlike manufacturing or the provision of retail goods and services, health care deals directly with people's lives, and mistakes carry a high price. Doing things right is tantamount to every nurse's professional standard and receives the appropriate emphasis in all of our training. Beyond the correct performance of a procedure, however, is another question regarding efficiency: did the right person do the job? We have repeatedly stated that "things ain't the way they used to be," and this certainly applies to the resources available to us as health care providers. It is imperative, then, that we make every effort to determine that the individual who best meets the requirements of the job to be done is the one assigned to do the job. As nurses, it is our responsibility to the patients we care for to ensure that they receive the best that we can offer by delegating wisely.

Effectiveness, or doing the right things, will be apparent when outcomes are what we desired them to be. Reducing length of stays, eliminating admissions 24 hours post discharge, reducing the need for amputations due to poorly managed foot care of diabetics, and restoring autonomy to patients who have been dependent on others to meet their basic needs are all outcomes we can plan for and achieve.

If periodic evaluation (we recommend daily) does not reveal the desired results, review each of the steps of the process that you used to determine what needed to be done and by whom. In your analysis, be sure to consider input from other members of the team, as well as the patients.

CHECKPOINT 6–8

Review how you currently start your shift on the job. Do you set aside time for planning? Who do you include in this time? Are there ways that this could be improved, or do you feel satisfied with the information received, and are you able to plan effectively and be organized regarding what needs to be done?

SUMMARY

There is so much to be done, and there are only a limited number of people to do the job. How do you best plan to delegate appropriately, while ensuring efficiency and effectiveness? Remember to use the nursing process: assessing, planning, implementing, and evaluating your practice. Focus on outcomes and an awareness that evaluation of the achievement of those outcomes will increase nursing's visibility in all areas. Prioritize care, using the parameters of *"life-threatening," "safety,"* and *"essential to the medical/nursing plan of care,"* and delegate by matching the correct individual to the job based on a simple job analysis.

By realizing your part in the determination of what needs to be done, you are allowing yourself the time to practice the professional component of nursing—the implementation of the nursing process. Your extensive knowledge and sound judgment are the key ingredients to planning and delivering quality patient care.

ANSWERS TO CHECKPOINTS

6–1. a

6–2.

The PTA Model	Professional *"the whole picture"*	Technical *"expert skill level"*	Amenity *"the caring touch"*
Example 1	discharge planning	passing medications	changing linen
Visible to	colleagues	physicians/patient	patient/family
How Measured	length of stay	medication errors	patient surveys/letters
Example 2	diabetic teaching in the home setting	giving insulin injection	fixing a snack for the patient's family
Visible to	patient, family, physician	patient, colleagues	family
How Measured	pt behavior, follows rx	# of attempts	patient survey, response
Example 3	medication instructions	changing a dressing	changing ice water
Visible to	patient, family, physician	physician, pt, colleagues	patient, family
How Measured	patient behavior	healing status	pt/family comments
Example 4	your choice		
Visible to			
How Measured			

6–4.
1. Life threatening
2. Essential to care plan
3. Essential to care plan
4. Nice
5. Safety
6. Safety

6–5.
1. Assessment of AM vital signs:
    a) knowledge—how to take pulse, temperature, respirations, and blood pressures
    b) skills—math, ability to work electronic or mercury thermometer, electronic or manual sphygmomanometer
    c) traits—conscientious, friendly, organized
    d) who—nursing assistant or any trained unlicensed assistive personnel would be best choice
2. Teaching insulin administration
    a) knowledge—process of administration, side effects and desirable effects of insulin and the various types, sites for injection
    b) skills—ability to give a subcutaneous injection, psychomotor skill
    c) traits—calm, confident, reassuring
    d) who—LPN or RN

6–6.
1. yes
2. no, maybe to an LPN
3. yes
4. no
5. yes
6. yes

REFERENCES

American Nurses Association. 1993. Press release, October 13.

Brider, P. 1992. The move to patient focused care. *American Journal of Nursing* 92: 27–33.

Donahue, M.P. 1985. *Nursing: The finest art*. St. Louis: C. V. Mosby Company.

E. J. Murphy, Ltd. 1992. Headlines—RNs do 93 different jobs. *American Journal of Nursing* 92: 9.

Hanrahan, T. 1991. New approach to caregiving. *Healthcare Forum Journal* 34: 33–37.

Joint Commission on Accreditation for Healthcare Organizations (JCAHO). 1994. *Accreditation manual for hospitals*.

Manthey, M. 1991. A pragmatic concern. *Nursing Management* 22: 27–28.

Mason, D. J. and S. W. Talbott. 1985. *Political action handbook for nurses.* Menlo Park, Calif.: Addison-Wesley.

McCloskey, J. C. and G. Bulechek. 1992. *Nursing interventions classification.* St. Louis: Mosby-Year Book.

National Council of State Boards of Nursing (NCSBN). 1990. *Concept paper on delegation.* Chicago.

Chapter 7

Know Your Delegate: How Can I Determine the Right Delegate for the Job?

Ruth I. Hansten and Marilynn J. Washburn

"Sometimes we are assigned a float nurse in our very specialized ophthalmology day surgery area. Some do okay, others are frightening to work with because they just don't know what they don't know! How can I feel comfortable working with these people? The way I understand the supervision clause in the state nurse practice act, I need to know the competencies of those to whom I delegate."

We've put a bit of energy into examining ourselves. We've looked at what needs to be done and how the RN is accountable for leading the team to achieving outcomes. Now it's time to examine the other most pivotal person in the delegation process: the delegate. For those nurses who have been used to doing all their patient care without help, trusting some of the tasks to another person is difficult at best. But it is possible to *know* that delegate, just as we get to *know* those we serve.

As an example of how we get to know those to whom we delegate, think of the family. Whether you must hearken back to your family of origin or have a family now, think about how you've found out about the strengths, weaknesses, motivation, and preferences of those in your family. If you tell a 10-year-old to clean out the kitty litter box or fix dinner while you are at work, chances are the assignment will be incomplete or, worse yet, forgotten unless you supervise on a one-to-one basis. If you go to work, and a parent or a responsible young adult son or daughter is at home during the day, chances are they won't even have to be told to do the breakfast dishes or get dinner in the oven. Within your work group, you may see variations in the need for supervision and also many differ-

151

ent manifestations of strengths and weaknesses (more politically correct, "areas for improvement") in your staff, as well as how they fulfill the requirements of their job descriptions.

In this chapter, we'll briefly revisit the fundamental importance of state practice acts, explore job descriptions and competencies, and then identify strategies to clarify the personal expectations you may hold for your coworkers. Then we'll examine how we can best assess each delegate's strengths, weaknesses, motivation, and preferences, and how these combine to give you the information you need to match the best delegate to the work at hand.

WHO ARE THE DELEGATES?

Who do you delegate to on a daily basis?

_____

_____

Here are some of the answers we've heard from nurses throughout the country:

- Student nurses
- New personnel (RNs)
- LPNs, LVNs
- Nursing assistants
- Orderlies
- Home health aides
- Respiratory therapists (or speech, occupational, or physical therapy)
- Pharmacy people
- Secretaries
- Volunteers
- Social workers
- Medical students
- Doctors (Nurses report asking doctors, especially medical students, to do some of the care!)
- Psychologists
- Medical technologists

- Phlebotomists
- OR technicians

Whether we are delegating to all of these people in the strict sense of the nurse practice act or asking them to do things for our clients as we coordinate the care, the same principles apply.

Those nurses who are attempting to find a workplace in which there is no delegation may need to think twice. How frequently do you find yourself in a supervisory role as a delegator?

ASSESSING THE ROLES PLAYED BY EACH DELEGATE

What was it like in your family? Did your mom do the cleaning and the cooking and the yard work? Did Dad or Grandpa or Uncle fix the car? Roles that were standard in the "Leave It to Beaver" era are no longer useful in the present family configurations. But no matter how your family or "significant other group" is formulated, each person has certain roles. The analogy of the family situation may not fit for all of us as we compare it to work life, but the new flexibility and resiliency we find in the 1990s in family or social roles are characteristics that are also required of us in our organizations as we explore new methods and caregiver job descriptions.

What was your job description in your family of origin? It may not have been written, but it was certainly present. In our health care organizations, we must pay close attention to the written as well as the "unwritten" roles given to each worker.

OFFICIAL EXPECTATIONS OF EACH ROLE

Before we explore the underlying issues of what people really are expecting of each other in your workplace, let's take a closer look at the official documents. In Chapter 3, we asked you to examine the practice act for those with whom you work each day. Do you know the job descriptions for all the workers in your facility, and how your state's practice statutes are reflected in the organization's policies? Is it clear what each person is expected to do? How does each role reflect the values and mission of your organization?

CHECKPOINT 7–1

❏ I have located the mission and/or a values statement for my organization.

❏ I have also located recently revised job descriptions for those I work with, as well as my own job description.

❏ I have called the state board of nursing and have obtained current copies of the regulations, rules, and administrative code for RNs, LPNs (LVNs), CNAs, medical assistants, or other health care workers in my facility.

Reviewing these documents now, I can answer the following questions:

1. I know what type of health care professional (which job description and practice act) is allowed to:
   a) pierce the skin to perform procedures
   b) start IVs
   c) monitor IVs
   d) perform the nursing process
   e) gather data for the nurse as she or he performs the assessment, nursing diagnosis, planning, intervention, and evaluation
   f) perform hygienic care
   g) deliver medications
   h) be "in charge" of coordinating patients' care in my health care setting
   i) educate the patient
2. I can locate several competencies in our job descriptions that reflect our mission and the values of the organization.

With the practice statutes, your organization's mission and/or values statement, and your job descriptions by your side, let's examine how these documents determine the official expectations of each role.

PRACTICE ACTS AND REGULATIONS

As we discussed in Chapter 3, the fundamental expectations of each health care worker's job are based on state regulations and rules. In assessing your delegate, these statutes are the necessary framework on which you base your supervision and assignment of the delegate.

It's really not legal (or common!) for an organization or facility to assign duties in job descriptions that are beyond the scope of legal practice as determined by the practice acts of your state. More frequently, however, facilities may interpret regulations differently, or limit scope of legal practice within their organization, or individuals may attempt to practice beyond the legal and official boundaries. As the supervisory RN, you must know whether the tasks your delegate agrees to complete are within the state practice act as well as the facility's job descriptions.

As you examined your state practice acts and your facility job descriptions, did you find any questions or inconsistencies? (If you are a student, ask your clinical experience facilities for examples of their job descriptions.) If you found some discrepancies, take time now to answer your questions by initiating a phone call to your state regulatory board or discuss the issue with administrative personnel.

CHECKPOINT 7–2

Pat reviewed his state practice act for LPNs and found that there was nothing specified as to IV therapy. It also stated that the LPN acts as an assistant to the RN in completing the nursing process. However, he noted that LPNs were monitoring IVs and giving IV medications in his hospital. Many LPNs functioned just like RNs as primary caregivers. He wondered how this could be possible or legal.

What do you think may be occurring in this hospital? What should Pat do?

See the end of the chapter for the answers.

JOB DESCRIPTIONS

Job descriptions come in many forms: based on competencies or standards, performance criteria, the nursing process, or specific required behaviors or responsibilities. These documents may double as competency checklists or as performance review tools. Job descriptions may be considered a type of contract between the employee and the management team to perform a given role as specified within the written information, which will include such topics as the necessary qualifications, reporting relationships, scope of responsibilities, and a position summary discussing the overall role. In unionized environments, the union contract for each type of worker will also influence the roles played by each union employee, and should be in agreement with the job description.

For our purposes here, turn now to the job summaries and lists of duties or responsibilities you've assembled from your clinical areas. Generally, RN job descriptions will contain such descriptors as

- provides patient care, utilizing the nursing process
- assists in coordinating patient care activities
- acts as a communication liaison among departments and with physicians
- functions in a leadership role
- is accountable for the standards of nursing care
- assesses, plans, implements, evaluates, teaches

As organizations are revising care delivery systems, job descriptions for the RN are beginning to include such statements as

- delegates appropriately and directs the activities of other team members
- effectively supervises team members
- evaluates care given by team members and gives feedback
- actively engages in solving problems in the organization

Job descriptions of assistive personnel reflect their dependence on the leadership of the RN:

- works under the supervision of the RN and receives written and/or verbal assignments and direction
- gathers data for planning the care of the team's patients
- reports appropriately and in a timely manner to the RN who is accountable for the care of those patients
- performs various patient care and attendant activities under the direction of the RN

- participates in planning, implementation, evaluation, and modification of the plan of care by sharing information and reviewing care administered

Duties or specific responsibilities are often outlined. These lists will help you determine what tasks can be assigned to a specific delegate once competency and understanding of the assignment are ascertained.

Examples of some of the duties listed for assistive personnel may be:

- performs oral/nasal suctioning
- assists with admission, transfer, or discharge as determined by the RN
- measures and records intake, output, and vital signs
- performs tasks such as bathing, feeding, and providing postmortem care
- assists in sponge count procedures as instituted by the RN
- observes patient carefully for significant changes
- maintains and orders equipment and supplies
- performs CPR under supervision of an RN or MD
- assists with bowel and bladder retraining

If the job descriptions in your organization do not reflect what is actually happening in your department or facility with your patients, ask some questions!

VALIDATED COMPETENCIES

Many of you may have enjoyed the opportunity to supervise the completion of a competency checklist for a peer, an orienting employee, or for assistive personnel. These checklists are based on what the state law says about scope of practice, how the organization interprets those rules within its system in the form of job descriptions, and the education or orientation attended by the employee. The portion of the state regulatory information that describes the subject matter for the educational program, and standards and competencies expected for the beginning graduate of an educational program, may provide a starting point for competency checklists for new employees.

For an example of what is commonly required in some assistive roles, let's review the State of Arizona's project in which the Arizona Department of Education (1985) published a validated competency list for nursing assistants, LPNs, and associate degree RNs. Fifty competencies were expected for the beginning nursing assistant, each divided into more specific behaviors. In this document, nursing assistants were expected to be competent in such skills as

- collecting sputum and stool specimens
- testing urine using routine methods
- applying protective restraints, ace bandages, flexible abdominal binders
- applying ostomy appliances and irrigating established colostomies
- taking vital signs
- giving a cleansing enema

These competencies are consistent with the *Standards of Function for the Nurse Aide* published by the National Council of State Boards of Nursing (NCSBN) in 1990. The NCSBN warns that enemas may be delegated to nursing assistants but that sterile procedures should not be delegated (NCSBN, 1990).

Validated competencies (Arizona Department of Education, 1985) for LPNs numbered 72, and included such skills as

- sterile technique
- administering medications and IVs, including calculating infusing rate and regulation of gavages and irrigates using previously inserted GI tubes
- timing contractions and measuring and recording fetal heart tones
- performing normal newborn care
- recognizing substance abuse in the child and adolescent (Arizona Department of Education, 1985)

We are often asked by seminar participants clarifying questions such as, "Since Mrs. Fujini's bowel was perforated when Sally gave her that enema, how can I support or document that I was correct in asking Sally to perform that procedure?" When you are familiar with the job descriptions of a nursing assistant in your organization and when you also know that Sally was "checked off" on giving a cleansing enema, the job descriptions and competency checklist are your documentation. If Sally had also been performing enemas without problems, and if in fact you recently observed Sally's technique when you happened to make a home visit while Sally was performing this skill, even better! Since you had not assessed any potential problem with the patient, your decision to ask Sally to give Mrs. Fujini the enema followed the delegation process to the letter.

Some facilities ask new personnel to keep their competency checklist with them, especially during orientation, as an aide to the delegating RN. Other organizations have developed so many new, multiskilled worker roles that they have created a laminated skills checklist for these crosstrained workers to keep in their pockets at work.

THE IMPACT OF THE MISSION ON JOB ROLES

We've spent a fair amount of time focusing on job responsibilities and the details of roles within your team. Earlier in the chapter, we asked you to determine how the mission was reflected in your job descriptions.

As discussed in Chapter 4, a mission statement may include such phrases as the following:

- providing high-quality, cost-effective, integrated health services that support independence and are responsive to the needs of individuals, families, and the community
- promotion of wellness, absence of disease, comfort, education, and independence by the collaborative health care team, in an environment that is responsive to the needs of the public, as well as fiscal accountability and responsibility

Values statements may include such concepts as

- the respect and dignity afforded patients, the public, and employees, with an emphasis on communication skills
- a culture of professional growth
- proactive leadership in shaping change

Examine your facility's mission and/or values. Do you see an emphasis on collaboration, high quality, cost effectiveness? Is the quality of personal relationships among the interdisciplinary team inferred, if not directly stated? If so, you'll recognize the related performance criteria in the job descriptions translated as:

- demonstrates positive interpersonal communication skills that enhance patient care and the functioning of the interdisciplinary team
- uses assertive language in interpersonal relationships
- participates actively in solving problems
- maintains confidentiality
- effectively utilizes human and material resources in planning and implementing care
- responds positively to guidance and feedback
- performs assigned work without discrimination on the basis of age, sexual preference, national origin, race, economic position, religion, disability, or disease

Why are we spending time detailing these parts of the official roles? Because you, as the supervisory RN, must understand fully the impact of the job descriptions and other organizational policies as you match jobs to the delegates and evaluate their performance. This information is necessary not only for making assignments but for giving feedback to your team.

CHECKPOINT 7–3

You've been working with a new multiskilled worker in your neonatal ICU. This person is a respiratory therapist who has been cross-trained as a phlebotomist and nursing assistant. He is in school for LPN licensure. He seems to be doing quite well clinically but has been avoiding performing the care of infants who are HIV-positive or are the babies of "crack" mothers (cocaine abusers). How does this employee's performance reflect that he is not fulfilling his job description if he were working in your facility?

See the end of the chapter for the answers.

UNOFFICIAL EXPECTATIONS OF EACH ROLE

In addition to the official expectations based on the state laws or regulations are the *real* expectations within your facility. If there is a discrepancy between what the state regulations say, what the job descriptions explain, and what really happens, there is a serious problem. Workers should *not* be performing *beyond* their roles in any case. Keep in mind the supervisory and evaluative responsibilities that are present in your state nurse practice act and that were discussed in Chapter 3.

However, there are often other "gray areas" concerning what each individual may expect of his or her coworkers. For example, if you as an RN expect that the home health aide will telephone you immediately if the patient is complaining that the current pain control isn't effective, and if that doesn't happen, you will be justifiably angry. The operational definition of anger is *"unmet expectations."* (We covered this in detail when we talked about the grief process in Chapter 5. This reminder is for those of you who skip around when you read a book.) If a nursing assistant in the long-term care facility expects that you as an RN will be physically involved in helping him or her with hygienic care on a regular basis and you aren't doing that, he or she will be angry also. In the acute care arena, unresolved issues such as these below will continue to cause conflict:

- Who is responsible for answering the phone?
- Who is responsible for answering the call lights?
- Who is responsible for talking with the physician?
- Who is responsible for communicating with the family members about code status decisions?
- Who has the right to sit at the nursing station? For what reason?
- Whose patients are these, really?
- Who communicates what to whom, when?
- Who really has the authority to "make" you do what you are asked to do?
- Who should clean up the equipment or break rooms?

Understanding what each job entails, discussing your expectations within the group, and being realistic about what's reasonable to expect will go a long way to promoting better teamwork.

There is a practical strategy for resolving these issues of "unofficial expectations." Each group must define its expectations of the other groups, and discuss them in an open forum. We suggest that this be done within a staff meeting. If you are unable to do this in a more public and less threatening way (such as in a team meeting), then you must clarify expectations on a personal basis. For example, consider the last few times you've been angry or frustrated with a coworker. What expectation wasn't met by that coworker? It's time to clear the air and clarify what you expect. For example, "When you left the unit today with three patients left on their bedpans and didn't tell anyone, I felt concerned about the patient's skin breakdown. Tell me about what happened today." (Listen to response.) "I was expecting that you would come to tell me before you left for break or ask someone else to help those patients. Let's talk about how you can be certain that patients are not left without someone responsible for getting them off the bedpan." (See Chapter 8 on assertive communication.)

If you feel someone is angry with you, clarify his or her expectations. For example, "I noticed a few minutes ago that you sighed loudly when I gave you the same assignment as yesterday. I am confused about whether you are unhappy with the assignment or if something else is wrong. Let's talk about it so we're all on the same wavelength."

You may wish to use Checkpoint 7–4 in your staff meeting, sharing the responses. You'll find that some people focus on the very concrete tasks ("passes medications"), some will discuss issues that relate to organizational values ("shows respect to the public and coworkers; calls me by name"). You may wish to ask the following questions of each other within your work group on a personal basis.

The following list shows of some of the most common responses that have been given by RNs and CNAs concerning their expectations of RNs:

- Competence
- Do your job
- Be a troubleshooter
- Be an advocate
- Call workers by name
- Respect team members
- Communicate progress and inform team
- Sit at the desk: means RN is doing charting, coordination of care, problem solving
- Share plan for shift clearly
- Instructions should be clear and complete

CHECKPOINT 7-4

(Fill in the blanks now for your own information, and plan to do this exercise as a group.)

I expect RNs to _____

_____

I expect LPNs to _____

_____

I expect CNAs to _____

_____

I expect patient care assistants to _____

_____

I expect the secretary to _____

_____

I expect ___ (fill in the blank) to _____

_____

I expect our boss to _____

_____

On a person-to-person basis:

1. Have I been performing the way you expect me to?
2. Are there things I have or haven't been doing that sometimes bother you?
3. In what ways am I doing a great job?
4. In what ways could I improve the way I do my job?
5. How could I help you perform your job better by the way I do mine?
6. Have you been disappointed about anything in your job?

- Answer lights
- Be courteous
- Teach other team members
- Assess
- Evaluate
- Plan
- Chart
- Trust others
- Organize care
- Give feedback
- Give clear, concise report

The following are some expectations of CNAs reported by CNAs and RNs:

- Respect each other
- Attend report
- Find out if you have questions
- Communicate progress, changes
- Take initiative, but ask questions
- Answer lights
- Be an extra pair of hands
- Be honest
- Trust
- Be motivated
- Follow RN orders
- Be positive and cooperative
- Work as team
- Be part of problem solving
- Organize work
- Beds
- Baths
- Vital signs
- Don't talk to patient about diagnosis or teach
- Don't have to clean up after RNs in kitchen or break room
- Okay to sit at desk if patient work is done or to chart

Talking about these personal expectation issues may seem like a risky process. However, not much is gained without risk. Throughout this process, you will find yourself understanding each other more fully. You'll clarify what each other's jobs should be, and you'll find many fewer conflicts will be getting in the way of excellent care of your patients or clients. Change frustration and anger to relief as you deal with those trying situations that make your job more difficult than it has to be!

ASSESSING THE DELEGATE'S STRENGTHS

Think back to your family. Do you know the strengths of your family members? Who was best at doing the vacuuming? Certainly you had years to get to know each other, and this lengthy process is not always available in health care. In each case, as we look at assessing the qualities of the delegate, we'll focus on how to determine the competencies of those you work with daily and those who are "short-term" help.

Before we consider methods of assessing strengths, it's important to remember *why* we are doing this. Think now of one reason you'd like to know your delegate's best qualities.

_____

_____

Perhaps asking this basic question seems too obvious. When we ask nurses around the country this question, it's common for participants to consider the good of the patients but rare for them to consider the positive effects for themselves or their delegates. You may have come up with other reasons, but we think several are compelling for all of us engaged in treating or caring for patients. The first, most obvious reason is that when people are using their strengths to perform their care duties, the outcomes for the clients are the most effective. The second reason is that people grow when their strengths are recognized and utilized for the good of patient care. The third reason is that your ability to lead is enhanced because there are fewer needless worries each day when people are working within their areas of competency. Let's look at a couple of examples.

1. Do you remember the last time your supervisor gave you an evaluation or yearly performance review? What do you remember most about it? We are willing to bet you remember the competencies your supervisor checked as "needs improvement." Human beings tend to remember the

critical before they remember the positive. Think back, though, about a well-earned compliment you were given. Perhaps your boss or colleague said, "I've noticed that in your caseload you are especially effective in working with families of those who are dying. All of us are impressed with your ability to communicate clearly with them and help them through the grief process." That feels pretty good, doesn't it? And the next time you take care of another similar case, you'll find that you redouble your efforts to do a fine job. You may even think more about the methods you use to be so effective and find that you are able to help others apply the same principles.

2. At Memorial Hospital, a nursing assistant had worked for years on the plastic surgery and burn floor. When she began to float, she was able to alert the RNs on the other floors to special procedures and information she'd learned as "tricks of the trade" in her past clinical areas. Although many of these were less experienced nurses and could have been threatened by her knowledge, they were anxious to learn from the CNA. This sharing of information encouraged a climate of mutual respect in a situation that could have been difficult.

3. The Visiting Nurse Service employed a nurse who had been quite negative in her outlook for years. She had been married now for the third time to a person with a substance abuse problem. But she finally realized there was a pattern to her life, and joined Al-Anon (a program for the families of alcohol-dependent persons). She learned about her codependent tendencies and further delved into all the literature about alcoholism and the community support available. Because of her specialized knowledge, she became the "group expert" on alcoholism, from treatment of the D.T.s (delirium tremens) to the best programs for aftercare in the area. As she found that her home life was improving and as she found herself to be a valued member of the team, her entire attitude changed. She was "making lemonade" out of the lemons she had collected during her life, and it helped her grow as she shared from her experience.

DETERMINING STRENGTHS

We are clear on all the reasons why strengths are important. When you reflected on how you are utilizing your own strengths and those of your delegates, you may have wondered how to discover the "gems under the rough-hewn exteriors" of those with whom you work. How do we determine those sterling qualities? As we discussed in our family example, we determine them from what we observe and hear. You see that Bob is a better cook and enjoys doing the cooking. On your unit or within your work group, if you have not been able to observe strengths in action, then *ask*. You may first ask someone, "What do you *like* to do best?" This is often a good indication of what that person believes he or she does best. If you haven't received enough information yet, ask the delegate, "What do you feel the most comfortable doing? What are you *best* at doing?"

For "short-term" workers such as floats, agency people, or those you may work with only for a short period of time, remember to just come out with it. Ask them what they are good at. Most people know.

A caveat is necessary, however. We have spent time focusing on the strengths, and we have established they certainly are important. However, if a person *always* does what they feel comfortable doing, they will not grow. Be careful not to get into a rut and allow people to become apathetic from a lack of challenge. (We realize that health care is not a boring, slow job and is full of challenges daily, but we felt it necessary to remind people of the potential hazards of becoming too comfortable in one way of doing things.)

Another warning. Some people perceive that they *are* skilled at tasks or processes, but we may observe that they aren't. The RN who is supervising the group cannot afford to take a statement of "I'm good at doing brain surgery" at face value. You may also find yourself falling into the trap of the "halo or horn" effect. That person who seems to be an all-out super crackerjack cannot be perfect in *all* areas. The delegate whose personality rubs you the wrong way is not really the devil in disguise. He or she has at least one or two strengths also. *All of the assessment data regarding the delegate, the patient situation, and the work that needs to be completed is essential for your decision making.*

CHECKPOINT 7–5

How then, are you now utilizing your own and your coworkers' strengths in the way you divide and apportion your work now? Think about your last week of work and a few examples of how your delegates' strengths were used effectively.

If you were unable to come up with situations, spend a few moments thinking about the strengths of each of your coworkers and how they could be utilized for positive future impact.

ASSESSING THE DELEGATE'S WEAKNESSES

The potential weaknesses of the delegates are the most frightening aspect for the RNs we've talked with across the United States. They are afraid that "their license is on the line" and that they will be losing their licensure if a mistake is made by one of their delegates.

Remember that supervision means you will provide guidance for the accomplishment of a nursing task or activity, with initial direction and periodic inspection of the actual task or activity, and that the total nursing care of the individual remains the responsibility and accountability of the RN. The burden of determining the competency of the person who will perform the work and of evaluating the situation remains with the licensed nurse (NCSBN, 1990).

So it is very important to determine a delegate's competency, strengths, and weaknesses. We have already addressed the state regulations limiting practice, the job descriptions of your facility, and the competency checklists that may be used by your organization. These are all excellent guides for your decision making.

At this point, however, the RN must determine the competency of that one individual for a specific set of circumstances for one day, one shift, one caseload. There is no exacting scientific formula for this. Once again, your decision rests on your *nursing judgment*. Your nursing judgment is based on your assessment of the delegate and the situation, your past experience, and is one of the reasons you are being paid as a professional. There is not a profession on this earth that allows its practitioners to avoid making these kinds of decisions. An attorney's decision to plea bargain or to try for acquittal for his client based on his knowledge of the situation affects all involved. A CPA's decision to try a new tactic to use impending tax laws to the client's best advantage, drawing up a limited partnership agreement, is based on her best judgment of the future and her past education and experience. As a professional RN, you are called upon daily to make these types of decisions many times. You decide when to call the physician, when to approach the family for a code status, how to plan therapy for the newly diagnosed schizophrenic, how much IV pressor to administer to reduce the potential for renal insufficiency.

For the short-term worker within your organization, the person that you don't *know* as well, you may ask the following questions: "What do you feel you are best at doing? Have you completed these kinds of procedures before at our facility? There is a new procedure written up for this task. I'll get it for you and we'll go over it. Do you have any questions now? Let me tell you about our patients in more detail. I'm on this beeper if you have any questions later on."

Some organizations that use floats or short-term help frequently have developed "float cards" or other evaluative tools for the agency or internal float pool. These allow the RN to give written information to the person's immediate boss for positive and negative feedback or to determine learning needs. They are not a substitute for verbal discussion with the delegate at that time, however. Feedback and communication will be covered in more detail in Chapters 10 and 11.

For those colleagues who are within your work force on a general basis, how have you assessed their weaknesses in the past? You may be aware of their weaknesses from several sources:

- from personal observation as you have supervised them or followed them
- from the competency checklist
- from asking them for input as to what they feel uncomfortable doing or what they need to learn more about
- from the "grapevine"

Let's look first at the "grapevine." The grapevine can be valuable in that you may be aware of a potential need for increased supervision if you have heard that someone is "a quart low on energy." However, *beware* of the grapevine. Most nurses have heard of situations in which a new staff member was branded by a person who didn't like students or didn't approve of some aspect of the staff member's personality, and a negative image was spread across the organization. Remember that an open but observant and listening attitude is the most useful.

Asking the person for input is extremely important and can be the most simple way to uncover potential problems. An atmosphere that allows people to be imperfect, having some space for growth, is essential. This kind of communication will reap rewards in the future. For example, a new graduate may be frightened to death of patients with tracheotomies, but after being guided in caring for them, that staff member may be the most careful and the most well prepared to work with that type of client. Use your experience and judgment, and open your mouth and *ask* people if they are uncomfortable with any aspects of their assignments. For example, if you're working on a pediatric unit and there is a cerebral palsy patient who has a special feeding and needs to be fed, what will you ask the nursing assistant who is going to help with feedings today? "Have you ever worked with dysphagia feeding before? I'll show you today, and we'll do it together until you are comfortable with it. I'll have to check on the suction apparatus as well."

Use your competency checklists and job descriptions! Find a place for team members to keep them so they can be responsible for having them available for your discussions.

What about the problems that you've seen with delegates because you've followed them, or observed or heard their actions? These shortcomings generally fall into the following categories:

1. They don't understand what is expected of them.
2. They don't understand that their perception of their activities does not fit within your acceptable parameters for behavior.
3. They may have unmet educational needs.
4. They may need more supervision and guidance.
5. They may not care.

Let's look at each of these underlying reasons for performance weaknesses, often aptly called "areas for improvement and growth," and determine your course of action with each.

1. *They don't understand what is expected of them.* Understanding expectations is essential. Although we have covered this in detail previously in this chapter, when someone doesn't know that it isn't okay to sit at the desk and eat chocolates while others are performing CPR, he or she needs to be told. Some people truly need to be told things that we may suspect "should be" common knowledge. Remember, don't "should" on each other. Clear communication about your expectations is essential. "I expect you to be answering lights when you are not directly involved in the code situation."

2. *They don't understand that their perception of their activity and your assessment do not directly coincide.* As we discussed when we evaluated delegates' strengths, delegates may not recognize that they are not doing their job the way you believe it should be done. When you find this is the problem, remember to focus on *outcomes.* Does it make any difference to the

patient outcome that John does the bath in a different order, or that Pat's charting on the intake and output chart is done after break? It may or may not be significant. Just realize that some of us tend to be a bit "set in our ways" and have difficulty seeing things done differently, even if it doesn't affect the outcome in any way. Be clear about what you expect and *why* it makes a difference.

If patient welfare or safety is involved, *immediate* action must be taken. If you see a CNA giving a medication to a patient (in most states this is not acceptable except in certain long-term care arenas with specially certified CNAs), you should immediately ask her to step out of the room and talk about unlicensed practice, and bring this to the attention of the manager.

3. *They don't know, understand, or have sufficient information.* Some weaknesses may be educational needs. Perhaps the delegate doesn't want to care for AIDS patients because he or she is afraid. If the staff member understands more about the transmission of the disease and attends the mandatory education about HIV, there will be a change in the delegate's behavior and acceptance of the assignment.

4. *They need additional guidance and supervision.* As we discussed in our example of family roles, there are those in our family or social group who need more supervision than others. The spouse who goes to the grocery store and picks up the children at the soccer game may need exact directions and a specific list of items to buy at the supermarket. The roommate who pays the electricity bill may need a reminder when it is due, whereas other roommates may clean out the tub without being reminded. Some of your delegates will take more energy than others in terms of your time and observation.

Remember that there is a bell curve of performance. The majority of people are on the competent level. Some are overachieving "stars" as they go above and beyond the most highly competent and superior ratings in their job descriptions. But there are a few that waver at the marginal performance line. These individuals cause us the most consternation, but since we can't eliminate the possibility that we'll always have one or two (or more) within our staff, we must address how to deal with these marginal performers.

As we talk with nurses across this country, they often tell us that the most difficult part of their work life is dealing with this type of delegate. They often express anger at the managers: "Why doesn't the manager fire this person! She (he) should know that this person isn't performing well!"

We then ask, "What have *you* done about the problem?" Part of your professional role is as patient advocate. You are required to report and to deal with any behavior that would adversely affect your charges: your patients. The nurse manager or other supervisory person must be given the exact data that will assist him or her in dealing effectively with the performance problem. As an RN who supervises others, you must confront any performance that does not fall within legal parameters or job descriptions, or could be detrimental to the patient. Changing the bed in a certain way may be just a personal preference issue, but leaving a confused patient in a bed with the side rails down and in high position is unacceptable from a safety standpoint. Again focusing on potential outcomes, how will these behaviors affect the patient care or organizational goals?

As we'll discuss in more detail in Chapter 10, RNs must give their perceptions of the performance to the delegate and send on any information that will be necessary to the manager involved in formal performance counseling.

Let's discuss a difficult situation: that of the staff member who is wavering on the line of competent/incompetent while being assisted to either improve her performance or be counseled into another position (one perhaps that won't involve live human beings!). How does the RN supervise this delegate? *Very carefully!* This person will not be assigned tasks or processes that have been problematic in the past, and will often be buddied with another, competent person who understands the limitations. The RN must then be very careful to check on the progress of this delegate, observing, assessing, asking questions, and obtaining report information from the delegate more frequently. This type of staff member poses special problems when the staffing is low. Remember that there are other methods of care delivery. If this person can handle vital signs and other housekeeping tasks well, perhaps that is what they should be assigned. This situation, although rare, challenges RNs to use all their creativity and innovative approaches to encourage the marginal delegate to use all of his or her strengths for the best possible patient care and safety.

5. What about the person who *doesn't seem to care?* This brings us to another parameter we need to be aware of as we assess the delegates: What makes them tick? What motivates them to do their job? We'll explore the delegate's motivation after this checkpoint.

CHECKPOINT 7–6

1. You have noted that Joy, a new LPN (LVN) telephoned a physician for orders yesterday. This is not recognized as the LPN's role in this organization. You realize that Joy:
   a) may not know the role expectations in this facility.
   b) may have done this in past jobs and feels competent to do so, no matter what you say about this.
   c) probably won't do this again, and you decide not to mention it to her.
   d) will need to be told about the expectations and that you may need to give feedback also to the nurse manager, depending on her response.
5. Zachary, the secretary, has made several transcribing errors today as new residents are being admitted to your Alzheimer's unit. You, as supervisory nurse to Zachary, decide to:
   a) wait until the facility director of nurses hears about the problem.
   b) tell the director of nurses.
   c) find out if Zach's problem is an educational need.
   d) recommend action to the director after first discussing it with Zach.
5. Patty, an experienced worker in your outpatient surgery area, has the combined job of nursing assistant and environmental services (housekeeping). She often interacts with the public, and you've noticed that she sighs loudly as she bends over, making groaning noises that disturb the families. She also seems to need constant direction. You decide to:
   a) let it go. She's not your problem.
   b) ask her about her behavior. Find out if she's having back trouble, and find out if she knows her job description.

continues

CHECKPOINT 7–6 *continued*

    c) determine why she is having trouble finding things to do when there is so much work needing to be done, without accusing her or putting her down.

    d) discuss your findings with her and ask her for some ideas for solutions. Share your conversations with the supervisor.

5. A float nurse has just come to work with you on your unit. Your nurse manager had given you the feedback that this person has made several errors and is being helped with her problems through the clinical nurse specialist. How will you assess what this person will be able to do today?

    a) ask her for her competency checklist.

    b) tell her you're having her work in a nursing assistant role and that's that.

    c) question her carefully on what she's done before, what she feels comfortable doing. Arrange for someone to be available and for specific checkup times for assessing and assisting.

    d) call the supervisor and demand a competent person to care for your patients.

See the end of the chapter for the answers.

ASSESSING THE DELEGATE'S MOTIVATION

How often have you traveled home from your workplace, wondering *why* Sue or John ever showed up to work today at all? Why do they bother to come to work when their apparent lack of commitment and energy forces us to push and pull them through the day? The motivation of our coworkers becomes a significant issue for the quality of our work lives, and certainly becomes essential for our ability to assess our delegates and match them with the work that needs to be done.

Return to your past knowledge of Maslow's hierarchy of needs (Maslow, 1970). In clinical situations, we know that if a family needs food and shelter, these basic needs must be supplied before we educate them about their child's diabetes, for example. In the work situation, we may all come to work for different reasons each day, and often these reasons are related to where we are currently functioning on the hierarchy of needs. Exhibit 7–1 shows these different levels of need and your possible response, as a supervisor, to employees functioning at these levels.

The first step of the hierarchy of needs is that of safety and security needs. Few of us are independently wealthy, and most of us certainly would notice if our paychecks were to disappear. But most of us have other reasons for working in the type of job we choose. Coworkers who are working *only* for their paycheck so that they can put food on the table and keep a roof over their heads will need to be supervised differently from those who chose health care because they feel an affinity for it. If the *only* thing that motivates people is getting that paycheck, they need to know that they must fulfill their job expectations for performance in order to remain employed. Although this may seem to be a "hard-nosed" point to emphasize, as RNs supervising others, you must be prepared for such employees. They must know that if they do not fulfill the job requirements, they won't get their paycheck.

When there has been a recent reduction in force, or layoff of nursing personnel, many staff are concerned only about taking care of the safety and security needs. Few nurses will volunteer for a special committee or become excited about a quality management program when they are

Exhibit 7–1 Levels of Employee Needs and Supervisory Responses

Functioning Level	*Your Response*	*Examples*
Self- fulfillment	Encourage involvement in dept. functioning, variety and new challenge Keep eye on vision and purpose	Volunteering to head a new committee to discuss new care delivery design
Ego	Positive feedback (necessary for all motivation stages)	Saying thanks Detailed feedback
Social or belonging	Use social strengths for patients who need it, may need to observe progress closely	Potlucks, celebrations of the outcomes of a difficult case
Safety and security	Safe, secure climate; close supervision	Clear expectations Security guards in parking lot

worried about having a job at all. If it's impossible for your night shift workers to find enough warm, nutritious food at night when your diet kitchen is closed down, don't expect they'll have gone out of their way to get a start on the oncoming shift's work.

Motivation comes from within the person. You can provide an environment that will encourage growth and excitement, but you can't force a person to be engaged and enthusiastic about the teamwork and the outcomes you are all achieving together. Keep in mind each person's individual reason for being at work, and use this to your best advantage for the best patient care. As staff become more confident that their basic needs will be fulfilled, they may catch the excitement and climb to a higher level of motivation. We all waver in our motivational levels in a manner related to our personal life and how we perceive our impact on the world through work and other institutions.

The second level of motivation is that of social or affiliative needs. Many of us find fulfillment from the personal relationships we enjoy in health care, whether with each other or with those we serve. The staff who are significantly motivated at this level may be those who love to talk and to organize the baby showers or social events. They may hold very dear the time that they have to interact with their clients on a one-to-one basis. This staff member may be the perfect person to assign to the elderly client who requires more interpersonal time. He or she may also be buddied with a coworker who is very goal directed but gives the affiliative-need partner much positive feedback.

The third level of motivation is that of ego needs for self-respect or status leading to self-esteem. Staff who would like recognition and job growth may be motivated from this level. As RNs assign work or supervise staff at the ego level, the use of positive feedback, opportunities to be involved in task forces, recognition in the form of clinical ladders, and educational opportunities may be the most energizing. A CNA who is functioning primarily at this level may want to care for patients who have different diagnoses, which he or she can research and use in their care.

A note of caution here. When nurses or other health care professionals identify themselves too closely with their job description, so that they themselves become interchangeable with what they do (i.e., what I do equals who I am and my value as a human being), and then their job roles change, they will be most disturbed. If asked who you are, how do you respond? Do you immediately think, "I'm John Jones, an oncology home health RN"? You as a human being have value beyond what you do for employment or as a profession. Be aware of this tendency when changes rock your workplace, and be especially good to yourself as you cope with the changes.

The fourth level of Maslow's hierarchy is that of self-fulfillment or self-actualization. As professionals, we hope that many of you are doing your job because you are aware of how your role affects the lives of others and that you are aware of how you affect your own growth and the growth of those you serve by what you do. Staff who are motivated at this stage are a joy to work with since they often help you, as supervising RN, look beyond the daily frustrations to the real reasons that you do your job.

YOUR RESPONSIBILITY FOR THE "GENERAL CLIMATE" OF MOTIVATION

Whether you are currently working in the role of a student nurse, staff RN, charge nurse, or nurse manager in any portion of the health care system, you have an influence on the environment in which you work. It is true that you can't be in control of others' behavior, but you can behave in a way that will affect others positively.

Multiple studies have been done—within health care, with nurses, and in business—about what motivates workers. Most researchers would agree that the significance of the work being done, the degree of autonomy or decision making within the job, and the feedback given to workers affect job satisfaction and motivation. The types of relationships among workers also influence the climate of motivation within a group.

Research has also proven a positive correlation between productivity, commitment to the organization, and job satisfaction. Specific leadership behaviors have been proven to directly influence productivity, commitment, and job satisfaction. The critical behaviors of "inspiring a shared vision, enabling others to act, modeling the way, challenging the process, and encouraging the heart are all positively related" to the results you want to achieve in establishing a climate of motivation in your team (McNeese-Smith, 1992).

Your communication with others is fundamental to building relationships in your facility. When you tackle problems with a proactive, positive outlook, others want to be around you. (How many people follow leaders, or want to be around colleagues, who consistently express feelings of defeat, discouragement, and gloom?)

A climate of achievement is promoted when everyone understands what he or she is expected to do and where he or she is going. Reinforcing expectations, making goals clear, and encouraging everyone to participate in decision making as much as possible will provide a basis for clear and open communication. With that open communication, trust will develop. Reminding people of *why* they are doing what they are doing (your mission) will energize them as they recognize how what they are doing contributes to the group's goals. Positive feedback (discussed in detail in Chapter 10) is one of the most powerful motivators in your formulary.

You may not be the CEO of the organization, and you may not sign the paychecks. However, pay raises are short-lived as motivators. Long-lasting motivation comes from being involved, feeling appreciated, and being clear about what you are to do and why. Each of you, every member of the team, is an integral part of establishing the climate of motivation in your facility.

ASSESSING THE DELEGATE'S PREFERENCES

You may be surprised that it's taken us so long to get to the point of assessing the delegate's preferences. You will note that this is not the first of the criteria on the assessment list. This is because, all too often, the most aggressive delegate's preferences determine the assignments given to all the delegates. When it's possible, and reflects your best judgment clinically, delegates appreciate doing the tasks they like best. However, again there may be an issue of whether the comfort zone is the best choice, and if it seems unfair that "Railroad Rita" has an easier assignment and avoids caring for Mr. Difficult Patient once again, it's important to analyze the other criteria for matching the delegate to the assignment more carefully.

As RNs understand more clearly their responsibility and accountability for supervision of the delegates, they will be less likely to choose the course of least resistance when delegating care.

ASSESSING CULTURAL DIFFERENCES

As we work together to care for patients of diverse cultural backgrounds, we, the caregivers, are also influenced by our rainbow heritage of every hue of race, creed, color, gender, sexual preference, and age group. Even the community in which we grew up affects the way we communicate, prioritize and perform our work, and relate to each other.

A story illustrates the challenges we face as a multicultural team. A second-grade teacher announced to the class, "Boys and girls, there were four blackbirds on the limb of a tree. One was hit with a rock from a slingshot. How many were left?" One little boy immediately waved his hand and breathlessly shouted, "I know, teacher, I know! There were three blackbirds left!" A second boy interrupted. "No, there's not a chance any of those blackbirds would stick around! There were *zero* blackbirds left!" The first little boy placed a high priority on task, structure, and timely response to the teacher's question. The second little boy focused on reality and on relationships. Both were right.

This book is not a text on cultural diversity. However, we encourage readers to explore how the background of each of their coworkers affects their understanding of the communications they give and receive each day. Even the body language and eye contact used by certain cultural groups can be misunderstood by coworkers. To you, is lack of eye contact a sign of respect or of dishonesty? It depends on your cultural heritage.

The first step to overcoming the possible hazards of miscommunication because of cultural differences comes from recognizing that these differences are a reality of who we are and consequently are not negotiable. One could never find a totally homogeneous group with whom to work. Who would want to? Not only would it be boring, but there would be few variations to enrich the service we provide to our clients!

The second step is to embrace the differences. Ask questions of each other about backgrounds, such as "How did you handle conflict in your family?" Enjoy the attending special strengths that can be enjoyed with cultural diversity. A potluck with ethnic foods can be a tasty way to celebrate differences.

The most important step to is communicate, communicate, communicate. Clarify questions and perceptions. For example, "When I told you that the vital signs in that room were a high priority, I didn't tell you that I meant within five minutes. Did you have another priority that came up?" (This situation may occur with a cultural background that looks at time in a different way.) "When you didn't look me in the eye when we were speaking together, I wondered if you were understanding me." (This type of clarification may assist you in learning that eye contact is not polite in the staff member's culture.)

Again, just as we must *know* our patients in order to care for them effectively, we must *know* our delegates.

CHECKPOINT 7–7

1. Knowing a delegate's motivation is important because:
   a) It is one of the assessment parameters that will allow me to make the correct decision about matching the delegate with the correct assignment.
   b) It will help me understand how to help him or her grow as we provide safe, effective patient care.
   c) I need to know how closely I will need to supervise this person.
   d) It's not important because no one could possibly take the time to know all this stuff about the people they work with.
   e) Understanding my coworkers better decreases the frustrations I may have to face each day.
6. I keep asking for feedback from Lew, but I can't seem to get an answer. She also asks someone else to do any personal care to any males. I can't decide if she's lazy or what!
   a) Both of these issues could be a cultural barrier we need to discuss.
   b) She may not be motivated to do the job.
   c) I will speak about this to her.
   d) I will just understand this is who she is and forget about straightening it out.
5. A student nurse will be caring for my patient who has a tracheotomy and a feeding tube. I will ask the following questions:
   a) Nothing. The instructor should be there for all of the care. It's his problem.
   b) I'll ask the student what parts of the care she is planning to do.
   c) I'll ask about whether she's done any of this care before.
   d) I'll ask her detailed questions about positioning, suctioning, tube feedings, and trach cuffs, and will be involved in the care of this patient all day.

continues

CHECKPOINT 7–7 *continued*

5. Return to the questions we asked at the beginning of the chapter. Which type of health care professional in your organization can perform the following procedures?
   a) pierce the skin to perform procedures
   b) start IVs
   c) monitor IVs
   d) perform the nursing process
   e) gather data for the RN as she or he performs the assessment, nursing diagnosis, planning, intervention, and evaluation
   f) perform hygienic care
   g) deliver medications
   h) be in charge of coordinating care in your health care setting
   i) educate the patient

See the end of the chapter for the answers.

SUMMARY

Let's return to that pesky question nurses ask, "What about my license?"

When you as the RN are following the supervision clause in your nurse practice act, when you are delegating appropriately, you

- know the job descriptions and official rules and regulations for yourself and delegates
- know delegates' strengths, weaknesses, motivation, and preferences
- know the patients and clients based on your assessment, diagnosis, planning, intervention, and evaluation
- use your professional judgment to match delegates to the work that needs to be done
- continually supervise, evaluate, and give feedback to delegates

When you do these things, you are using your professional judgment and being responsible and accountable. The delegates themselves are accountable for their own actions as they perform their roles within their legal and organizational limitations. As much as you would like to control every one of their actions and protect patients from any mistakes, you cannot do that any more than you can prevent mistakes from happening within an all-RN staff. Delegates are accountable for their mistakes as they act within their job descriptions and practice limitations. You as an RN are accountable for the total care of the patient and for correcting the effects of the error. You must also address the cause of the delegate's error, be certain that charting and other paperwork (such as the Unusual Occurrence Report) is completed, and pass on the information to those who need to know (possibly the manager, and the next shift). You have acted with excellent nursing judgment. Although you could not control every action of those you supervised, you followed professional standards to be accountable for your supervisory duties.

Getting to know delegates' qualities, just as you get to know qualities of family members, allows you to match delegates to the work that needs to be done for more effective patient care. In the next chapter, we'll discuss how to communicate your delegation decisions to the members of your team and how to keep the group from becoming a dysfunctional family!

ANSWERS TO CHECKPOINTS

7-2. Pat needs to consult with an administrative person to determine what steps were taken as the hospital decided to introduce IV therapy into the LPN role. (Hopefully, they contacted the state board for an advisory opinion, which determined that LPNs could monitor IV therapy and administer some IV medications if educated in this area. Competency would have to be determined and "checked off" after the education program was completed.) As for LPNs as "primary nurses," the LPNs may be functioning nearly independently because RNs do not understand their own accountability by law. Pat needs to discuss his concerns about LPN supervision with his manager and help solve this problem. This hospital needs to determine the methods by which RNs will supervise LPN practice. RN's assessments and/or care planning involvement should be documented on the patient record as well.

7–3. This multidisciplinary worker may be discriminating based on disease. Or he may need some more education about HIV and how to treat crack babies. He may not be aware of the pattern of his behavior. (Read more about performance problems and giving feedback in Chapter 10.)

7–6.
   1. a, b, d
   2. c, d
   3. b, c, d
   4. a, c

7–7.
   1. a, b, c, e
   2. a, b (but probably not), c
   3. b, c, d
   4. We suspect that only RNs can perform d and h! Refer to your state practice act and organizational job descriptions to determine your answers.

REFERENCES

Arizona Department of Education. 1985. *Inventory of validated competencies and skills for nursing assistant, practical nurse, and associate degree nurse graduates.* Phoenix, Ariz.

Maslow, A. H. 1970. *Motivation and personality.* 2nd ed. New York: Harper & Row.

McNeese-Smith, D. 1992. The Impact of leadership on productivity. *Nursing Economics* 10, no. 6: 396.

National Council of State Boards of Nursing (NCSBN). 1990. *Model nurse aide administrative rules by the Subcommittee for Model Nurse Aide Language and the Nursing Practice and Education Committee.* Chicago.

Chapter 8

How Can I Communicate So That the Work Gets Done Right?

Loretta O'Neill

"Believe me, I'd love to delegate more of my routine care. I've tried in the past, but it hasn't been worth the effort. I get anxious about asking someone else for help because I'm concerned that they will think I can't handle my assignment. Then when I'm really bogged down and do delegate something, I spend time worrying if it is getting done right or done at all, following up, finding out that it wasn't even done, and finally doing it myself. It seems I save a lot of energy by just doing it myself in the first place!"

Sound familiar? You can probably see the need for delegating in your workplace. You think it is important, but somehow in the thousands of details that make up your work day, learning the skill of delegation isn't at the top of your "to do" list. When you delegate, you entrust another to act in your place for that particular task or cluster of tasks. You are still responsible for the delivery of the task. How can you be sure it will be done satisfactorily and on time? Notice that the criteria for successful delegation are satisfactory accomplishment of the task (which includes important safety and patient interaction components) and on-time completion. Since the delegate is not you, he or she may not perform the task the exact way you would.

A key to successful delegation is in understanding, first, that delegation is an investment of time and energy that doesn't always have immediate returns, and second, that delegation is a skill, which implies that it has discrete steps or components, that it requires practice to improve, and that repeated practice of it will facilitate improvement.

185

DELEGATE RESPONSES

Assuming that the task(s) delegated and the delegate selected were appropriate, your request may receive a number of responses, all of which are probably familiar to you. Here we are assuming that your communication instructions have been *clear* and *complete*. The delegate's responses may fall into one of the following three categories: agreement, refusal, and absence.

Agreement Response

This represents the happy scenario of a delegated task willingly accepted. You delegate a task, and the delegate agrees to perform it. The response is basically, "Yes, I'll do it." You have delegated the authority to the delegate to complete the task. You have also indicated time frames for completion and situational boundaries for which you need to be notified.

Possible results of agreement response are:

1. You monitor the delegate's progress and find out that the task(s) has been accomplished satisfactorily and on time.
2. The initial willingness of the delegate to perform the task leads to partially satisfactory results. The task may actually be completed but not satisfactorily, or it may be done correctly but not in the appropriate time frame. Many nurses habitually "fix it" when faced with this scenario. They complete the partially accomplished work or redo the incorrect work of their delegate. This has a number of negative effects. First, "plugging the gap" circumvents the accountability of the delegate to perform the agreed-upon task satisfactorily. The delegate needs feedback regarding what is and is not acceptable in the completion of the task. Without this feedback, the delegate is not likely to improve. Second, the delegating nurse becomes hypervigilant, checking, rechecking, and possibly redoing work that he or she thought was being done. This hypervigilance can lead to resentment toward the delegate, deterioration in the working relationship, and an unbearable workload for the nurse.
3. A frustrating variation on this scenario of initial agreement to perform the delegated task is the delegate who willingly and cheerfully agrees to do the task but does not actually perform it. When you follow up on the delegate's progress or lack thereof, you may hear, "I

forgot," "I asked someone else to do that for me" (the delegate becomes a second delegator), "I got too busy with my patients," "I'm getting to it," or some other reason for nonperformance.

Once again, the delegating nurse will often reclaim the task and complete it him- or herself. Some of the rationales given by the nurse for this action include urgent need for patient data to be collected; concern that the treatment or therapy needs to be done on schedule; and concern that the delegate will be angry or upset with the nurse if confronted and will make a scene, take his or her feelings out on the patient, or make an error.

In possible results 2 and 3, the delegating nurse shares responsibility for creating the delegation problem, usually by failing to monitor the delegate's progress until the deadline, then taking the task back. In doing so, the nurse participates in setting up a frustrating cycle: delegation; unsatisfactory accomplishment of the task by the delegate; reclaiming of the task by the delegating nurse; resentment and/or anger for both parties; recommitment to "doing it all myself"; work overload for nurse; attempted delegation. This cycle fails to motivate or develop the skill level of the delegate in doing the task or of the delegating nurse in holding the delegate accountable. It can also frustrate and stress both the nurse and the delegate unnecessarily.

Refusal Response

This represents the unhappy scenario when the nurse attempts to delegate a task and the delegate indicates verbally or nonverbally, "No, I won't/can't do it." This may be accompanied by a number of reasons for the refusal. The reasons offered may be rational and based on stated but conflicting goals. For example, the nurses' aide can't stay at the bedside of a confused and fall-prone patient while simultaneously helping to pass out meal trays. Or the refusal may be due to an inability or lack of knowledge about how to perform the requested task.

On the other hand, nonrational reasons based on hidden and unstated goals may be behind the refusal. The intended delegate's desire for personal power, prestige, or revenge may be motivating the refusal response. For example, a delegating nurse, on her way to administer a pain medication to a patient, stops and requests another staff member to help one of the nurse's patients on the bedpan. The intended delegate places her hands on her hips, glares at the nurse, and states in a loud voice, "I am not your slave!" and walks away. This refusal of a delegated task is based on a desire to equalize a power imbalance in the relationship between the delegating nurse and the delegate.

Absence Response

In addition to the responses of "Yes, I'll do it," "No, I won't/can't do it," and a nonrational "attack," there is another scenario, that of the missing delegate. Nurses, desirous of delegating routine and noncomplex tasks to others, note that some of their ancillary staff are "missing in action." It is indeed difficult to delegate to someone who is avoiding the additional work. As in a bad game of Tag, you are forever "it" because you can't find the delegate who is off the unit, hiding in an empty room, or otherwise occupied and unavailable to be tagged with a delegated task.

COMMUNICATION STYLES

How do you, as the delegating nurse, deal appropriately with this wide scope of possible behaviors? How can you find the right words to communicate to the delegate, to keep communication channels open, and to resist the temptation to just do it all yourself? The words you choose and the way in which they are delivered to the delegate make the difference between a successful and a frustrating episode in delegation. Your communication choices fall into one of three general categories: passive, aggressive, or assertive. Let's take a look at each of the three possible styles, taking passive first.

Passive or Nonassertive

After listening to reports, you make out the shift assignments, based on the acuity of the patients and the skill level of the staff available today. The LPN counts up each person's patient load and says, "I have all of the heaviest patients. I think this should be divided up evenly between the RNs and LPNs, since LPNs do everything but IVs." You think the assignment is appropriate, based on the previous criteria, but this particular LPN can be quite difficult to work with and you don't want to start the shift with a scene, so you say, "Oh, here. I'll take one of your patients in 334. I have the other patient in that room and will be in there a lot anyway."

This is a typically passive or nonassertive response, also termed avoidance. Although it is not advisable or even possible to deal with every conflict situation, a habitually passive response stems from a number of feelings, including fear, anxiety, timidity, inhibition, hurt, self-denial, helplessness, and physical and emotional stress. If words are spoken they are often not reflective of the actual thoughts or feelings of the passive individual, adding an element of emotional dishonesty to the communication. Internally, an intense dialogue rages, with repeated replaying of the situation and various alternate responses that the passive person could have given.

The costs of habitually passive behavior include lowering of self-esteem and self-confidence, a negative self-image, avoidance of responsibility for the quality of one's relationships and life, and lost opportunities to develop skills in managing conflict and resolving issues. Problems are not faced or solved. Consequently they multiply at the feet of the passive communicator. Effective delegation become impossible and the delegator ends up doing more and more work him- or herself. If the delegator's passivity is excessive, the delegates may become even less cooperative and control the amount and quality of work done.

Through constant acquiescence, the goals of others get accomplished, not the goals of the passive person. In addition, nonassertive behavior can engender feelings of pity, disgust, irritation, confusion, and anger in others.

Why on earth would anyone choose this communication style when the results seem so negative? A passive response is based on the fear of rejection and retaliation caused by displeasing others. Conflict is avoided at the price of denying one's own feelings and needs. The reward is immediate avoidance of an unpleasant situation and the attendant feelings of tension. Eventually this strategy backfires because feelings stay suppressed only for a time. Like a toxic chemical solution buried in a rusty drum, feelings of anger and resentment begin to leak out. These negative feelings show up in subtle, hostile behaviors and quiet ways of punishing or manipulating others such as forgetting, unconscious sabotage, withdrawal, sulking, or crying. So the helpless, withdrawn, silent martyr actually has a method of communicating, though it is indirect and manipulative.

Aggressive

You and two nursing assistants are working the night shift. One assistant on the Alzheimer's unit is off the unit on an errand. You are already behind schedule in giving medications when you find that a patient, Mr. Smith, has untied his restraints, been incontinent of urine, and slipped and fallen on the floor. You go to the desk and see the remaining aide reading a magazine with his feet up on the desk. When you request his help, he replies, "This is not my side of the hall" and returns to his reading. You lose your cool and in no uncertain terms tell him, through clenched teeth, in a low and angry voice, "I don't really care whose side of the hall it is, you worthless, lazy bum. This patient needs help, and you are going to help me get him back to bed and cleaned up right now. I'm tired of seeing you sit around here when these people need help. You do this every night. Get out of that chair now and don't let me catch you sitting down the rest of the night!" You stomp off to Mr. Smith's room.

In this scenario, the nurse has no problem expressing her thoughts, feelings, and wants. She is expressive and her words honestly reflect the feelings she experiences. You can see that she is annoyed, stressed, impatient, and angry.

However, her direct communication comes at the expense of the other. Her words carry a tone of righteous superiority and "loaded" terms such as "worthless," "lazy," and "bum." Such phrases have not been known to engender cheerful acceptance of delegated tasks! The communication she uses in this aggressive response is riddled with "you" messages of blame and labeling. How do you imagine the nurses' aide feels about himself? Probably hurt and humiliated. His feelings about the nurse are likely to be angry and vengeful. She even throws in a general condemnation about how he has used his time previously. These characteristics of aggressive communication typify the verbal attack. Aggressive behavior is an encroachment or attack upon another and is almost always hostile in intent. The communication flows from the aggressive person outward. Little listening takes place while he or she talks at, not with, others. This style, long on criticism and short on praise, successfully suppresses ideas and feedback from others. Such a tension-filled relationship evokes passive aggressive behavior on the part of others, which perpetuates the cycle of overbearing authoritarianism and indirect aggression.

In another setting you may have witnessed aggressive behavior without actual speech. The pediatric clinical specialist who has just lost a neonate after a long fight may enter the nurses' station area with a flourish and then begin to throw charts or slam the telephone down on the hook when the lab doesn't respond immediately to his call.

The will of the aggressive person often prevails in the conflict situation. The goal is to dominate and hurt the other. The price of winning is the animosity of the recipients. During the verbal storm the aggressive person speaks as if he or she has no "mental filter" but says whatever is on his or her mind. This brutal directness fosters fear and resistance, sabotage and resentment in the listener. Delegating with an aggressive manner of communication often has the same ultimate result as a passive style, since real problems don't get solved and the delegator is avoided and ends up doing more work him- or herself.

Assertive

You assign a staff member to take postoperative vital signs on a C-section patient. When you go back to check on the readings, the last two sets are not on the flow sheet. The last set of vital signs charted is over an hour old. You find the staff member and say, "I was in Mrs. Miller's room and noticed that the last set of vital signs charted is from an hour ago. I am concerned about her blood pressure. Do you have a more recent set?" The staff member gives you vital signs written on a scrap paper in her pocket. You say, "These look fine. In the future, please chart them all on the bedside flow sheet. It will save us both time."

No one approach will be best for handling every delegation situation, but knowing how to express yourself assertively can help you with the people-related problems of delegation. Assertive communicators are confident and positive and lay claim to their own right to speak up for themselves. In the example above, the nurse is direct and expresses what she has observed, thinks, feels, and wants in this situation. The message is congruent with what she feels, so it is emotionally honest. She clearly addresses the problem without belittling herself or the other person. She knows what she wants and asks for it without apology. Assertive people feel good about themselves at the time they communicate and later. They are not ambushed by feelings of anger, resentment, or guilt. Because this style of communication addresses the problem in the situation, real problems get solved and stay solved.

Other people generally respect the assertive person because they themselves are treated with respect, not with deference, as in passivity, or with dominance, as in aggressiveness. And because the assertive person communicates directly when there is a problem, others can trust that problems will be shared with them and not inappropriately with others. This leads to the development of trust, an essential component of effective delegation.

At the heart of delegation is the skill of clear, effective, assertive communication. Improving your ability to express yourself can have a number of positive effects on your mental health and work life. Some benefits for you include increased feelings of self-confidence, improved communication with coworkers, resolution of problems, nonmanipulative negotiation for behavior changes, and the ability to act as an advocate for patients. A key strategy is to begin assertiveness practice in small nonemotional situations and build upon your success. The most difficult, negative staff member on the unit is not the ideal recipient of your first efforts. Start out small and practice. Assertive communication will become easier and more natural to you. Please complete Checkpoint 8–1 before reading on.

EFFECTIVE ASSIGNMENT GIVING

The first step in effective communication related to delegation is to be clear in your own mind about what you need to have done by the delegate. A handy mental checklist can be borrowed from journalists, who routinely use the *who, what, when, where, why,* and *how* format in getting the details of their stories. By taking the time to share each of these aspects of the assignment with the delegate, you are communicating your specific expectations regarding the performance of the task.

Let's look at each of these in turn, starting with who.

Who

Usually at least two people are involved in any patient care delegation situation: the intended delegate and the patient. Who is the delegate for this particular task? In Chapter 7, the process of identifying and assessing a delegate has been discussed at length. The delegate may be a nurses' aide, patient care technician, LPN/LVN, another RN, or someone outside the work group, such as a member of the patient's family. Be sure to specify the person who is your intended delegate. It is much clearer and more effective to say, "Mary, would you take this specimen to the lab?" than to generally announce, "Who has time to take this to the lab?"

CHECKPOINT 8-1

Determine what type of communication style is being used by the following personnel.

1. Rashad attended the team meeting with all the rest. When the topic of role clarification for assistive personnel came up, he stated that he thought part of his role was to anticipate the needs of the patients for toileting and personal hygienic care. Robin, one of the staff RNs in their psychiatric care group home, raised her voice as she firmly stated, "*You* are only an aide. *That* is in the RN role. We don't expect you to think, just to do what we tell you to when we tell you." Rashad sat quietly without responding because he needed to keep his job, but began his plan on how he'd make Robin pay for her statement. Maybe he wouldn't do *anything* without being told.

2. Pamela, one of the school nurses in a rural county, was following up on some vision and hearing testing done by one of the volunteers, Brigite. She was concerned about the accuracy of the work due to the readings as compared to previous readings. Instead of discussing this with Brigite, she decided to do it all herself and re-test everyone.

3. Rosa managed the ambulatory care surgical center for a large health care conglomerate. Mabel, one of the surgical technicians, told her that she would not consider scrubbing in any orthopedic cases. Her rationale was that they were too physically stressful. When Rosa discussed that although she wanted staff to work together as a team, with everyone using his or her strengths to bring the best care for the patients, being involved in orthopedic cases was a part of Mabel's job description, Mabel told her menacingly that she was the granddaughter of the chairman of the board and that she'd "get Rosa's head on a platter."

See the end of the chapter for the answers.

The second "who" is the patient or receiver of the task. This seems incredibly simple and obvious, but avoidance of patient care errors begins with correct identification of the patient. An example of being clear about who is to receive the service/task is as follows: "Tracy, would you please take Mrs. Miller [who] into exam room #2?"

What

What is the job/task to be done? Be clear and specific regarding the task or assignment that you are delegating. Unless you already know that the delegate understands the task, you need to take the time to explain the task thoroughly. Without adequate information, the chance that the task will be completed to your expectations is slim. What *exactly* do you want done? Here are three examples of being specific about the delegated task.

- "Sandy, could you go [what] to the Diet Kitchen and pick up [what] a late tray for Mr. Sams? Please check [what] that it is an 1800 ADA diet."
- "James, I've noticed that your documentation of patient teaching on eye surgery patients is clear and thorough. Would you be willing to review [what] the patient teaching sections of these ophthalmic surgery patients' standardized care plans for completeness and update [what] the references to reflect current practice?"
- "Patricia, will you please go [what] to Mrs. Paulson's home today instead of tomorrow to do her [what] hygienic care?"

At this point, many nurses feel and respond to their own overcrowded schedules. "I don't have time to explain what he (she) needs to do. It's easier and quicker for me to do it myself." This is probably accurate. Unfortunately it also ensures that you, and only you, are the one spending precious time on tasks that could be delegated. On the other hand, if you work with the same staff members often and begin to invest a little time in clearly delegating one new task at a time, you will develop delegates' repertoire of skills and expand the pool of competent persons.

Another method to communicate the "what" of the task to delegates is to show (teach) them rather than tell. Take the delegate with you the next time you'd like to delegate a task. Use this opportunity to show him or her what is to be done for the next time. Even experienced staff have gaps in their knowledge and might appreciate being shown exactly what needs to be done, saving them from admitting they do not know how to perform a task.

When

When, meaning what time or by when, do you want the task completed? And when, or under what circumstances, should the delegate notify you? Your communication of the time frame for completion of a delegated task is crucial to on-time completion. Only when you specify the time parameters will the delegate share your prioritization of the task. Examples of communicating the "when" follow.

- "Audrey, Mr. Pong needs to have his AM care done by 0730 because he is scheduled for an arteriogram this morning."
- "Angela, Mr. Phillips is back from surgery. I took the first set of vitals, so he gets three more q 15 minutes, starting now [when to do the task], then the rest of the routine schedule. Let me know if he has significant changes in BP or pulse or any bleeding on the dressing [when or how often to notify you.]"
- "If you receive a call on the answering machine about a poison control question, please notify me as soon [when] as I walk in the door."

Where

Communicating where you want a task done could mean either an anatomical location on the patient or a geographical location. For example:

- "Susan, when you take off the TED hose on Mr. Johnson, please clean the graft incision on the calf [where—anatomical location] with Betadine."
- "Mary Ellen, please ambulate Mrs. Darcy from her room to the patient dining area and back [where—geographical location or distance] twice this shift."

- "Liz, would you go to Materials Management and pick up a replacement sterile instrument kit? The department is on the first floor behind the cafeteria [where—location].

How

How do you want the task done? There is a large range or scope of possibilities in answer to this question. Essentially, ask yourself if you have any assumptions about how the task will be completed. If you do, it is important to communicate these specifics to the delegate. Two examples of communicating "how" follow:

- "Beth, Mr. Barnes is coming up from the ER. He has a rebreathing mask on, so when you do his admitting vital signs, he needs a rectal temp taken [how]."
- "Judy, please stay at the bedside with Mrs. Murphy and take her vital signs [how] before and after dangling. She has a history of fainting and subsequent fractures."

Why

Most delegates will tell you that they are able to accept delegated tasks more willingly if they are given information about why they are doing a task a certain way. So be sure to communicate why you need a task completed or carried out in a particular way.

For example, "Joan, Mr. Sanders needs to stay in bed today. He had a plasty done yesterday, and his 24 hours of bedrest aren't up until 4 PM this afternoon [why]."

All of these components (who, what, when, where, why, and how) may seem like a lot to remember and take ages to communicate, but such is not the case. It is actually a quick, clear, and thorough method to delegate successfully. For example, "Martha, [who—delegate] do you have 10–15 minutes to ambulate [what] Mr. Parker [who—patient] before lunch please? [when]. Good, thanks. He is slightly weak on his right side, so please walk on his left side [how] to give him support on his unaffected side [why]. See if you can get him to walk the length of the hall [where]. Thanks."

In four short sentences, you have explained exactly the who, what, when, where, why, and how of a delegated task! And although it may seem obvious, note that a liberal sprinkling of "pleases" and "thank yous" really make a difference to your coworkers!

CHECKPOINT 8–2

Decide how you would clearly communicate the following tasks to be completed:

1. You want Geraldine, a medical assistant in your office, to check the temperatures rectally of all the babies under three years when they come in for a well-child checkup.
2. Linnea, your secretary, must still complete the Medicare forms, or your rehab center will not receive reimbursement.
3. You'd like Antonia to pick up the psychiatrist's evaluation and referral from the homeless shelter on her way back from home visits.

See the end of the chapter for the answers.

ASSERTIVE FOLLOW-UP

So you have now clearly delegated a task. On the follow-up, you find that is has been done satisfactorily and on time, that it has been done partially satisfactorily, or that it has not been done. How can you respond in an assertive way, mindful of your needs and those of the delegate? How can you communicate assertively in all these situations? How can you think of the appropriate words when you are pressured for time and have strong feelings about the situation?

Step 1. "When You. . ." or "I Notice That. . ."

Here you describe the actual observable, verifiable behaviors that you have seen, heard, or noticed. Be specific and give as many concrete, specific details as you can recall, such as time, place, and frequency of action.

For example, "Melissa, I asked you to go to Admitting to pick up Mr. French 15 minutes ago. Since then I noticed that you have been on the phone discussing your plans for the evening. I am anxious to get the patient admitted. Please go to Admitting now and pick him up." Notice that this is a description of the events, not an assumption about Melissa's motivation or character flaws.

If you give others feedback about their behavior now, take note of your language choices. Do you use "you" messages, such as "You are late!" or "You forgot to ambulate Mr. Smith"? A "you" message sounds like an accusation and others may feel defensive and resistant to hearing your message. An important principle of assertive communication is the use of "I" messages, such as "I've noticed that. . ." or "I would like you to bathe Mrs. Dove."

Step 2. "I Feel. . ."

Here you describe an emotion. You communicate a great deal to others when you share the impact of their behavior on you. They can get a clearer picture of the effect on others. An example is, "When I asked you to float off the unit just now, you slammed the chart down on the desk and said, 'No way! I am not going to float up there.' I feel angry. Every staff nurse has taken a turn floating off the unit, and now it's your turn."

Step 3. "I Want. . ."

Here you specify what action you want the person to take or what behavior you want him or her to change. Your best bet is to start by requesting small changes of behavior, and only one or two changes at a time. But let's face it, by the time you have noticed a behavior significant enough for you to spend time, effort, and adrenaline to ask for a behavior change, you really want more than a small change. In your heart of hearts, you secretly wish for a complete conversion experience that totally reforms both the offending behavior and the accompanying attitude! And when you point out the problem, you want the person to say, "You are absolutely right! I am so grateful to you for showing me the light. I can't believe I didn't see this about myself. Believe me, from now on I'm going to be different. Thank you again." This is an entertaining but unlikely fantasy. Remember, it can take years to change an attitude. Focus on a small change in behavior related to your goal. An example is, "Jeff, you are late getting back to the unit. I expected you 20 minutes ago. The next time you get tied up in another department, I would appreciate it if you would call me [small behavior change] and let me know you are going to be late so I can plan for it."

CHECKPOINT 8–3

Using the 3 steps:

"**When you . . .**" or "**I notice that . . .,**"

"**I feel . . .,**" and

"**I want . . .,**"

Respond to the following situations:

1. The jail chaplain has once again intruded into a counseling session when you are discussing problems with one of the assistive workers from the clinic.
2. When the roster for your family planning class was finally located, it had been placed in the wrong public health nurse's mailbox by the agency secretary.
3. The rehabilitation aide has not charted the range of motion exercises for the last two days.
4. Patient call lights are blazing, but Joan is sitting at the desk eating chocolates.

See the end of the chapter for the answers.

NONVERBAL BEHAVIORS

What you say is very important, but how you say it carries even more weight. Research on human communication has shown repeatedly that the majority of the message we communicate comes from the nonverbal components. Nonverbal behaviors can either enhance or conflict with the verbal message. And when confronted with such a mixed message, most listeners choose to believe the nonverbal message is the "real" one. So paying attention to your nonverbal behaviors can strengthen your verbal message.

The assertive delegator uses a level, conversational tone of voice and audible volume appropriate to the situation. Words are enunciated firmly and confidently. The assertive delegator is also comfortable with silence and pauses after key points to allow others to process the information. These behaviors communicate that the speaker has the legitimate authority to delegate and that the delegator is respectful of the delegate.

Eye Contact

An assertive delegator has a relaxed, steady gaze into another person's eyes. Looking away or down while speaking is usually suggestive of lack of self-esteem or confidence, although there are cultural variations on this interpretation. Avoid staring, blinking, squinting, or excessive eye movements.

Body Posture

How you hold your body while speaking says a great deal about you and your message. Face the person you are speaking with and place yourself at the same level, sitting or standing appropriately close. Hold your head erect and avoid slumping. Lean forward slightly. If you are standing, avoid shifting your weight from one foot to another. These are attending behaviors that say you are paying attention to what is being said.

Gestures

While speaking assertively, maintain a relaxed use of hands and arms. Use gestures for emphasis but avoid gestures such as arms folded across the chest (defensive), making a clenched fist (threatening), or finger shaking (aggressive/shaming). Also avoid the myriad of other distracting nonassertive behaviors such as excessive head movement; covering your mouth with your hand while speaking; and playing with jewelry, coins, keys, hair, beard, clothing, and so on. This fidgeting distracts from your message.

Facial Expression

Your facial expression should be relaxed with a pleasant to neutral expression. Most importantly, be consistent with the verbal message. If you are angry or upset, do not smile since this nullifies your words. Relax the muscles in your face and maintain a neutral expression. Avoid a drawn, tight-lipped mouth, wrinkled forehead, repeated swallowing, or other nervous habits such as excessive throat clearing or lip licking.

Personal Space

Maintain an appropriate distance, not crowding or invading the personal space "bubble" of the other. Avoid wandering and pacing.

SUMMARY

Nurses have tremendous responsibilities and need to be able to delegate effectively through clear, assertive communication. Assertiveness is a learnable skill that improves with successful practice. Start out in small, low-emotion situations and gain skill and confidence.

Whether the response to your delegation is agreement, refusal, or absence, you can develop an assertive dialogue with your delegate that addresses the real problem and begins the process of resolution. And what is in it for you? Just increased feelings of self-confidence and self-respect, improved communication with coworkers, resolution of actual problems, above-board negotiation for behavior changes, and the ability to act as an advocate for yourself and patients.

ANSWERS TO CHECKPOINTS

8–1.

1. The psychiatric nurse was being aggressive. Rashad responded by being passive, but planned to be passive-aggressive in the future.

2. This school nurse was being nonassertive.

3. Mabel was aggressive. Her boss was being assertive.

8–2.

1. Geraldine, will you please take rectal temperatures on all patients who are under three years of age when you do their admission work for the next two weeks? Please let me know verbally before I go in to their physical assessment if any are over 100°F. I think we've had some problems recently with the accuracy of the tympanic electronic thermometer, and I'm sending it off to get it fixed. Any questions? Great! Thanks, I think we'll avoid giving sick kids their immunizations this way!

2. Linnea, I am concerned about this new Medicare paperwork. If we don't get it right and send it in before two days have elapsed post discharge, we won't be paid the full amount we have coming. Let's go over how to fill it out. Is there any reason you can't get these sent off the day they leave, or at least the day after? Great! I appreciate your help in keeping this place open!

3. Will you possibly have time to go by the Midtown Homeless Center before you come back to the office today after visits? Good! Mrs. Burn's psychiatric evaluation is waiting there at the front desk to be picked up. I'll call Sammy, the secretary there, and let her know you'll come about 3:30 to pick it up today. Thanks! We need this evaluation to do her team planning tomorrow morning.

8–3.

1. When you come into my office when I'm involved in a private conversation, I feel concerned about maintaining confidentiality, and I'd appreciate it if you'd knock before you come in.

2. I noticed that the class roster was in the wrong mailbox today. I felt panicked when I couldn't find it. Would you please put it in my inbox the next time? Thanks!

3. I noted that the charting on range of motion has not been completed the last few days, and I feel particularly frustrated by this since the state health department is visiting tomorrow. Please chart them now and plan to get them in the charts as soon as you can after completion. I appreciate it!

4. Joan, when there are patients who have put on their call lights for assistance and you are sitting at the desk eating chocolates, I feel angry, and concerned about patient safety. I want you to get up and help answer the call lights. (Please note: This is not *all* you might say

in these circumstances. We will be adding to this kind of communication when we discuss conflict resolution and giving feedback in the next chapters.)

RECOMMENDED READING

Anderson, K. 1993. *Getting what you want.* New York: Dutton Publishing.

Burley-Allen, M. 1983. *Managing assertively: How to improve your people skills.* New York: John Wiley & Sons.

Genua, R. 1992. *Managing your mouth.* New York: American Management Association.

Chapter 9

How Can I Get My Coworkers To Work with Me As a Team? Resolving Conflict

Ruth I. Hansten and Marilynn J. Washburn

CONFLICT AS A CONCEPT

"You may *tell* me to do this assignment, but that doesn't mean I'm going to do it. In fact, there's no way that I am going to care for Mrs. Smith, or work with Jerry!" In the last chapter, we discussed how to communicate clearly and assertively, and began to look at situations in which delegation may precipitate some uncomfortable interpersonal situations.

Conflict! It is definitely something most of us fear or avoid. However, when working with people, conflict of some kind is inevitable. Our attitude toward the possibility of conflict often influences the manner in which we delegate. "But if I tell someone to do something, or give them feedback, there's a chance they will disagree, and then there will be *conflict!*"

Conflict, although uncomfortable, must be accepted as a part of living and working together. If you consider the whole concept for a few moments, think about what life would be like without any conflict at all. (Those of you who are breathing a sigh of relief and envisioning a world with prancing Bambis and fluttering butterflies, read on!)

There would be no new ideas or inventions. Most of these arise from conflicts over which idea is better.

Some of us would not put in the required effort to improve our performance. If negative feedback is given to us, even though we may disagree and begin a discussion about our own perceptions, we will be more aware of our supervisor's perceptions and focus on those problem areas.

More open relationships and better communication occur when colleagues are not afraid to disagree. Each person's point of view can be considered, and patient care improves from sharing varying perspectives.

Procedures and systems can improve through conflict. When a member of the team argues that things need improvement and that his or her way is better, it offers a window for changing things that need to be changed.

Conflict *can* be constructive, depending on the way it is handled. As the energy from the conflict is channeled to making things better for all, staff performance and better patient care can result.

Unless you work totally alone, we know you probably have ample opportunity to experience conflict. You may have developed your own philosophy of the origins of conflict. To make certain that you've covered all the bases when you steam away in frustration at those difficult situations in your work setting, let's take a look at the more common sources of conflict.

SOURCES OF CONFLICT

Why bother to look at sources of conflict? As nurses, you know there are at least 100 horrible physiological events that begin to take place in the human body when a patient is immobile, and you've learned to expect them and take measures to avoid the negative sequelae of such conditions as constipation, pneumonia, or deep vein thrombosis. Similarly, if you understand the usual sources of conflict, you'll be able to anticipate them as normal, even healthy, phenomena. This mind-set will make dealing with those issues much less stressful, and you may even be able to take steps to plan for them.

Ambiguous Jurisdiction

Not knowing who should be doing what and how roles and duties overlap is a common cause of conflict. This is a common problem when new roles are undertaken and systems of care delivery change. Inherent in these conflicts are questions of responsibility and authority. Instead of wasting energy on unnecessary disagreement, clarify job descriptions, state practice acts, and role expectations to reduce this source of conflict.

Conflict of Interest

Where do you see these types of conflicts occurring in your health care setting? Everywhere! Whether an administration perceived by staff to be solely interested in "the bottom line" or whether staff seem to define quality of patient care by the numbers of patients they care for, we see conflict of interest each day. In your specific setting, you'll see delegates having a conflict about care methods or about priorities based on their own personal values. Recognizing conflicts of interest will help you begin the conflict resolution process by identifying what each party really wants. (This will be covered later in the chapter.)

Communication Barriers

Physical and time barriers abound in health care. The very nature of our work in acute and long-term care facilities requires shift work. The pharmacist who works in the third-level underground in the medical center may not have as clear a concept of the needs of the nursing department on the oncology floor as the pharmacist who works in a satellite on the twelfth story. The inpatient care coordinator may find that conflicts occur regularly with the outlying ambulatory care clinics. The French have a wonderful saying that translates as "He who understands all, forgives all." Our communication barriers prevent us from understanding each other, and conflict results.

Dependence of One Party on the Other Party

Delegation, from the physician to the nurse, the nurse to the assistive personnel, or the nursing care team to other departments, creates potential for disagreement and anger. When one party doesn't complete the job on time or correctly, righteous indignation blooms as the delegator sputters, "But I was counting on you! The patients were counting on you!" When one party is dependent on another and the process doesn't progress well, expect this kind of reaction. Anticipating it allows you to take steps to rectify the problem, and will encourage the necessary communication and supervision to be certain the work is completed as planned.

Association of the Parties

The dictator type of management, in which the supervisor does not request participation and input, is uncomfortable for staff and stifles creativity and job growth. However, as interaction increases among workers, the potential for disagreement also grows. We've stated previously that disagreement can be positive, and a climate that encourages participation is excellent for improving staff motivation and the overall products we produce. Increased association of the parties becomes a source of conflict when the parties are unable to tolerate disagreement, do not have the communication skills to deal with the disagreement positively, and are working in a pressure-cooker environment. Expect that you'll need to help resolve conflicts when all have been under particular stress and when some members of the team are not employing assertive communication skills.

Behavior Regulations

Standardized policies, procedures, and rules seem to do two things at once. These regulating mechanisms are intended to reduce conflict by providing guidelines for performance. In some circumstances, however, the individual who wants more autonomy and less structure will chafe under the organization's regulations. For example, if your state's nurse practice act allows an LPN (LVN) to perform many procedures that are prohibited by your organization's job description for LPNs, expect some annoyance from some of the LPN staff. This discomfort will certainly surface as conflict.

Unresolved Prior Conflicts

The most common cause of conflict is unresolved prior conflicts. Consider those people of whom you aren't extremely fond, and time how quickly a list of past insults or negative incidents arises in your memory. Human beings often store up data that reinforce their viewpoint of a given individual. This data storage has been called "gunny sacking," a process that promotes an aching back and head. When the offending person once again commits his or her crime, the gunny sacker finally dumps the overflowing bag onto the unprepared recipient. "You *never* listen to your assignments! You *always* act like a lazy bum!" The ability to deal with conflicts effectively as they arise allows both parties to feel better about themselves and their work, unencumbered by the weight of past, unresolved problems.

CHECKPOINT 9–1

Consider the conflicts you've encountered in the past two weeks in your work setting. Which source of conflict was responsible for each situation? In what ways could positive resolution of those conflicts be constructive for your team and your clients?

Let's take a look at how your past may be influencing your attitude toward conflict. Answer the following as true or false.

___ 1. I am afraid of conflict. In my family of origin, conflict meant people yelling and fighting, which always translated into heartache for someone.

___ 2. In our family, we argued for fun. The neighbors often thought we were really fighting, but it was our way of showing we cared about each other.

___ 3. My parents never raised their voices to each other. I never knew things weren't going well until they were ready to get a divorce.

___ 4. The people in our family didn't ever disagree until someone was really very angry. Then one little thing would put Dad (or Mom) into a screaming rage.

___ 5. I grew up in the only nondysfunctional family in our town. We all discussed any issues that bothered us openly and freely, and calm, insightful, respectful discussion was the norm.

Review statements 1–5 in the above checkpoint. Think about how the norm for handling conflict in your family of origin has affected the way you deal with, or avoid, conflict at work. Those of us who learned that any kind of disagreement was very painful may find it more difficult to respond to conflict in a positive, open manner. If significant others in our past modeled ineffective communication skills, which culminated in rearrangement or destruction of our family unit (whatever our definition may have been), we may be baffled and confused by those who enjoy a good argument and don't feel threatened when confronted by conflict. People who learned to keep quiet and passive, then fly into a rage, may find it more difficult to bring out issues that may trigger conflict until the situation becomes unbearable.

Now that we've had some time to reflect on the models of conflict management we've been exposed to throughout the years, let's look at how these past experiences may have shaped our current responses.

CHECKPOINT 9–2

Evaluate your attitude toward conflict and your strategic response repertoire by answering the questionnaire in Exhibit 9–1. Most people use different coping mechanisms in conflict situations depending on the setting and the future implications, but use your first reaction for the questionnaire.

STRATEGIES FOR CONFLICT RESOLUTION

Now that you have some idea of how you react to conflict, let's review how effective your preferred coping mechanism becomes in different situations. This section's adaptations of the Thomas-Kilmann Conflict Resolution grid show how attitudes toward conflict reflect our intensity toward our own interest and the self-interest of the other viewpoints.

Avoidance

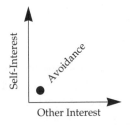

Source: Adapted from the Thomas-Kilmann Conflict Mode Instrument. Copyright © 1974, Xicom, Inc., Tuxedo, New York.

Exhibit 9–1 Conflict Questionnaire

	Very Unlikely	Unlikely	Likely	Very Likely
1. I am usually firm in pursuing my goals.				
2. I try to win my position.				
3. I give up some points in exchange for others.				
4. I feel that differences are not always worth worrying about.				
5. I try to find a position that is between hers and mine.				
6. In approaching negotiation, I try to consider the other person's wishes.				
7. I try to show the logic and benefits of my position.				
8. I always lean toward a direct discussion of a problem.				
9. I try to find a fair combination of gains and losses for both of us.				
10. I attempt to work through our differences immediately.				
11. I try to avoid creating unpleasantness for myself.				
12. I might try to soothe the other's feelings and preserve our relationship.				
13. I attempt to get all concerns and issues immediately out.				
14. I sometimes avoid taking positions that create controversy.				
15. I try not to hurt the other's feelings.				

SCORING: Very unlikely = 1, Unlikely = 2, Likely = 3, Very Likely = 4.

	ITEM	ITEM	ITEM	
COMPETING	1	2	7	TOTAL
COLLABORATING	8	10	13	TOTAL
COMPROMISING	3	5	9	TOTAL
AVOIDING	4	11	14	TOTAL
ACCOMMODATING	6	12	15	TOTAL

Source: Reprinted from Thomas, K.W., Toward Multi-dimensional Values in Teaching: The Example of Conflict Behaviors, *Academy of Management Review,* Vol. 2, p. 487, with permission of the Academy of Management, © 1977.

The first common strategy to resolving conflict is that of avoidance. Those who answered "Agree" on Question 1 in Checkpoint 9–1 may find avoidance to be an overused tool. It may be evidenced by the statements "I don't want to talk about it," "Let well enough alone," and "Don't rock the boat." Although avoidance works well in situations when you need more time to reflect, calm down, or get more information or input, it won't work for those situations that require your action and involvement.

A study of nurses' conflict resolution styles at three hospitals (Fowler et al., 1993) noted that nurses use withdrawal, or avoidance, as their most common coping mechanism when confronted with conflict. The authors stated that this indicated a willingness to remove themselves from relationships and possibly a lack of interest in the outcomes of the conflicts as well.

How do we decide whether to get involved? Certainly in health care it is easy for us to either brush conflict situations under the rug, leave it for the next shift or the next nurse, pass it off to a manager to take care of, or run in and save the day. It's certainly easy for us to put ourselves in a rescuer role when we don't need to be.

When making a decision about whether to get involved, focus on the intended outcomes. For example, what will happen if I do something about this issue? What will happen if I *don't* get involved? Examine the potential costs and potential benefits, and make your decision. Further, think about whether this situation affects your own safety, security, or goals. Does it affect the safety or welfare of those committed to your care? Does this conflict get in the way of achieving your group goals? If the answer to any of these questions is yes, then your strategy of avoidance had better remain an interim tactic only. You'll need to deal with this conflict.

Competition

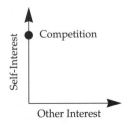

Source: Adapted from the Thomas-Kilmann Conflict Mode Instrument. Copyright © 1974, Xicom, Inc., Tuxedo, New York.

Competition as a method of solving conflicts shows a great amount of self-interest and low interest in whether the other party's viewpoints are considered. We see competition as an integral part of our society, of our business world, and of the games we play in the Western Hemisphere. In the past, boys were taught how to compete as they were raised, within the games and sports they played. Girls were encouraged to cooperate and be "nice" to everyone, and therefore women may not feel as comfortable with win-lose situations. As we enter into health care reform, we have discussed the idea of "managed competition" as compatible with the American way of business. The win-lose mentality works very well in some situations but is not satisfactory for making certain everyone's positions are considered and for promoting a long-term supervisory relationship.

For example, if a school nurse and a school secretary have had repeated discussions about the necessity of instructing the asthmatic children how to use their metered dose inhaler properly, but the secretary refuses to do it, and the nurse observes a child in real distress being merely handed the inhaler by the secretary as she glares at the RN, an "I win, you lose" or autocratic approach to resolving the conflict may be necessary for the short term. The nurse will want to intervene immediately to be certain the child's health is not at risk, and will have to overrule the secretary's actions with her own, discussing the problem later with the secretary in a private place. Certainly when a client's health is at risk, time is not wasted to ascertain the other party's position on the matter.

Partially as a result of the serious nature of health care and nursing, rules or policies are considered important guides for practice. Some rules are based on reason and excellent rationales. However, in some organizations the culture (or "the way things are done here") may encourage forced compliance when conflicts occur. This becomes a kind of "corporate competition" when rules are enforced without reasoning why the policy was written in the first place. When situations like this occur, the agency itself is the "we win, you lose" competitor. For example, it's necessary for the safety of all concerned when a hospital enforces a rule that no one (except security or police) will be allowed to carry concealed weapons when visiting patients, and in a case when a visitor brandishes an AK-47 assault rifle and is carried bodily from the ICU, the "we win, you lose" method of solving a conflict may be best. But when the rule against bringing pets into an acute care institution is considered written in stone and is adhered to, even though nurses advocate for a short visit from a dying patient's dog, the competitive method of resolving a conflict may not be the most effective method for all concerned.

Just as we discussed the necessity of using your nursing judgment when delegating care, choosing the correct method of solving problems rests on your assessment of the situation and what tactics would be the most effective.

Accommodation

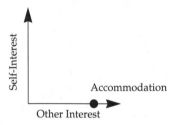

Source: Adapted from the Thomas-Kilmann Conflict Mode Instrument. Copyright © 1974, Xicom, Inc., Tuxedo, New York.

This style of resolving conflict develops when a person is much more interested in the other person's needs or desires than in maintaining his or her own point of view. Those whose answers scored high in accommodation may use this as a comfortable method of relating to others when there is some disagreement. Accommodation is effective in a situation that doesn't matter much to you. For example, if a delegate (a home health aide for example) states in a challenging manner that she is planning to rearrange her schedule of home visits, and this does not present a problem to you or to your clients, it's fine to be accommodating. (The nurse in charge may want to explore the situation more extensively and find out why the home health aide seems angry and challenging today also.) If, however, a scrub technician in your outpatient surgical center states that she doesn't think she'll provide the correct instruments for Dr. Jones' orthopedic patients today, it's not time to accommodate her wishes.

The message of accommodation is this: accommodate when it's truly okay with you. Use another method of conflict resolution if you are feeling uncomfortable or unhappy with the situation. (For those with codependent tendencies who tend to accommodate others, we recommend Question 71 in *The Nurse Manager's Answer Book* or *I'm Dying to Take Care of You* [Snow and Willard, 1989].)

Compromise

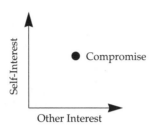

Source: Adapted from the Thomas-Kilmann Conflict Mode Instrument. Copyright © 1974, Xicom, Inc., Tuxedo, New York.

"I win some and lose some; you win some and lose some" is commonly used for conflict resolution in our society. The political process often uses compromise to come up with a reasonable middle ground as terribly complex issues are discussed by highly polarized groups. Each of these groups has principles or values that are ingrained to the core of each individual's personality and are at complete odds with each other. What is right and good and ethical will be very different for different individuals; therefore it is sometimes difficult to come up with a conflict resolution in which all people are completely satisfied. If you discovered in your conflict questionnaire that you compromise frequently, you may be aware of the very common human tendency to avoid flexibility and understanding the opposite viewpoint when your opponent is so obviously wrong and you are so obviously on the side of "good and all that is right."

Compromise allows us to move ahead in situations that are terribly complex or polarized. When changes must be made in the admissions processes for an acute care medical center, conflicting ideas and positions will occur since literally scores of departments and hundreds of people are affected. Even if all departments are involved in creating the changes in procedure, not all of the personnel may agree wholeheartedly with the end-product and may need to "give" a bit on their original position. Mutual consent that the decision is made, and all will implement it for the good of the whole, will allow the medical center to continue to function as smoothly as possible during the admission process.

You may experience compromise frequently in your work setting. For example, if a new admission is coming to your area but all staff are overloaded, the admission process could be divided up into parts and shared, with one RN coordinating the process. If a dialysis RN asked for Christmas Eve off for the last year but ended up having to take call, perhaps the dialysis tech would share call and get the work done more quickly.

Collaboration

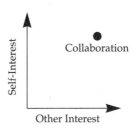

Source: Adapted from the Thomas-Kilmann Conflict Mode Instrument. Copyright © 1974, Xicom, Inc., Tuxedo, New York.

The "win-win" approach to conflict resolution, or collaboration, is founded on the ability of each party to focus on what each wants or needs, as well as their mutual goals. In collaboration, each party contributes to the problem-solving process so that views can be integrated. All relevant issues are discussed in an open and honest manner, with mutual respect for each individual's thoughts, feelings, and ideas. Both parties "win" since they have been heard and their ideas and needs have been considered and discussed. The final resolution should be acceptable, if not preferable, to all involved. This "win-win" approach will be discussed in more detail in the Hansten and Washburn Collaborative Resolution Process later in this chapter.

As you reviewed your organization's mission, we suspect you found some statements about treating those you serve with dignity and respect. These same precepts or values are necessary to work within a situation of conflict. Although all the methods can be used effectively within an appropriate problem situation, compromise and collaboration reflect a thorough consideration of each party's needs, emotions, and issues.

Collaboration is a time-consuming approach and should be used for those problems that require participative involvement for the success of a program, those where emotions are deep, and those where there is significant need for the relationship between the parties to grow and mature. Changing care delivery systems, adding new personnel, and redefining roles requires a true collaborative effort.

Let's look at a few issues and determine what method would be best used.

1Q: There is a conflict between the RN who supervises the oncology program in this ambulatory care setting and the medical assistant who
schedules the chemotherapy appointments and who often gives the
prechemotherapy nausea medication. The issue here is the timing of
the medication and the administration of the chemotherapy.

Conflict resolution method of choice _____

Why? _____

1A: Collaboration should be attempted first since there are significant
reasons to invest in this relationship: its quality will affect both individuals, the team, and the patients. Both individuals are driven by
the mutual goal of the most appropriate and effective patient treatment. It's possible that other personal needs are involved, and compromise may be necessary.

2Q: The rehabilitation team has worked extensively with a family regarding the home care plan for a paraplegic patient, Fred. However,
one of the family members strongly believes, from a religious standpoint, that Fred should not be completing his own self-catheteriza-
tion. Although this is viewpoint is difficult for the health care team,
there has been no change of attitude on the part of the caregiver, despite many reasoned discussions.

Conflict resolution method of choice _____

Why? _____

2A: Compromise may be necessary in this situation. Reality dictates that
if a procedure will not be completed due to pressure of a family member, another method may be needed. Perhaps the religious standpoint
could be further explored and the exact nature or rationale of the pro-
hibition could be discussed so that creative solutions could be applied. Perhaps the family member will not have to be involved in this
procedure. When deep values, such as religious teachings, are involved, it's difficult for everyone to be totally satisfied with solutions.

3Q: Sally was brought up by an abusive, alcoholic mother. When making
visits to the home of an alcoholic diabetic patient, she finds herself
unable to listen carefully to the concerns of this patient. When she allows herself to be honest, she figures that he's killing himself anyway

and that her time is wasted when she tells him to eat right and to take his insulin and medications as ordered. It's a constant argument, with Sally telling him what to do and Jack ignoring her.

Conflict resolution method of choice _____

Why? _____

3A: Unless Sally has already embarked on an effective personal counseling journey, it may be best for her to use avoidance and ask someone else to take over his care. Awareness of her inability to deal with the inevitable conflict successfully shows respect for herself and for Jack.

4Q: Pablo, a case manager for total hip patients throughout the health care continuum in a large health care conglomerate, notices that one of the subacute care facilities frequently sends total hip patients back to the ICU on the weekends and holidays. When he attempts to discuss this with the director of that department, she begins to shout about the level of staffing that is available during those periods.

Conflict resolution method of choice _____

Why? _____

4A: This situation calls for collaboration on the part of Pablo, who has legitimate concerns, and the department director, who seems frustrated at her staffing situation. A win-win solution will creatively address both individuals' concerns. Their mutual ground at this point is their need to assure patients' welfare.

5Q: Pat, an AIDS patient in a combined long-term care and hospice facility, has been very angry about the corporate visiting rules. She wishes to be married to her significant other, Kim, and wants to invite at least 50 friends. Her condition is declining. She is angry and shouts at you, the charge nurse for this shift, about the "anti-humane corporate policies."

Conflict resolution method of choice _____

Why? _____

5A: The charge nurse has every reason to accommodate Pat's need to go around the rules. The nurse may need to ask Pat to compromise some on the number of guests, but if possible, accommodate to Pat's wishes. The charge nurse has very little invested in the corporate rules in this situation, and will be even more satisfied if Pat "wins."

6Q: The Medic One ambulance has patched in a serious arrhythmia on the monitor. The patient is about 10 minutes away from your emergency room in the middle of a traffic jam on the highway. You have instructed the medic to give a bolus of lidocaine. He states he's just been to an update on arrhythmia treatment and that he thinks another choice of medication would be better. You have recently been through an advanced cardiac life support course and do not wish to argue as the patient's pressure drops.

Conflict resolution method of choice _____

Why? _____

6A: "I win, you lose" is the method of choice in this situation. The patient also wins if some antiarrhythmia treatment is given and is effective. You can be clear that you'll discuss the new treatment protocols later, but for now, *"Give the drug!"*

7Q: The materials management and environmental services departments have made a change in the location of the sharps containers for contaminated needles and other disposable instruments. These have been placed in the rooms of the patients and within the areas that nurses may need them. It is the evening shift, you are in charge, and you've been told that the containers will be moved during your shift to a central location on the unit. The materials management worker states sourly, "It's going to save $400 per day to have fewer containers to empty." Your obvious concern is safety.

Conflict resolution method of choice _____

Why? _____

7A: This situation calls for a collaborative approach in the long run. In the short run, the charge nurse may try competition ("I can't let you change them now because I am very concerned about patient, nurse, and environmental services workers' safety") or avoidance and compromise ("If you'll wait just one day, I'll get in touch with the department managers and we'll start a discussion about this change in procedure").

Before we move on to the Hansten and Washburn Collaborative Resolution Method, let's review the sources of conflict, the beneficial and destructive consequences, and the advantages to dealing with conflict appropriately to the given situation. Please review the flowchart in Figure 9-1.

INNOVATIVE ISSUE RESOLUTION PROCESS: A COLLABORATIVE METHOD

Exhibit 9–2 outlines the collaborative resolution method. Quickly review the process steps in the figure and then proceed to the discussion. We'll be asking you to apply the process in some clinical situation that you may have encountered.

The first step in resolving issues or conflicts is to be aware of your state of mind. If you are angry and upset, your mind will be closed to creativity. If you feel threatened, your "fight or flight" response will be operant, and things will not proceed as effectively. In health care, we don't have the luxury of wasting time and money on uncontrolled, unexamined emotions.

➡ 1. *Shift your focus.* Instead of thinking of how you're being wronged, or the negative characteristics of the Neanderthal person you're dealing with, blow out the flame of anger instead of adding fuel to it. There are several methods of remaining calm and logical as you attempt to resolve an issue.

Stimulate your right brain and creativity by thinking about what is *good* about the problem. (We encourage you to read Anthony Robbins' *Awaken the Giant Within* (1992) for more on positive problem solving.) For example, in the above problem (#7) of the sharps containers being moved away from where sharps are used, consider what could be positive about this issue arising.

Perhaps you are glad that this has happened on your shift since you feel so strongly about safety issues. Perhaps you are anxious to be more involved in interdepartmental planning and in "fixing" the system by which decisions affecting many departments are made. Perhaps this will allow you to get to know those support people better. This may sound like a Pollyanna part to collaboration, but it is essential to shift to a posi-

SOURCES OF CONFLICT

Ambiguous jurisdiction
Conflict of interest
Communication barriers
Dependence of one party
Association of the parties
Behavior regulations
Unresolved prior conflicts

CONFLICT

Resolution INAPPROPRIATE Techniques

Resolution COLLABORATIVE Techniques

NEGATIVE OUTCOMES

Destructive behaviors
Hostility
Professional stereotyping
Negative gossip
Burnout
Lack of professional growth
Frequent job changes
Lack of collaboration among
    professionals, increasing use of
    resources and suboptimal care

BENEFICIAL OUTCOMES

Better patient care
More open relationships
Personal & professional growth
Improved communication
Improved & innovative systems
Staff satisfaction
Professional growth
Collaboration
Patient satisfaction
Better use of resources
(LOS)

Dennis Burnside

Figure 9–1 Conflict Flowchart

Exhibit 9–2   Hansten and Washburn's Collaborative Resolution Method

 Shift Your Focus.

What is good about this issue?
Separate the person from the problem.
Determine exactly what you want.

 Create a Positive Open Attitude.

Listen and restate what the other party wants.
Be certain he or she feels heard.
Reflect and respect feelings expressed.

 State Your Perception.

Use assertive language.
Express what it is you want from a factual viewpoint.
Determine what you are willing to do, or give up, to get what you want.

 Establish Mutual Goals.

Determine what the other party is willing to do, or give up, to get what he or she
wants.
Propose a solution that reflects your understanding of both parties' needs/desires.
Summarize each party's agreed-on actions.

tive way of thinking so that the creativity necessary for problem solving
can be used.

Separate the person from the problem. This time-honored phrase has
been used as fundamental to conflict resolution since people began to
think about the process. Remember that the person who is removing the
sharps container is *not* the problem, but a *decision* that was made about
the sharps containers is the problem. This allows you to view the person
dispassionately, more as a pawn to circumstance than as someone who is
personally plotting against your happiness.

Determine exactly what you want. In order to do this, you must be
calm enough by this time to take the energy produced by those emotions
and harness it to think logically about what you'd like to reap from the

time you'll spend on this issue. *What is the bottom line result* you'd like to see? In this case, you probably want the sharps containers to be where they can be most safely and efficiently used by all personnel.

If you are still not calm enough to think about this problem logically, then take some time to relax and calm down. Deep breaths, counting to ten, prayer, and taking a short bathroom or coffee break are useful to some. Nurses have also told us that they use such techniques as creative visualization and directive self-talk. These are not auditory or visual hallucinations. In creative visualization, you think of yourself in a safe, calm place, whether it is by a rushing stream in the mountains, fly fishing, or on your couch at home in front of a crackling fire with a cup of herbal tea. Others visualize themselves or someone that they admire dealing with the issue in an effective manner. Some visualize the offending opposing person(s) with their pajamas on, with a clown nose, or in other less threatening attire. Many people direct their self-talk, that continuous running commentary in your brain, to be positive: "I know I can handle this, I will be calm, and besides, no one will remember this day a hundred years from now!"

⬆ 2. *Create a positive open attitude* by listening closely to what the other party is saying. By continuing to keep your focus shifted from your anger to what the other party's needs may be, and trying to fully understand his or her position, you are influencing the potential for a positive outcome to the discussion.

Listen carefully to what is being said. The materials worker who has stated that "it's going to save $400 per day to empty fewer containers" is probably discussing the rationale that he's heard for the change in procedure. As you restate what you've heard, you're clarifying and asking for more information. "So the idea here is to cut the material and personnel costs as a part of our money-saving plan? What else have you heard about why this decision was made?"

Be certain that the other party feels he or she has been fully heard and that his or her position has been understood. "If I hear you correctly, your department is doing this as a cost-savings idea, but you're also afraid that a few more of these ideas, and you won't have a job left to do?"

Reflect the feelings that have been expressed. In our example discussion, the worker has shared his concern about being laid off if he doesn't have enough to do. In many cases, people will not express their feelings clearly, and you may need to put yourself in their place, empathize, and then ask for confirmation. "You seem nervous and angry about this. I can certainly see where this would be of concern to you. Am I on target with how I think you are feeling about this?" Naming their emotions, fears, or concerns often allows people to be less guarded, discuss the issues without hidden agendas, and solve problems more effectively. If the other party is very angry or upset, stating that you've received that message will help take the wind out of their sails. "I can see this is upsetting for you and you seem to be feeling quite concerned. We understand that this was an order given to you and that you didn't make the rule yourself. Let's talk about what we can do together to solve it."

Respect all feelings that are expressed. Nurses are great empathizers; we may know how *we* would feel in the same circumstance. However, the range of human emotions and thoughts are varied, and whatever feelings are expressed must be respected as such. Judging whether a feeling is right, wrong, or justified is not helpful and only serves to further isolate the two parties. (Behaviors, however, are subject to feedback and comment. Discussion of methods of giving feedback will be discussed in Chapter 10.)

➡ 3. *State your perception of the problem.* In this step, you are again sharing your viewpoint and what you'd like to accomplish by your discussion. Think back to our last chapter on assertiveness and use your "when you, I feel, I want" recipe as needed. For example, you may state, "When one department makes a decision that affects another, such as changing the location of the sharps containers, the other department feels left out and devalued, and I'd like all of us to work together to determine a better system for interdepartmental decision making." This statement focuses on the long-term results and the reason you are feeling distressed. "For now, however, it seems that you've been given an order by your department that isn't one you like, either. I will talk with your supervisor so that you don't get into trouble, but I am asking you not to move those containers until we can find a better solution. The safety of the nurses, other health care personnel, and the patients may be adversely affected by moving those disposal bins."

In the above discussion, the nurse in charge has looked at the problem in two ways: one a short-term resolution (don't move the containers) and the other a long-term one (how can we find a better system to avoid these problems?). The nurse has used assertive language to express feelings, and expressed what he or she wanted from a factual viewpoint. The nurse has also determined that he or she is willing to do at least one thing to resolve it: take on the responsibility of calling the materials supervisor about these concerns and thus providing some assistance to assuage the materials worker's anxieties.

What else may the RN plan to do to get started on resolving the long-term issue? Certainly he or she would be willing to alert the manager to the issue so that follow-up can continue. Perhaps he or she would be willing to be on a task force for determining the safest and most cost-effective manner to dispose of sharps. Perhaps the materials worker would want to join that committee as well. The RN might also want to research current methods of discussing and resolving interdepartmental issues, and help solve this recurring problem within the organization.

◀▶ 4. *Establish mutual goals.* In any area of health care, the patient or client's service or care must be the mutual, bottom-line objective of all parties involved. When people are reminded of their shared goals, it is much less difficult to obtain participation. "Since all of us are here for safe, quality patient care, we all have to think about safety along with the costs."

Determine what the other party is willing to do, or give up, to be a part of the solution. "Will you be willing to stop the process of changing the containers if I call your supervisor to explain?"

Propose a solution that reflects your understanding of the needs and desires of the other party as well as your own, and then review what each party has agreed to do.

"So you'll leave the sharps bins where they are, and please explain our discussion and our concerns with your supervisor also. You're also willing to be on a committee to solve these interdepartmental problems, and at the same time, you can think of ways to keep your job through added responsibilities, if necessary. I'll call your supervisor for tonight to explain why we don't want this done right now, and I'll discuss ways in which we can solve the short-term problem of the sharps disposal as well as what each of us can do to keep these interdepartmental issues from cropping up due to lack of understanding. We each have a couple of things to do but it's worth it to keep us all safe and employed! Is this all okay with you? Great!"

This step allows us to clarify whether each party has remained clear and whether the parties are currently in agreement on a course of action. Each party has "won" and will be invested in the solutions.

Although the process of collaborative resolution seems intricate and involved, there are really four main issues:

1. Shift your focus to what's possible and away from the negative feelings.

2. Create a positive open attitude by listening and respecting the other party's position.

3. State your perception and position assertively, clearly, and factually.

4. Establish mutual goals and actions based on input and participation from both parties. Use the imagery of the arrows to help you remember.

CASE STUDY ANALYSIS OF COLLABORATIVE RESOLUTION

Jamal is a jail nurse for a men's work release center. He has had some concerns about some nagging coughs that he's heard, particularly during the night and early morning hours. Although most of his clients have been smokers, some also had positive PPDs (TB skin tests) in the past without preventive drug therapy. He's read about the growing prevalence of a multidrug-resistant tuberculosis and wonders whether all of prisoners would be infected with the current ventilation system. He's brought the concerns and a plan for follow-up PPDs, chest films, and sputum samples to the physician advisor, Dr. Richards. Dr. Richards, who is also responsible for the budget of the facility, reacts angrily: "Jamal, you are just like a mother hen! I am tired of hearing about all the real or imagined ills of 'your patients!' These people are heavy smokers, have been drug abusers, and are in horrible health all around. They are going to cough in the morning, for heaven's sake! Don't you have enough to do? We can't afford to do all those tests on these people!"

Follow the process to help Jamal respond to Dr. Richards. Write down your thoughts as well as your dialogue in this situation.

1. Shift your focus.

_____

_____

_____

_____

2. Create a positive open attitude.

_____

_____

_____

_____

3. State your perception.

_____

_____

_____

_____

4. Establish mutual goals.

_____

_____

_____

_____

1. In shifting your focus, you wonder what is good about this problem. Perhaps this gives Jamal a chance to prove his clinical expertise and judgment, or an opportunity to clarify his role expectations with Dr. Richards, since they seem to be in conflict. It's certainly good that Dr. Richards is reacting at all, since he rarely seems to have an opinion on anything. Besides, it's necessary to get him involved in this potentially serious situation. In separating the person from the problem, you've identified that the real problem is the health of these coughing patients. What you want is an opportunity to further assess the etiology of these coughs and rule out TB or other infectious disease agent.

2. What is Dr. Richards saying here? Is he afraid that he can't really affect the wellness of the inmates without it costing too much? Does he feel out of control of their health due to the myriad of other risk factors? He's obviously irritated. Jamal might respond, "Dr. Richards, I can see this is a frustration for you as it is for me. These people have just about destroyed their bodies before they get to us, and certainly we don't have enough money to give them all bionic parts! It's hard

for us, me especially, to determine where I can best be of help to them all. Do you ever feel that way?"

3. Dr. Richards has verified this feeling of helplessness, now it's time for Jamal to share his position. "As frustrating as it may be, I am even more concerned when I hear the increasingly loud racket of productive coughs during the night and early morning hours. Some of the inmates are complaining of night sweats also, and were never followed up on their positive skin tests. When I am confronted with all of these symptoms, I feel increasingly frightened for their safety as well as ours, and I want your help in deciding what kind of follow-up should be done with respect to efficacy as well as cost. The cost would be astronomical, both in terms of treatment and in terms of public outrage, if we had a TB problem and did nothing about it. I am willing to do overtime or whatever it takes, including getting the advice of the public health department experts."

4. Since Dr. Richards seems to be responding well to the facts now that Jamal has outlined them effectively, as well as being cognizant of the risks involved with not acting, it's time to remind him of the mutual goals. "After all, our jobs here, as I see it, are to assure the optimal health of these clients, given the cost constraints and the material we are given to work with! We are certainly working together for the same goals, right?"

After Jamal asks Dr. Richards for suggestions, Richards determines he'll call an old friend at the health department for some input. He'd like Jamal to call the TB nurse specialist and find out how they could help. As the conversation continues, Jamal wants to restate the plan. "So I will call the TB nurse specialist for assistance, and you'll talk with your friend who's been involved in the program, and we'll get together to discuss this on Friday at noon? Great! I feel better checking this out. There are just too many indications to avoid exploring the cough problem!" Jamal also knows there is a long-term problem left to solve. How can he determine whether he is fulfilling Dr. Richards's expectations or if there is a problem? Is he really a "mother hen," or was that response a result of Dr. Richards's frustration? "You know, Dick, I am wondering if we could also discuss how you feel I am doing in my job. I'm not sure how to interpret the comments you made earlier in the conversation, so could you think about this and we'll discuss it on Friday? I want to be able to present my concerns to you and to do my job overall, in the most effective manner, and I'd like some feedback." The physician may or may not respond now, but Jamal potentially will find out how he can better get his attention without having to resolve a conflict.

CHECKPOINT 9–3: CONFLICT PRACTICE

To feel competent in dealing with the Collaborative Resolution Process, it's necessary to practice it continually. As often as we've taught these communication skills, it is still difficult for us to use them in every situation. We recommend that you think about a recent issue or conflict and role play resolving it with a friend. If you feel uncomfortable doing that, make yourself a "skill card" with the process, and keep it in your backpack, purse, or pocket to use before you are planning to solve an interpersonal problem. After a conflict situation, use the process to evaluate how well you have done and where you may have needed to concentrate. Many nurses have found it effective to teach the process to their children or spouses and learn it better from teaching it.

Here are a few situations you can use to test your understanding. For further practice, look over the conflict issues in the last checkpoint of this chapter.

1. You've assigned a nursing assistant to complete a task. She reacts, angrily, that you've been of no support or help to her, she's been working like a demon all day, and she is just too tired to consider taking on another assignment.
2. You return from a break and you notice that one of your psychiatric patients is having a serious problem because you see a code cart and several security guards by the door. One of your coworkers is on the telephone, talking about a date that is being planned for this evening. You motion for her to get off the phone and help with the other patients, and she glares and turns her back, continuing her conversation.

continues

CHECKPOINT 9–3 *continued*

3. You and your supervisor have had a disagreement about your caseload and the home health aides and rehabilitation aides working with your patients. You feel overwhelmed and unable to take on more work, and you aren't happy with the performance of your assistants. Your supervisor is adamant, and the entire agency is under terrible financial stress.

4. You are an ambulatory care nurse working with several physicians. One of the physicians you work with has displayed some erratic behavior that may indicate he is being affected by a chemical dependency or some other intense personal problem. It has affected his work with the patients. You approach the senior physician, and she reacts angrily that you should keep quiet about this, and that she is sure the other physician has "everything under control."

See the end of the chapter for the answers.

SUMMARY

Conflict, and our response to it, will always determine if we move ahead as a profession, or if we will become paralyzed victims of circumstance, unwilling to take the risk conflict demands. We have seen countless nurses literally stopped in their tracks, victims at the mercy of everyone else's control as they perceive the potential for conflict too great to take the chance. We have also observed many nurses who see conflict as a process of life, and who have developed their skills in dealing with disagreement, just as you have mastered numerous clinical skills.

Nursing is in the people business. And people don't always agree. Appreciating the benefits of that disagreement and being confident in your ability to resolve conflict will position you for the most satisfying career you can imagine. Secure in your understanding of the basic four-step process of conflict resolution as outlined in this chapter, you will find yourself taking control of both your personal and professional growth. Isn't that the best outcome of all?

ANSWERS TO CHECKPOINT

9–3. Scenarios: suggested dialogue:

1. In shifting your focus, you realize that the real problem is not this nursing assistant, but the fact that there is a task to be done, and no one agreeing to do it. You consider what is good about this problem: perhaps you are glad to have the chance to interact with this CNA, who has expressed her concerns about overwork before. Perhaps you are rested today and feel energetic about using your new conflict resolution method! What you want is to find someone to take over the task assignment and to find out what's wrong with this CNA. To create a positive open attitude, you'll respond: "Wow, Mei, I can see that you are really overwhelmed! And I am sorry that I haven't been as available as I'd like to have been to help you. We've had a pretty rough day." In stating your perception, you may say, "But Mei, when I come to ask you for help, and you react by throwing the linens on the floor, I feel hurt. I'd like us to look at the assignments and figure out what ideas you have for who can do this work. Some one has to complete it, and I know three of us will be overtime already." Mei may discuss with you that she needs to have foot surgery and that she isn't feeling well. (You should certainly respond to this with a few caring comments.) You may also express that you've looked at the assignments and are unable to find anyone with time on her hands, and that you can't take on any more work yourself with Mr. Smith being so critical. In establishing mutual goals, you may also state: "Mei, I know we all want the patients to get quality care and we also all want to get home and put up our feet. Would you be willing to assist with this task if I ask the next shift to finish whatever else you have to do at 3:45? I'll get 15 minutes of overtime authorized for all of us." Mei agrees. The next day, when time allows, discuss the long-term problem of Mei's feet and how you and she could interact more positively regarding her assignments and supporting her as charge nurse. Clarification of expectations, another concept covered earlier, will be helpful.

2. In shifting your focus, you take a few deep breaths. (If you have a split second of time, you may consider that what is good about the problem is that you finally have some objective evidence that this coworker is not performing. Usually she just disappears!) You know the real problem at hand is getting adequate assistance in the code

and with the other patients, who will be very upset. This is time for using "competition" as a mode of resolution until you can work out a long-term solution. You may lightly touch your coworker and state, "Sue, *now*, I am going to help with the code. You must check on the other patients. *Now*." Or, after you ascertain that the code situation was under control, you may return to Sue. You may use your assertive language and say, "I understand that it's important for you to have some time on the phone with your friends, but when I come back to the unit after break and you are on the phone talking about a date while an emergency is going on, and you ignore me, I feel angry, and frightened about the safety of the patients." You've determined what you really want: that Sue will participate in the emergencies on the unit. You've determined that what you are willing to do is to make a point of resolving the issue and discussing it with Sue. Your mutual goals in this situation are safe patient care. Sue may have the additional goal of getting break time or free time to resolve personal issues. If that is the case, you can discuss how she can also get those needs taken care of during breaks. A solution will certainly include all individuals being involved in caring for the patients during emergencies.

3. You begin by shifting your focus. What is good about this problem is that it has finally come to a head and that you'll be dealing with it for the good of all involved. You determine that what you want is to be able to do the work as required, but to have some impact on the way you supervise and evaluate the assistive personnel. You begin by discussing with the supervisor: "I know it's very tough financially here and we all want to do our best and keep the agency open, and keep our jobs. You've got your hands full helping us to maintain productivity. But when I'm asked to do more than I'm sure I can do well, without having adequately trained assistants, I feel absolutely overwhelmed, and frankly, I am afraid. I'm not sure my patients are getting the care they need unless I have more time to supervise and teach these new assistants. I'm willing to take any suggestions you may have." As your supervisor understands that you are trying to work things out, she'll be able to interact with you more positively. "What I'd really like from you are some ideas on how to make certain I can supervise, train, and evaluate them and still do the necessary caseload." As the discussion continues, your supervisor may give you many worthwhile ideas, may assist in

training or supervising your assistive personnel, or may modify your assignment. Remember to summarize each other's agreed-upon actions.

4. What's good about this problem? You've used your excellent powers of observation as a patient advocate. The problem here is the potential for unsafe care due to an MD's behavior. What you want is for someone to find out what is going on with him and to take action to protect the patients. You have another meeting with the senior physician, Maria Menendez. You begin by saying, "Maria, I know you are good friends with Dr. Putz, and it's tough to think there could be a problem. It's scary for all of us. But we all want to protect the patients if my concerns are valid. When you seemed to dismiss my objective examples of his erratic behavior yesterday, I felt even more concerned. I've lost sleep over this situation. This is definitely a matter that could go to the state board if you find there is a problem. In fact, this is our professional duty. I am willing to be involved in the discussion with him, if you'd like, or be of support to you when you talk with him. Are you willing to discuss it with him? Good. Will you let me know when you've talked with him, then?" Although we haven't added the responses of Dr. Menendez, she is aware that she must deal with the situation and determine what needs to be done. She also knows you aren't going to let the problem simmer when patient safety is involved. Good job!

REFERENCES

Fowler, A. R. Jr., et al. 1993. *Health Progress* 74, no. 5: 25–29.

Hansten, R., and Washburn, M. 1993. *The nurse manager's answer book.* Gaithersburg, Md: Aspen Publishers, Inc.

Robbins, A. 1992. *Awaken the giant within.* New York: Simon & Schuster.

Snow, C., and D. Willard.1989. *I'm dying to take care of you: Nurses and codependence and breaking the cycles.* Redmond, Wash: Professional Counselor Books.

Weeks, D. 1992. *The eight essential steps to conflict resolution.* New York: Jeremy T. Tarcher, Inc.

RECOMMENDED READING

Anderson, K. 1993. *Getting what you want: How to reach agreement and resolve conflict every time.* New York: Penguin Books.

Fisher, R., et al. 1991. *Getting to yes.* 2nd ed. Boston: Houghton Mifflin Co. ·

Rusk, T., with D. P. Miller. 1993. *The power of ethical persuasion.* New York: Viking Penguin.

Chapter 10

Know How To Give Feedback: What Do Delegates Really Want?

Ruth I. Hansten and Marilynn J. Washburn

In Chapter 7 we discussed the need to know your delegates in terms of their strengths, weaknesses, motivation, cultural differences, and preferences. Communication is an essential skill in assessing your delegates in these areas, and the specific process of feedback will allow you to maintain a continuous cycle of effective communication that will not only assess the progress of the delegate but *motivate* that performance as well.

Feedback is the final note in the circular process of delegation. Foregoing feedback is similar to singing the notes of the scale: do, re, mi, fa, so, la, ti.... Everyone is waiting to hear "do," the last note, your words that will complete the cycle and will set the tone for the next time you work together. If they are left unspoken, you have failed to close the loop and to provide a solid foundation for the working relationship with your delegate. Lacking your feedback, the delegate may be making assumptions, filling in his own note.

The next time you work together, the delegate will be functioning with an unknown evaluation, and performance will be adversely affected by his or her unanswered questions. "Did I do ok? Does she think I'm a good worker? Does she even notice what I do?" Or the delegate will have formed an opinion of YOU: "She never notices, doesn't even say thank you after I've worked like a demon for her." "He never seems that busy, always sitting at the desk, talking to docs while I'm running around like crazy, I hate to work with him." Or, worse yet, "I hope I don't do anything wrong, but who knows? I never get any feedback, so what does it matter?" Closing that loop by sharing some honest feedback during and at the end of the shift can go a long way in preventing this type of working relationship from developing. Isn't it worth the time?

Giving and receiving feedback takes courage. It's difficult to tell people what's going wrong, easier to talk about what is going well. It may be harder still to ask your delegate for an appraisal of your performance, and you may feel that this is unnecessary in your role. When it seems that giving and receiving feedback is the absolute last thing you want to do, it's helpful to think about the possible benefits to you and the delegate.

CHECKPOINT 10–1

Think about the benefits you will realize from learning a process for giving effective feedback to your delegates. Jot down a few thoughts.

_____

_____

If delegates felt comfortable giving you some constructive feedback on your communication skills, leadership, or performance, how would that benefit you and your performance?

_____

_____

BENEFITS OF GIVING AND RECEIVING FEEDBACK

Some of the following responses are most commonly given to us by nurses. We hope that you identified similar benefits, as well as some that are particular to you:

- You learn how to better lead the team.
- Personal growth for both the RN and the delegate provides improved job opportunities for the future.
- The delegate learns and grows, and is thus motivated to a more energetic effort.

- Positive performance is reinforced.
- Individual and team performance improves.
- Open communication helps overall teamwork.
- Patients receive better care.
- Besides, haven't you always wondered what your delegates and co-workers thought about *your* performance?

THE POWER OF FEEDBACK

The value and benefit of feedback as a motivator cannot be stressed enough. Research studies repeatedly show that recognition, feedback, and constructive criticism are high-ranking factors in enhancing productivity and performance. When asked to rank work factors in terms of importance, the majority will list "appreciation of work" and "a feeling of being in on things" as more important factors than the amount of pay, the loyalty from the supervisor, or the physical conditions of the job (Jenks and Kelly, 1985). Figure 10–1 demonstrates the importance of feedback when considering multiple factors in job satisfaction and motivation.

Feedback in the form of recognition is a significant factor to most of us. In a survey of nurses in the midwest, 92 percent ranked recognition as important to job satisfaction, but 28 percent perceived this recognition to be seldom or never given. Verbal feedback was described as the most significant form of recognition, and many looked to their head nurse, nurse executive, patient, coworker, physician, and hospital department heads for this feedback (Goode et al., 1993). Unfortunately, studies show that head nurses often do not see the process of motivating staff (giving positive feedback) as one of their tasks (O'Neil and Gajdostik, 1989). No wonder we perceive that something that is so important to all of us is so sadly lacking! What an opportunity you have as a fellow colleague, knowing that a simple "thank you" or "good job" can take so little time to say and yet can have such a tremendous impact!

CHECKPOINT 10–2

Recall the last time someone recognized your efforts on the job or at home. How did you feel?

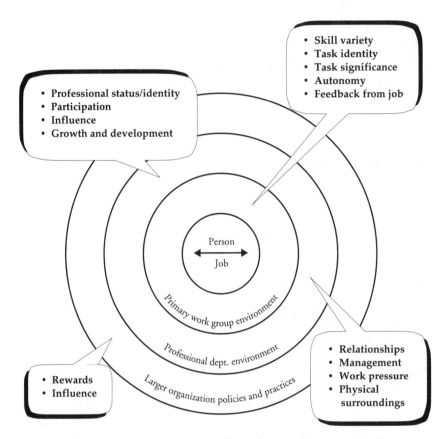

Figure 10–1 Factors that Affect Job Status and Motivation. *Source:* reprinted from Henderson and Williams, The People Side of Patient Care Redesign, *Healthcare Forum Journal*, July–August 1991, p. 46, with permission of Healthcare Forum, © 1991.

THE PROCESS

Many nurses would like to leave the process of feedback to the manager, believing perhaps that it is out of their realm of responsibilities and that the manager has more time to devote to evaluating and supervising employees. However, in the process of delegation, The National Council of State Boards of Nursing (NCSBN) states,

The delegating nurse is accountable for assessing the situation and is responsible for the decision to delegate. *Monitoring, outcome evaluation and follow-up* are necessary supervisory activities that follow delegation.... The delegator would be expected to provide supervisory follow-up such as intervention on the behalf of the client and *corrective action* (1990, p. 3).

The feedback that you are required to give as a delegator involves some preparation in terms of assessment and analysis. The following basic questions will be helpful in preparing you to follow up with your delegate:

- What do I see? Is the delegate having difficulty with the task? Is the information not where I expected it to be (daily weight not on the graphic sheet)?
- How does it affect me? Is it making my job easier or more difficult?
- What can I do about it? Can I offer additional training for the task he seems to be unable to do? Can I encourage him to share this skill with other members of the team?

When you are providing feedback to your delegates, the information shared will usually be one of the following four types (Hersey and Duldt, 1989):

1. Clarifying: this will involve restating your instructions, making certain that any confusion regarding the assignment is cleared up so that you both are in agreement regarding parameters for reporting and the expectations of performance that you both have. "Please get the vital signs from the new post op in room 101 and report them to me immediately."
2. Interpretive: this particular type of feedback involves making an observation of the delegates' behavior and making assumptions about the meaning. "When I could not find you on the unit, I thought you were out on the deck smoking as usual." Be careful about this type of feedback—check your assumptions first!
3. Judgmental: similar to interpretive feedback, this form also involves drawing conclusions, this time in the form of a value judgment regarding behavior. "You're such a slob! How can we get any work done when you never clean up the treatment room?"
4. Personal reaction: when you provide the delegate with information about your personal feelings you are giving a strong message of how

he or she is coming across. "I feel relieved when you are working with me because you do such a good job and I can count on you."

CHECKPOINT 10–3

Can you recall times when you have given feedback to coworkers that was (1) clarifying? (2) interpreting? (3) judgmental? (4) a personal reaction? How did you feel on each of these occasions? Which type was most effective for you?

GIVING FEEDBACK TO THE DELEGATE

It is easy to see by reviewing the types of feedback that one can potentially do more harm than good. You can increase the defensiveness of the delegate and further alienate the members of the team if a few simple criteria are not followed. In further preparing your feedback message, consider the following criteria (LaMonica, 1983):

- It is specific rather than general.
- It is directed toward behavior the receiver can do something about.
- It considers the needs of both the receiver and the giver of the feedback.
- It is solicited, rather than imposed.
- It is well timed.
- It is checked to ensure clear communication by asking the receiver to rephrase the message to make certain he understands.

Keeping these criteria in mind, let's look at a method for giving feedback. Our proposed recipe can be used for both positive or negative feedback. For our example, let's use the situation of a new student nurse who has been working with you. You've noticed that Brenda does an excellent job in working with those patients who have been diagnosed with cancer and are in the beginning stages of the grief process. You'd like to comment on how wonderful it has been to work with Brenda.

Who needs to be told this information? Brenda, certainly, needs to know how you feel. It would be helpful for Brenda if your evaluation of

Brenda's expertise were shared with her instructor as well. When you have positive feedback to share, feel free to shout it from the rooftops and tell everyone. Letting others know about Brenda's performance is certainly positive to the general atmosphere of the work setting. However, if the feedback is negative, then only Brenda should hear the news. It may, of course, be necessary for the manager and the instructor to hear about problems. (Be sure to tell any person that you'll be sharing the information with the manager or supervisory person prior to doing so.) Resist telling stories to others about the errors others have made. Adlai Stevenson said, "If you throw mud, you get dirty." Confidentiality in performance feedback of a negative nature is essential, and betraying confidences will cause the speaker to look bad as well.

When the feedback discussion takes place is also essential. As soon as you are aware that feedback needs to be shared, then time should be planned to make certain it occurs. If emergency circumstances dictate that feedback will need to wait, then tell the person as soon as possible that you'll need to talk with him or her and set up a time. It is human nature to avoid the unpleasant, but in health care we do not have the luxury of avoiding giving performance feedback of a negative nature since human lives are at stake. (Think of late feedback you've been given about a circumstance that took place several months ago. It isn't effective for learning or for motivational purposes either.)

Where the feedback session occurs is also important for the success of the discussion. Obviously, negative feedback is never given in public, whereas praise is wonderful to hear in any setting. Negative feedback given without discretion to the time and place will belittle the importance of the message and be ineffective since the receiver will generally react defensively due to the shame of being reprimanded in public. Instead of being useful, this is destructive to the results intended.

THE FEEDBACK MODEL

1. Get the delegate's input before proceeding.
2. Give credit for the delegate's efforts.
3. Share your perception of what you have observed, read, assessed.
4. Explore the situation more fully with the delegate: discuss gaps in perceptions, causes of the problem.
5. Get the delegate's solution to the problem.
6. Agree on an action plan.
7. Set a time to check on progress.

APPLICATION TO THE DELEGATION PROCESS

As Susan, an RN, plans to give feedback to Brenda, she will first decide when and where it would be appropriate to discuss this with Brenda. She'll also plan how she'll share this with the instructor. She has chosen the setting of the coffee room, in private, when they go together on break.

CHECKPOINT 10–4

Fill in the blanks below with your proposed responses.

1. Get the delegate's input before proceeding.	"Brenda, how do you feel things have been going?"
2. Give credit for the delegate's efforts.	
3. Share your perception of what you have observed, read, assessed.	
4. Explore the situation more fully with the delegate: discuss gaps in perceptions, causes of the problem.	
5. Get the delegate's solution or input.	
6. Agree on an action plan.	
7. Set a time to check on progress.	

Now, using the steps of the feedback model, refer to the suggested dialogue that follows.

1. Getting the delegate's input is essential and is the step that people often miss. In this case, Brenda responded that she felt that she wasn't getting enough direction from Susan, and that sometimes she felt that she might not be doing as well as she wanted to in understanding the effects of the chemotherapy and explaining them. If Susan had charged in with her positive feedback and glowing assessment, she might not have known that Brenda had these concerns about her supervision. The pair were able to discuss that Susan had gained trust in her, that Brenda had always asked questions appropriately, and that Susan was assessing the patients' understanding of their chemotherapy herself.

2. There is no substitute for giving credit for others' efforts. When nurses work as hard as they do every day, it's frustrating when everything accomplished is overlooked, but a small detail is criticized. "I realize several patients have expired today and you've had three codes, but your charting is behind!" Avoid the negative consequences of focusing only on the negative. This is the sandwich principle: When giving negative feedback, be certain to give positive feedback before and after the negative. It makes the news somewhat easier to swallow! In this case, Susan tells Brenda how much she appreciates how well she is prepared each day before coming to clinical.

3. It's now time to share the perceptions Susan has had. She tells Brenda that she has been very impressed with how well she has been communicating with the newly diagnosed cancer patients and their families. They seem to be pretty upbeat and are retaining treatment information well.

How information is shared will make a huge difference in how the discussion is perceived and acted upon. Being tactful and providing thoughtful, objective feedback without being judgmental, is essential if the feedback is to achieve your desired goal. Maintain and preserve the self-respect of delegates by being respectful in your manner and speech. Asking yourself what you want delegates to remember from the conversation will help you to set the correct tone. Do you want them to remember how angry and upset you were? If so, be prepared for the situation to repeat itself as a display of anger will allow delegates to focus on your behavior, not theirs. It's a fact of human behavior that we tend to remember process, *how* something was said, much more readily than *what* was said. A calm, objective manner will overcome that tendency and keep the focus on the message, not your emotions.

4. As the situation is explored, Susan shares her assessment of Brenda's performance, stating that she has observed Brenda's patients to be much more knowledgeable about their treatment and better prepared for dis-

charge. Brenda appreciates this appraisal but still feels that she is not giving adequate information to the patients.

5. Getting input and discussion from the delegate, Brenda responds that she didn't know her patients had been responding better than most, but she thought it had to do with the statistics she gave them and the discussion she had with them about their own participation in treatment. She states she has read a lot about the difference that attitude makes in treatment and gives Susan the names of several books.

As input is received from the delegate in a negative performance conversation, remember that performance problems are generally due to a combination of several factors: delegates may not understand their role or your expectations. They may not know that the way they are performing their role does not correlate with what you desire, or that it doesn't measure up. There may be barriers present in the environment (those systems problems), or they may not understand how to do their job or why it is supposed to be done the way you want it to be. They may need further education, closer supervision. Or they may lack the necessary motivation to do the job right.

6. Susan asks Brenda if she'd feel comfortable sharing her ideas with the regular staff. Brenda agrees to bring it all up at report and see if anyone is interested in having an inservice on what's she's learned. She may even be able to get extra credit for it! This action plan will begin on the next clinical day.

7. Setting a time to check progress, Susan will facilitate the discussion during the next report and check with Brenda as the plan emerges to share Brenda's success with others.

Let's now use the feedback model process to give *negative* feedback.

Grant is in charge of the post-anesthesia care unit today. The unit has been very busy and they are short a secretary. Several patients have had rocky recoveries, and two were sent back to the OR. Pat, the OR supervisor, stops in and sees order sheets stacked up and the phone ringing without being answered. Pat is normally a very perceptive and caring individual, but today she walks by Grant and tells him, "Get your act together, the JCAHO (Joint Commission) surveyors are on their way!" Without waiting for a response, she walks briskly from the room.

Grant knows he must give feedback to Pat about this incident. However, he knows that he'll have to wait to do this until after the emergencies are taken care of and after the staffing supervisor calls in the secretary she's been promising to reach.

When Grant talks with Pat the next day, this is the way the conversation proceeds.

Grant: Pat, can we talk over here in private for a few moments? Good. Well, I was wondering how the JCAHO survey went yesterday. How did your day go, considering all that stress?

Pat: Well, I haven't consumed that many antacids for a long time. I was very worried that they'd come in here and see the chaos.

Grant: How do you think we do here, overall, in keeping our act together?

Pat: Well, generally things seem to be very organized, and the transfer of patients is excellently orchestrated. You do a wonderful job in keeping all these people alive and caring for the most critically ill. There haven't been many problems at all. Why do you ask?

Grant: Pat, I know you have worked very hard to make this unit the success it is. You were here long before I came to work in this area. The reason I ask is that yesterday I was concerned about your conversation with me prior to the survey. When you saw the situation and said, "Get your act together" without asking me what was going on, I knew you were very busy and under stress, but I felt invisible. I wanted to tell you that we were short a secretary, how busy things had been, and that I'd taken care of the situation by getting help to come in. I felt pretty awful about your response, even though I understood your pressure.

Pat: Well, I guess I didn't realize how I came across! I knew that you would have taken care of the tight staffing as best you could and that you had things under control, you always do! I was reacting to my own concerns, I guess. I probably don't tell you enough how much I do rely on your excellent leadership and judgment.

Grant: Thanks! I'm glad to know that. You are right, we need to figure out a method to give each other feedback more frequently so that these types of interchanges don't cause problems or concerns in our relationship. We have enough other concerns just keeping this place going!

Pat: Let's use our monthly meeting together for that purpose. I'll try to let you know when I'm stressed out, and if you'll let me know right away if I say something that's confusing, I'll be sure to let you know right away if I have any concerns. If I don't say anything, be sure to know I'm still extremely happy with your performance.

Grant: Thanks, Pat, I feel better knowing that you're not harboring some secret worries about how I am doing and how well this place runs during my period in charge.

CHECKPOINT 10–5

Review Grant and Pat's conversation and match the steps of the performance feedback process on the following chart:

1. Get the delegate's input before proceeding.	"How did your day go? How do you think we do here?"
2. Give credit for the delegate's efforts.	"You've worked very hard to make this unit the success it is."
3. Share your perception of what you have observed, read, assessed.	
4. Explore the situation more fully with the delegate: discuss gaps in perceptions, causes of the problem.	
5. Get the delegate's solution or input.	
6. Agree on an action plan.	
7. Set a time to check on progress.	

Now give feedback to your secretary, Joe. His job description states that he will organize the clothing room of your residential psychiatric facility. Although he has been told repeatedly in the last two weeks that this task needs to be done, he has not completed the job. You've noted that he seems to have time on his hands since he's been playing cards with the residents.

Follow the process or role play a feedback session. Describe the setting. Then follow the steps of the feedback process.

A possible conversation would proceed as follows:

"Joe, how have things been going for you here with respect to your role and work?"

"Pretty well, Marion, but I feel a bit like my skills are being underutilized. You know I want to become a mental health professional instead of a secretary. Otherwise, I think the job is okay."

"I'm glad to know you want to keep working in psychiatry, Joe, and I have very much appreciated how well you interact with the patients. You have a gift for talking with even the most disturbed without being afraid of them. I'd like to talk to you more about your plans to become a mental health professional. Since you feel underemployed, I can see why you aren't too excited about cleaning the clothing room. It doesn't seem like a priority, but it really does need to be done. When I ask you to do something several times, and then I see you playing cards with a resident, I feel frustrated. Unfortunately, this is something within your job description, and as much as it is not the most fun job, it doesn't make sense for the other members of the team to be doing that type of work either. They are also concerned because clothes have been lost and they have had to spend time searching for things for the residents or their families. How do you think this should be resolved?"

"Marion, as much as I hate to clean, I guess I have been procrastinating. I can see how it would be frustrating for you all. Maybe this is like starting at the bottom and working up?"

"Yes, Joe, I think it would work best if you did the job. I'd like it done once every week. You can determine when will work out best, but please be certain it is done. In fact, it may be best if you mark it on the sheet that we use to record the inventory in that room. Then the others will know it is being done regularly."

"Plus you can tell if I am getting it done, right?"

"Right! Let's plan to talk more about your MHP plans when we evaluate the clothing room issue, too. I'll get some information together for you at our next monthly meeting, okay?"

Practice Feedback Scenarios

1. In your family planning clinic, one of the assistants who also performs secretarial work has decided to telephone the patients their HIV test results before consulting with you, the RN who generally counsels patients about these issues.
2. You have observed a new colleague drawing blood without using gloves. Someone needs to talk with her.
3. A medical assistant has been discussing confidential information about patients in the coffee room.
4. The psychiatric case worker talked with a patient's family to plan aftercare. After the case worker left, the family complained about the "condescending attitude" that was displayed.
5. A physician who is the consultant for the school nurses' immunization clinic met with some of the community leaders at an evening holiday open house. He had evidently had something alcoholic to drink because his breath smelled quite strong, although his behavior didn't seem altered. One of the community leaders asked, "Is this clinic run by someone with a drinking problem? I think that drinking alcohol is a bad example for the people of this community, where substance abuse is very high. You need to tell the doctor we don't want to smell alcohol on his breath again!" Margaret, one of the school nurses, has to decide whether to give this feedback to the physician, but is afraid of the impact to the clinic if she doesn't.
6. Maria, the nursing assistant on the night shift at the long-term care center, routinely complains about having to turn patients who are "just going to die anyway."
7. Greta has come in to work late several times in the last week.

REQUESTING AND RECEIVING FEEDBACK

As you can see from our model, feedback requires an exchange of information to be most effective. You can give recognition (and we certainly recommend it!) in a one-way communication format and still have a positive impact. However, allowing the delegate to offer input too will set up a two-way communication process that is much more meaningful and can lead to longer lasting results. When the delegate feels that his or her input is valued, you are building trust and a positive working relationship. The input you receive can help you to further improve your performance as well and make working together easier and more beneficial for the patient.

Great supervisors ask for feedback from their staff not only in terms of clinical data or reports on how the systems are working in their area but on their own performance. RNs who ask for input on their personal performance from their delegates will soon capture the respect and admiration of their teammates. Receiving feedback graciously allows the RN to hear the other person's point of view without being defensive or angry. The RN can further explore the points being made and decide whether the feedback is something that he or she can use to improve his or her performance or behavior in the job setting.

It is important to understand that some delegates may have difficulty in participating in a two-way communication process. Others may welcome the chance and overwhelm you with their opinions! To make certain the process stays on track, you may want to review what is expected (clarifying expectations again) so that you foster an environment in which you are all working together to improve your delivery of care.

On a periodic basis, it's important to ask such questions as

- How did these assignments work for you?
- Is there anything I could have done that would have made the day/ shift/case better for you?
- How am I doing, in your perception?
- What am I doing that works well?
- What should I be working on, in your opinion?
- What ideas do you have that I could use to make things work better here?
- Did the instructions I give you help, or was there a better way for me to communicate with you?

Being open to such feedback allows your delegates to know you think you are human too, and fallible. They will feel less defensive themselves when you must give them negative feedback or criticism when they know you are willing to receive it yourself. And certainly everyone will feel more free to give the positive feedback needed to keep everyone's self-esteem and motivation at the highest level.

CHECKPOINT 10–6

Consider the following situations:

1. Why is it so important, as an RN, to ask for feedback from others on the team?
2. Think about a situation in which you've been delegating to others. What questions could you ask to determine how you are doing?
3. Arlene, a school nurse, has given many instructions to the parents who help out in the high school when she's out in another one of the schools in her area. The school secretary tells Arlene that one of the parents was assisting when a girl came in with some concerns, and then the girl left the office sobbing. The secretary overheard the assisting parent telling the girl loudly that "you should have just said no! Well, you'd better call your parents about this pregnancy or I will!" How would you give feedback and further instructions to the assisting parent?
4. Frank, a nurse working in a poison control center, has trained a new assistant. This nurse is relatively inexperienced, and Frank is quite concerned about the first few times that she'll be on alone. How can Frank receive some feedback from his new assistant about the training process and his supervision style while giving feedback to the new nurse?

See the end of the chapter for the answers.

UPWARD FEEDBACK

Most of our discussion so far has been on providing information to the delegates in terms of their performance, to ensure their competency in performing delegated tasks. When soliciting feedback from the delegate, you are, in effect, asking them to provide "upward feedback," or evaluative information to a superior. This can be difficult for many, since the fear of reprisal may hinder their desire to be honest. Consider your own situation—are you comfortable in providing feedback to your supervisor—as was discussed in Grant and Pat's OR situation?

We have unfortunately worked with some organizations where the "chain of command" was strictly enforced and communication flowed only in one direction. This top-down approach has a significant negative impact on teamwork, morale, and productivity. It is sad to see such outdated management practices in any organization, but there are ways around the limitations imposed by such a command/control environment.

If you find yourself in a situation where providing feedback to a superior is forbidden and you must continue to work in that setting, you can speak to these individuals using the assertive strategy of "I messages." Rather than focusing on "*you* are never around when I need you," consider rephrasing the message as "*I* need to know where *I* can reach you if we get another admission." If you are not getting any feedback from this supervisor and would like to find out how you are doing, don't criticize him or her for lack of performance ("You never give me any feedback—how am I supposed to know how I'm doing?"). Instead, use the I-message technique and state, "*I* need to have some information from you about how I am doing. I have been here at the clinic for three months now, and I'd like to know if I am performing okay."

CHECKPOINT 10–7

Using I messages, give upward feedback in the following situations.

1. The charge nurse frequently gives you more patients with a higher acuity than anyone else's assignment. Other members on the team have noticed this but are reluctant to say anything on your behalf.
2. The evening supervisor was yelling loudly at you in front of patients and staff. This is something he does frequently, but no one will discuss it with him.

Often nurses allow position and chain of command to foster a helpless, "victim" mentality. As professional nurses, you are accountable for the safety of your patients, and working conditions such as those above may hamper your ability to provide that care. It is essential to be able to provide feedback to those persons who are in a position to affect your ability to provide safe care.

In Situation 1 above, if you are feeling overloaded and you question your ability to provide adequate care to the patients in this assignment, you must give this feedback to the charge nurse. Consider using an I message such as "I am concerned about this assignment. I will need some assistance with Mr. Smith when I do his dressing, and I will need someone to watch the rest of my patients when I begin the initial chemotherapy on Mrs. Blake. Will you be available?" Without being directly confrontational, or offering judgmental feedback on the charge nurse's ability to make fair assignments, you *have* let her know your specific concerns and that you will need assistance throughout the shift.

Situation 2 involves a situation that makes the work setting less than pleasant when allowed to continue. Taking control of the situation, you may consider using an I message to redirect the supervisor to another location: "I appreciate your comments and would like to have further feedback, but I need to step into the medication room to get an IV." Once removed from the public arena, you may continue your discussion with additional assertive techniques (see Chapter 8). As time and the situation dictate, using the entire feedback model to give upward feedback is also effective.

SUMMARY

Giving and receiving feedback can be risky business, but the potential for building more positive working relationships outweighs these risks. Remembering the step-by-step process and preparing your message before you speak will help you to make this a more meaningful part of your role as a professional nurse. From the impact of a simple "thank you" to the detailed exchange of the evaluation of the performance of a new task, feedback closes the loop of the delegation process. As a result, you are fulfilling your legal obligation to monitor, evaluate, and follow up, and the patients are reaping the benefits. Good job!

ANSWERS TO CHECKPOINTS

10–6.
   1. The RN, as leader of the team, must set the stage for listening to other's perceptions, being open to growth, and being nondefensive.

You will engender the respect of your coworkers as you teach them how to give and receive feedback. Your nurse practice act states that you must supervise your delegates, and this means giving feedback on their performance. They'll accept feedback from you much more happily if you are able to accept it yourself. You can grow and learn from constructive information sharing.

2. Use the questions preceding this checkpoint or others that fit your situation exactly.

3. Follow the feedback model, being certain that you get input from the parent first. You may have to explain the school district's policy on confidentiality.

4. Follow the feedback model. Be prepared with a few questions for your new assistant that would, when answered correctly, help you feel more comfortable with her knowledge. Be certain to listen to how well you've been orienting her.

REFERENCES

Goode, C., et al. 1993. "What kind of recognition do staff nurses want?" *American Journal of Nursing* 93: 64–68.

Hersey, P., and B.W. Duldt. 1989. *Situational leadership in nursing*. Norwalk, Conn.: Appleton & Lange.

Jenks, J. M., and J. M. Kelly. 1985. *Don't do—delegate!* New York: Franklin Watts.

LaMonica, E. 1983. *Nursing leadership and management, an experiential approach*. Monterey, Calif.: Wadsworth Health Sciences Division, 139.

National Council of State Boards of Nursing. 1990. *Concept paper on delegation*. Chicago.

O'Neil, K. K., and K.L. Gajdostik. 1989. The head nurse's managerial role. *Nursing Management* 20: 39–42.

Chapter 11

Know How To Evaluate:
How Well Has the Delegation
Process Produced the Outcomes
I Wanted To Achieve?

Ruth I. Hansten and Marilynn J. Washburn

It's 6 AM on a medical surgical acute care nursing unit. A nursing assistant who was assigned to answer call lights reports to the charge RN, "Oh, by the way, about midnight Mr. Peterson in Room 555 complained of chest pain and was diaphoretic. I decided it was because he'd been coughing too much and asked the other RN to give him a sleeping pill. I think he's okay." The charge nurse races down to the room, finds that Mr. Peterson is, in fact, having a myocardial infarction, and rushes him, monitored, to the cardiac unit (Hansten, 1991).

CHECKPOINT 11–1

Keeping in mind what you have learned about the delegation process, what went wrong in this situation?

_____

_____

_____

_____

As in any situation involving people and judgment, there are several possible problems as well as several times when the error could have been caught before it was too late for the patient. In this case, one would expect the nursing assistant to have known that all complaints of chest pain must be immediately reported to the nurse in charge. She was definitely overstepping her job description by diagnosing the origin of the pain and taking her own interventions. However, was this the first time throughout the entire shift that the charge nurse and the assistants crossed paths to discuss the patients? Where was the supervision by the charge nurse? Third, did the charge nurse make rounds and check the patients herself? An "eyeball" assessment of a sleeping patient often yields the necessary information to avoid a tragedy; in this case, however, the patient was stable and did not reflect the minor arrhythmias and ischemia his heart was certainly experiencing. A fourth issue is present: what about the second nurse who administered a sleeping pill without assessing the reasons for it? One wonders if the patient was experiencing the chest pain as he or she gave the medication.

EVALUATION: CONTINUOUS, PROBLEM RELATED, AND PERIODIC

Evaluation is a familiar word and process to all RNs. Evaluation, as a part of the nursing process, is continuous, as we consider whether our interventions are achieving the projected *outcomes* for each nursing diagnosis. In this chapter, we'll be discussing evaluation of the delegation process itself. How well the process is working will yield important information on the performance of the systems we have created and the people to whom we delegate. Evaluation will allow us to give useful feedback, both positive and negative, and to learn from the feedback that is given to us by our coworkers. In this chapter we'll cover some of the issues that we have discovered commonly interfere with successful completion of the process.

One of the most productive stages of the delegation process includes the portion covered in this chapter: evaluation of the results of the process, with a careful analysis of each step of the process to ensure that the cycle of delegation has been complete and effective. In the situation above, evaluation of a problem situation yields important information for the growth of the personnel involved and for improving the quality of the care delivered. Often, when evaluating, we discover that we've missed some essential points from preceding parts of the process. There were many errors in the "chest pain" incident:

- Before we question the people involved and find out more, we can at least assume that the delegate did not report appropriately.

- We can also guess that the charge nurse did not make a practice of giving and receiving feedback frequently throughout the shift.

- In this case, an evaluation of a particular incident (a problem evaluation) reveals that the shorter term, ongoing evaluation throughout the shift may not have been proceeding as effectively as it could have been.

- Checkpoints between the supervising RN and the delegate were missing.

- A long-term view of the situation will certainly reveal that the nursing assistant's performance must be evaluated and feedback given with relationship to her past performance.

- The communication systems used in this unit's selected care delivery system may need some changing.

Within any organizational setting, there is the need for both continuous (ongoing), incident-related, and periodic evaluation. Whether it is broken down on a shift-by-shift, daily, case, product line, program, or delegate basis, evaluation is integral. Just as the nursing process of assessment, planning, intervention, and evaluation is a circular, never-ending continuum, evaluation is a continuous part of the delegation process as the delegating nurse constantly checks reality with what was projected in terms of job descriptions, expected behaviors, and outcomes.

The feedback related to the process of evaluation is received in two forms:

1. Data reporting and the RN's personal assessment of the client situation and the actual process by which care is delivered will yield some of the information necessary to evaluate the process and the people performing the process.
2. Performance feedback (see Chapter 10) is a two-way, reciprocal action in which the RN coaches and guides the delegates, and receives feedback from them related to the RN's performance as well.

Evaluation of specific problems or situations, whether they have to do with personal performance or systems performance, will consistently be a part of the RN's job in his or her appraisal during the delegation process. Feedback must be given, and problem solving, both short-term and long-term, is necessary.

Periodic evaluation considers the effects of systems and people performance on the overall goal achievement of the team. What outcomes have been expected, and what outcomes have been evidenced? The RN looks for what is working well, and what problems or trends need attention to improve the quality of care, and takes steps to resolve recurring issues. Periodic evaluation of the performance of the team members is also a part of this type of evaluation.

The evaluation phase of the delegation process is represented graphically in Figure 11–1.

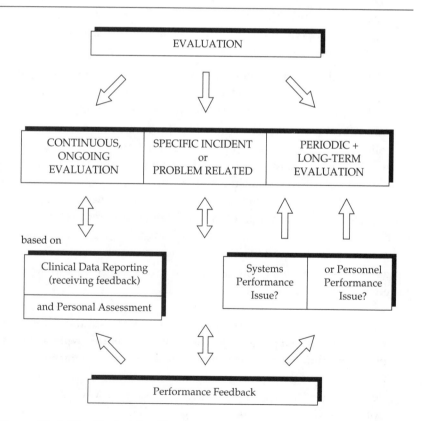

Figure 11–1 The Evaluation Process

CONTINUOUS EVALUATION

Checkpoints, Time Lines, and Parameters for Reporting

Depending on the health care setting where you work, you have integrated a method by which you can receive and give feedback or share information and clinical data on a regular, ongoing basis in your clinical work. The communication is two-way: to and from you as the RN and to and from the delegates. This data sharing makes it possible for you to evaluate the clinical situation and to make decisions about further assessment and interventions that may be necessary for a specific patient or case. In a psychiatric day care setting, for example, the supervising RN may receive data from assistive personnel several times throughout the day about a client who is experiencing an acute depressive episode. She or he may also spend one-on-one time with that patient to make decisions about further treatment modalities. Getting the necessary data in a timely manner from the assistive personnel depends on having checkpoints, time lines, and parameters for reporting.

As we have discussed previously in this book, it's essential for you to know what you want. Knowing what kinds of things you need to find out from assistive personnel is fundamental to your own ability to clearly discuss your requirements to the delegates. We again review the journalist's list of questions necessary for evaluation: *who, what, when, where, how,* and *why?*

Be clear with the delegate about:

- *Who* should be doing which tasks, and to *whom*
- *What* kinds of data are necessary
- *When, where,* and *how* it will be reported to you

This is basic information that is often assumed to be understood, and the expectation is not shared by all delegates and supervisors. (Is it okay to chart only essential information? What kinds of data are important?) *Why* shows the delegate what kinds of things you are concerned about and helps them grow while they become another set of eyes and ears. For example, in acute care, if a delegate is assigned a group of tasks, including data collection such as vital signs, he or she needs to know when he or she should report to you any vital signs that are abnormal, and what constitutes "abnormal"? Parameters for reporting are essential and are often forgotten, especially when you delegate to another RN who is floating to your area. Keep in mind that when you became a renal nurse specialist, you didn't know how much urine to expect the first 48 hours post transplant, and the float RN or assistive personnel won't know either. Guidelines for reporting help avoid unpleasant surprises. Wherever you work, take time to think about how you implement the following and whether the communication is in a written and/or verbal format.

- *Checkpoints:* How often do you get together to share data? (This is a two-way street, as shown by the double arrows in Figure 11–1.) Before people go to breaks or meals, knowing what has been happening is essential. Where and how can delegates find you if needed?

- *Timelines:* Are all personnel certain of when to report which data? Which are okay merely to chart and which need immediate attention? How often should the delegate expect that you'll report changes or update them on the client's situation? Are you clear about this expectation when delegating?

- *Parameters for Reporting:* Are you worried about the bleeding on the dressing or in the chest tube with Mrs. Smith? If so, how much bleeding should be expected in the next two hours? Are you wondering whether Mr. Potter's daughter has been in the home with him to discuss transport to the rehabilitation center for PT? How soon do you need to know about the travel arrangements that have been made? Just as you appreciate (and need!) specific parameters for reporting patient condition changes to the physician, your delegates need specific parameters as well. Do you provide them?

As you tried to answer the questions above, if the answers were difficult to come by or if the questions raised some concerns about whether information is being shared appropriately and in a timely manner, *now* is the time to determine what can be done about interruptions in the continuous flow of important information among the members of the health care team. As we discuss the problems that may become evident as a part of your evaluation process, you can use some of the suggestions to help you proceed with solving the communication flow issue.

Learning and Communication Styles

As you thought about how you are giving and receiving clinical information and feedback continuously with members of your health care team in order to evaluate whether outcomes have been achieved, you may have overlooked the importance of understanding how people best learn. This one issue commonly creates problems in the delegation process that become evident as you gather data and evaluate, and it is closely related to how well you assessed your delegate and acted on those assessment data.

People have preferred modes of learning that may affect their ability to retain and implement your instructions to them. Let's take a closer look at how learning and communication styles may influence the manner in which you discussed the work to be done with the delegates, and in the achievement of outcomes.

Global versus Linear Learning

Some of the delegates need to know the total, overall goals and the global picture before they are able to begin working most effectively; others want more detailed instructions of the steps to be accomplished, with less regard for the total view. When discussing the work at hand, it's best to give the overall outcomes to be achieved for the motivational value and for those who need that type of information to get started, while giving more detailed information to those who need it. For example, if you are discussing an assignment in a long-term care setting, you will want to tell the group about the outcomes you wish to achieve with Mrs. Ventelli: "The multidisciplinary team group, along with the patient and family, determined that we'd all work for the goal of getting her home by Christmas with a home health aide coming in several times a week for chores and personal care. [Overall picture for the global learners]. This means we'll be gradually increasing her PT and ambulation by 10 minutes three times per day. The rehabilitation aides will use this graph in the room to chart Mrs. Ventelli's responses. Let me know before afternoon break how well it's gone today." [More detail for the linear learners]. In this way, each person on the team is more clear about the work he or she needs to do and what kind of information you are expecting in return.

Visual, Auditory, and Kinesthetic Learning

Those of you who were very glad that we've included graphic representations and models to aid in your assimilation and integration of the material are probably visual learners. Very observant, these people may have difficulty understanding or remembering verbal directions. (Have you ever been given directions verbally at the convenience store or gas station when what you really wanted was a map of the area?) It is very frustrating for visual learners to hear directions only. These people will be able to do their jobs more effectively if given written directions, and even better when the care map or plan is visually represented by symbols or in a graph-like format. Visual delegates may want to make up their own assignment sheets or write up personal notes (often called "brains" in many settings) to make certain they are organized and will give appropriate feedback to the RN in a timely manner. It's best when written information on assignments, reporting timelines, and so on is available, for clarity and legal reasons as well as to facilitate the accomplishment of the process. We'll discuss the topic of documentation more fully later on in this chapter.

Many organizations have specific (written) policies for reporting times, checkpoints, and so on. Certainly all health care organizations across the continuum expect some kind of formal charting on patients' responses and of other clinical data. Computerized patient clinical data may be available in a real-time manner; however, it is not a substitute for the RN's interpretation and discussion of the implications with the delegates.

Auditory learners need to hear from you. They won't be satisfied with a written assignment, but will want to discuss it with you. This is their preferred method of communication, and despite the time it takes to talk about what needs to be done and how, it's essential to save time later by being clear in asking for and receiving feedback or clinical data reporting. We have observed negative consequences in systems where delegates were given only written instructions to be followed, without discussion, before beginning their work. Since health care in any setting is a dynamic process, what is written as an instruction one minute may be inaccurate at best, dangerous at worst, in the next minute. Relying on "routine" in any setting has created many problems. Be aware that some of the problems may be related to the necessity of auditory learners to personally hear from you.

With so many delegates learning English as a second language, it's important to understand the necessity of clarity in both written and verbal communication. When determining delegates' ability to understand, get immediate feedback from them by asking them what their plan for the day/shift/case is. Although it is uncomfortable to determine these issues, it's even more uncomfortable when unclear communication causes a patient problem. Many organizations use written universal symbols to help multilingual patients, staff, and families understand each other.

Kinesthetic learners are those that need to "do" rather than hear about it. Some delegates may feel comfortable with trying to complete a task with verbal instruction, but kinesthetic learners will need to experience an active learning process of watching and helping with the task or procedure, then doing it with a supervising nurse. When giving instructions such as parameters for reporting, it may not suffice for this delegate to be told that "the dressing should not have more than 1 or 2 more centimeters of bleeding on it, and please let me know the amount of additional drainage before you go to break." For these delegates, you may need to go with them to the patient's room and describe and show them what you mean. When asking a delegate to complete the patient's clothing checklist, paying special attention to suicide prevention articles, it won't suffice for them to read the procedure and discuss it with you. They'll have to work through it in a patient situation with a supervising nurse to feel comfortable with the process.

Since all of us have a combination of preferences of learning modes, it's best to use as many of them as possible when communicating and asking for feedback in the form of data reporting. Keep in mind that just because a delegate may have a combination of styles that is different from yours doesn't mean it will detract from his or her ability to do the job. It does mean, however, that you will need to adjust your methods of communication as you learn what works best with that staff member. As a supervising (delegating) nurse, you'll often find yourself using the same skills you've used with patients (assessing their readiness and preferred learning and communication methods) with your delegates and coworkers. If it works for the RN to adapt to the patient's needs, it is certainly effective to utilize the same skills with the other members of the health care team. (For additional information on learning styles and the principles of learning, we recommend Anderson's (1990) *Patient Teaching and Communicating in an Information Age*.) Before you proceed, turn to Checkpoint 11–2 and complete it.

Importance of Personal Assessment

Although we have mentioned this previously, whether you are evaluating achievement of outcomes on a patient-by-patient basis, doing ongoing evaluation as the shift progresses, evaluating a specific unusual occurrence, or completing a more global evaluation of the processes and systems you are using for delivery of care, *nothing can substitute for your own personal assessment and evaluation*. Using assistive personnel has al-

CHECKPOINT 11–2

1. Thinking about your communication links in the system in your workplace, how do you make certain you respond to the preferred learning and communication styles of those with whom you work?

_____

_____

2. Have you ever been frustrated with those with different learning styles? For example, what would the following example lead you to believe? (Use information you have learned in all the preceding chapters.)

   I have *told* Delegate A several times today that she needs to empty the dirty linen cart, and it hasn't been done yet. Is Delegate A

   a) lazy?
   b) hard of hearing?
   c) new to the English language, so that she may not have understood?
   d) a visual or kinesthetic learner who needs written in-structions or actual demonstration?
   e) of a culture that differs from yours, so that she may not interpret your instructions as a priority due to your method of communication?
   f) lacking motivation and being resentful and subordi-nate?
   g) misunderstanding what you expect?

Looking at this example, it would seem that further assess-ment and evaluation is necessary to determine what is re-ally going on here. Does the RN have the extra time and en-ergy to spend in frustration and anger, or would time be better spent finding out what's the real issue behind this? (You have learned many skills for working with these issues: the assertiveness formula, the collaborative resolution model, and the feedback process. You have also learned how to assess the delegate to determine how to delegate effectively based on your appraisal.)

lowed RNs to gather data with the additional eyes and ears of others, leaving more time for the RNs to perform professional nursing tasks and processes more thoroughly. However, keep in mind that the RN is the supervising authority. You are being paid to use the nursing process, solve problems, and think about maintaining and improving the quality of the care or service provided to your clients on a short-term and long-term basis. Nothing can substitute for the time you spend evaluating the situations you are faced with each day.

Besides evaluating the results achieved by your interventions according to your treatment plan as in the nursing process, you must evaluate the efficacy of the delegation process and the performance of the delegates. If you are a public health nurse who has been examining the data of the growing rate of tuberculosis and AIDS in your community, and has reviewed reports of specific cases from many assistive personnel, nothing can substitute for some on-site assessment and evaluation of selected patient cases. If you work in ambulatory care, and a medical assistant or LPN often gives the injections in your well-baby clinics, supervising the process and observing and evaluating his or her ability to perform the functions of the job description is essential to your ability to evaluate the systems you are using as well as the performance of the delegates. If you work in home health care and you've made a home assessment visit, you know that there is no other professional or assistant that can put together the medical, psychological, social, and practical aspects of the patient and family's life to determine the plan of care and how to best capitalize on the patient's strengths.

If you work in acute or long-term care and you are so busy at the desk being "in charge" that you never actually see the patients, you are missing a valuable and essential part of your job. You are able, in a moment's time, to "eyeball" a patient and observe very quickly any changes in condition. In a few seconds, you have taken in the patient's respiratory rate, depth, and comfort, his skin color and moisture, his body habitus and expression, all the visual and auditory cues; asking a short question will allow you to make a preliminary assessment of cognitive functioning, as well. Combining your observations with the clinical data and your experience with your scientific knowledge is a part of the art of nursing. You use this special art to evaluate, decide what more data are needed, and come to a conclusion about what needs to be done further. This patient assessment and/or evaluation data that you complete by your clinical assessment also yield valuable information about the delegation process and how well it is going. Is care being completed by the delegates? Are changes in condition being appropriately reported? How does the environment appear? Where have the assistive personnel been concentrating their efforts? How are we proceeding as a team in achieving the planned *outcomes*?

CHECKPOINT 11–3

Consider your own work environment. What kinds of information about the effectiveness of the delegation process and the performance of the delegates can be obtained from your own personal assessment? What kinds of information do you retrieve from your evaluation of the patient, the chart, or other written materials?

_____

_____

_____

Evaluation is another part of the delegation process that encourages you to make decisions about what data can be gathered by others and what data must be generated by your own senses. Again, nursing judgment must be used in each specific situation to determine how much of the evaluation can be based on reports and data collected by others, just as which tasks to delegate and the amount and type of supervision needed were determined in each situation in the beginning of the delegation process. A neonatal nurse specialist at a receiving hospital is the very best person to determine which questions to ask nurses at another hospital before transport of a critical infant can take place, even if a secretary calls with a cursory report. Nothing can substitute for the "eyeball" assessment and evaluation of the situation by another nurse. Even though this book is dedicated to helping nurses make the very best use of assistive personnel, we wish to caution all nurses to maintain patient contact so that the delegation process, and assistive personnel, can best be evaluated.

Give yourselves credit for that art of nursing, the judgment based on your experience and scientific knowledge. Think about how often we use it in our daily lives: when you and a friend are at the mall and you see someone walking past and you comment: "Boy, that person has COPD: looks like he left the oxygen at home!" or "My goodness, that pregnant woman has 4+ pitting edema up to her calf, and with that flushed face I wonder if she's had her pressure taken recently?" or, in conversation with a friend at church or the grocery store, "With the sleep and appetite disturbances, I wonder if he's tried drugs or psychotherapy for that depression. Has he ever said anything about feeling like he'd like to never wake up? Any other suicidal ideation?" It's impossible to take the nursing process or the "art" out of a nurse at any age or in any setting. Since your nursing abilities are second nature, don't assume that all humans are endowed with these special abilities, but instead, give yourselves credit for your expertise and use it for evaluating and improving the care we provide!

SPECIFIC INCIDENT OR PROBLEM-RELATED EVALUATION

Since you are the supervising nurse, incidents or problems will definitely occur, if not daily, then at least frequently enough that these "unusual occurrences" will consume a fair amount of your time. Evaluating the situation is essential for resolving the problem or situation. In the first situation we discussed (the case of the chest pain), there were many possible errors, and several times when the problem could have been resolved. For example, ongoing checkpoints and two-way feedback were missing. The other RN might not have assessed the patient before giving the sedative. The nursing assistant could have reported the problem.

The charge RN stepped in immediately when the information was shared to solve the short-term problem: finding out whether the patient had an MI, and what kind of treatment was necessary to provide immediately. After the emergency issues were resolved, there remained another concern. Why did this problem occur, and how could it be prevented from happening again? In this case, evaluation of the problem uncovered the need for more information from the other RN (to determine what steps would be necessary) and for performance feedback for the nursing assistant. (In Chapter 10, we discussed the process of performance feedback. As Figure 11–1 illustrates, performance feedback supports the entire evaluation process.) Now let's take a closer look at the RN's responsibility for evaluating incidents and resolving problems.

Many nurses have reported to us that they wish that their managers were better at resolving problems and incidents. They often share their frustration with the slow progress they've seen in improving and repairing systems and personnel's performance. These RNs have clearly evaluated specific incidents or have determined trends or recurring problems. They have begun the evaluation and problem-solving process by analyzing situations and coming up with ideas of what is wrong and what should be done. Most of the work in resolving the problem is already complete! Ideas like these should be shared and used with the managers of the departments to improve the quality of care and outcomes achieved, instead of being kept bottled up in individual and collective frustration! The managers cannot possibly "fix" everything (including people's performance) alone. Each RN has the accountability to be involved in the short-term and long-term improvement of care.

As discussed in Question 52 of *The Nurse Manager's Answer Book* (Hansten and Washburn, 1993), there is a step-by-step process to use when evaluating an incident or problem. We will first discuss the process and then use additional examples for practice. Remember to consult with a manager for assistance as needed.

1. What signs cause you to think there is a problem? (Patients who have an MI need to go to the CCU. A patient didn't get appropriate care because the RN didn't know about his symptoms. The symptoms weren't reported.)
2. What is good about this situation? (Remember Collaborative Resolution? This step allows the creative juices to flow. The good things about the situation are numerous: the patient didn't die; this incident allows us to teach the assistant and the other nurses and to look more closely at our methods of communicating clinical data.)
3. If everything would have gone well, what would have happened? (The nursing assistant would have reported the pain, the patient would have been transferred to CCU, the other RN would have assessed him further or at least asked if the charge nurse had time to assess him before the sedative was given.)
4. Decide if you need to do something about this incident or problem.
   a) Does it affect me, or my unit/department/organization, or those for whom we care? (Yes!)
   b) What will happen if I don't do anything about this? (Another patient could die. This is a good reason to deal with the incident.)
   c) What will happen if I try to resolve this problem? (Don't let concerns about conflict get in your way. You know how to deal with that. Keep your mind on what may happen that will be better: if

this communication problem is solved, perhaps lives will be saved.)

d) Can I live with this situation, or is it a real problem I shouldn't let continue? (The incident above is not a situation to let go; it is a serious problem that could endanger lives.)

e) Am I the person that can solve this problem (or prevent this type of incident from occurring in the future) or should this problem be dealt with by another person or department? (In the "chest pain incident," the short-term situation definitely required the action of the charge nurse. The long-term solution for this problem will rest with the charge nurse as well as the manager. The errors are too serious to leave for quick, undocumented verbal feedback.)

5. Determine the exact nature of the problem by asking what isn't the way you want it to be. Are there objective criteria that you could use that would determine when the problem is solved or that the errors that produced the incident are absent? (One of the most glaring problems here is that an assistive person did not report serious data in a timely manner. She made a decision about the implications of the patient's complaint and decided to make an intervention on her own. We would be able to tell that the problem were resolved if this staff member reported appropriately at all times. Another problem was the lack of checkpoints and sharing of information throughout the shift. If a system were set up by which that could occur, then information would be shared on an ongoing basis each shift. The outcomes for the patients would ultimately be avoidance of complications and, potentially, discharge as planned. In this situation, absence of lawsuits based on poor quality of care could be another outcome.)

6. What can we do about these problems? Without judging the feasibility of each idea, list some possible plans for resolving the problem. (The charge nurse may list such ideas as: (1) fire the nursing assistant (that would require the manager's help); (2) educate the nursing assistant about what to report; (3) plan for checkpoints and evaluation at intervals throughout the shift; (4) ask other charge nurses for ideas; (5) research the situation more fully, and get some feedback from all the people involved; (6) talk to the manager about this, and give him or her a list of possible alternatives.)

7. Determine the positives and negatives of each alternative plan. What should be done first? (In this case, the charge nurse decides to get more information from the others, then talk to the nurse manager.

The manager will need to know about this very soon because of the risks inherent in the situation, and will want to be involved. The charge nurse will also think of how to better supervise in an ongoing manner and report the plan to the manager at the same time.)

8. Plan the steps for implementation of the solutions or follow-up, keeping in mind the positive results you will enjoy because of your efforts. Remember the necessity of involvement of all individuals that will be affected when changes are made. (Depending on the amount of responsibility given to charge nurses in the job description, the charge nurse will be working with the manager to give performance feedback to the assistant and the other nurse. The charge nurse will be implementing the plan for better supervision. The manager (or perhaps the charge nurse if he or she has a "hiring/firing" supervisory role) will probably be engaged in the progressive discipline process for the assistive person. Don't forget to implement this excellent plan!

9. Evaluate your results by the objective criteria you designed. Is the situation/problem vanishing? (Is the nursing assistant reporting all information? How is your system of checkpoints working? Are you getting the information you need from the assistive personnel?)

10. If the related incidents continue to occur, the solutions aren't working and a new plan needs to be developed. (Perhaps this nursing assistant will never report appropriately and it's time to progress to a different job.) It's possible that the real problem hasn't been defined, or that the symptoms you saw were caused by something else. Perhaps the facts weren't fully disclosed or you did not fully research the incident. Maybe communication with all those that needed to be involved hasn't occurred. Or the solutions haven't been given enough time to do their magic!

We encourage each professional nurse to complete as much of the problem-solving process as is authorized in his or her work setting. As we have noted, managers must be notified of problems and should be involved in developing and carrying out the solutions. But as reforms in our national system continue, and health care adopts the business trend of flattened hierarchies, increased accountability and responsibility will be granted to each employee. Each RN will become more empowered to act in the best interests of the patients for whom he or she cares, and will be more involved in activities that once were considered the province of managers.

The ten-step process of evaluation and follow-up for specific incidents or problem situations can be applied to any clinical setting. To review the steps just outlined, see Exhibit 11–1.

The process of evaluation of a specific situation or incident includes many of the principles of the conflict management process as well as the nursing process. Evaluation must focus on the short-term situation as well as how the problem could be avoided in the future.

CHECKPOINT 11–4

Think of a problem incident or situation that has occurred in your facility or work setting in the last month. Was it related to the delegation process? Was it related to problems within the system or with the performance of personnel, or both? How did you go about helping to solve it, immediately and long-term?

Exhibit 11–1 Questions for Problem Evaluation and Follow-Up

1. What signs tell you that something is wrong here?

2. What is good about this situation?

3. What should be happening instead of what did happen?

4. Do I need to do something about it?
   Does it affect me, my patients, or our team goals?
   What will happen if I don't do something about this?
   What could happen if I do?
   Should I be solving this problem or should someone else be involved?

5. What is the exact nature of the problem, incident, or error? What objective criteria will tell me if the problem is solved?

6. What can be done about it? Get input. (In many organizations, this is where the staff RN would ask for assistance from supervisory or management people.)

7. Think about the positives and negatives regarding each possible solution. Discuss with others.

8. Plan the steps and implement the short-term and long-term plans.

9. Evaluate short-term results.

10. Evaluate long-term results and decide if more action is required.

PERIODIC EVALUATION

Whether you are a staff nurse working with assistive personnel, a charge nurse, or involved in upper management, you will need to take some time for periodic evaluation of the work and how the delegation process has been proceeding. Depending on the site in which you work, this may be on a shift-by-shift basis, as each case is finished, or every several months. Again, as an RN you'll need to use your nursing judgment, as well as consulting the policies, to decide when your periodic evaluation needs to occur.

We worked with one subacute care facility that had recently changed shift times for the professional nurses and the assistive personnel. When their shift was completed, assistants went home without reporting what had happened during those eight hours. It's obvious that this created some difficult situations as the RNs attempted to find out what had been done, how the patients responded, and what was left to be completed. The RNs spent a lot of time looking for charted information and asking the patients or family members. Although their observations within the patient's rooms and their rounding afforded them valuable information as to the performance of their delegates, some of the information could have been handled much more efficiently by verbal communication. It's obvious that evaluation needed to be done on a shift-by-shift basis at a minimum, in addition to checkpoints throughout the shift.

One community care agency developed a policy that required RNs to meet with the home health aides and rehabilitation aides twice a month to discuss progress on the long-term cases. Nurses who at first complained about the amount of time this would take discovered that it actually saved them time when they reflected on whether the plan of care was working, gave and received feedback from their delegates, and decided whether the system and the personnel were performing as required. The team were able to celebrate the outcomes they achieved with their patients as well!

An ambulatory respiratory rehabilitation clinic employed respiratory therapists, physical therapy/occupational therapy aides, a secretary/receptionist, and an LPN (LVN), all supervised by an RN. In this situation, the team met at the beginning and end of each case to plan the care and evaluate outcomes, but also to evaluate their process of delegation. Often personnel performance issues were discussed and feedback was given. Each time, the RN asked for feedback about how the system was working for the delegates, and ultimately for the patients and their families. When the clinic expanded its services to include general respiratory patients who were receiving ongoing outpatient care from the pulmonologists, some of whom were being referred to the rehabilitation clinic, the periodic evaluation of the system and personnel performance changed. Personnel were evaluated on a quarterly basis by the managing RN, and systems functioning was discussed in the staff meetings every month. The case-by-case evaluation of outcomes for the rehabilitation clinic patients continued. The staff handled personnel performance issues as they came up by using the feedback process, as we discussed in the previous chapter.

Overall evaluation includes asking some questions related to the delegation process. At the end of a shift, for example, an RN may ask the questions listed in Exhibit 11–2. When you have reviewed these questions, proceed to Checkpoint 11–5.

CHECKPOINT 11–5

All but two of the personnel in an acute care surgical unit were overtime this shift. Although the number of staff assigned matched what had been designated by the department's acuity system, all the RNs were behind and didn't have breaks. Joe and Marty, unit aides, completed their work early and were ready to go home on time. What possibly could have gone wrong with the delegation process in this case?

See the end of the chapter for the answers.

CASE STUDY ANALYSIS OF EVALUATION

In this case study, we will review the three types of evaluation (continuous, specific problem related, and periodic) and setting up timelines, checkpoints, and parameters for reporting in a community health setting.

Continuous Evaluation: Bob, a visiting nurse in a large metropolitan area, is supervising a challenging child abuse case. The mother has had two previous children who were mentally disabled from what has been surmised to have been head trauma. Since the charges were unproved previously, the judge awarded custody of her new twins to this natural mother, despite the concerns of the social worker, child welfare worker,

Exhibit 11–2 Questions for Overall Evaluation

1. Did we accomplish our goals? What patient outcomes have been achieved?
2. If so, did the outcomes have anything to do with the manner in which work was delegated and assigned? If so, what worked well so that I can use it again the next time?
3. What didn't work? Why?
4. If there was a problem, did it have anything to do with how I delegated?
   a. Did I know my own job description, roles, and responsibilities?
   b. Did I allow any personal barriers to get in the way?
   c. Did I know the roles, job descriptions, and characteristics of my delegates?
   d. Did I match the jobs to the delegates appropriately? Were jobs prioritized?
   e. Did I communicate clearly and assertively?
   f. Was conflict handled?
   g. Did I use checkpoints, timelines, and parameters for reporting?
   h. Have I given feedback as needed, both negative and positive?

mental health professional, and mental health worker. Until the case can be appealed, Bob is attempting to coordinate the team's activities as well as supervising the work of a chore worker who has been placed in the home to help do the food purchase and preparation and provide some assistance with feeding the babies. How will Bob best evaluate and give necessary instructions to Evelyn, the chore worker?

_____

_____

_____

Discussion: Bob will discuss the overall case with the chore worker and plan to visit at least twice weekly himself. The chore worker, Evelyn, will understand the global picture in terms of the desired outcomes (the twins to be healthy and safe and the mother to be able to handle the situation) and will be given details, both written and verbal, about what to look for: signs that would indicate Mom is not coping well, problems with the infants, and how to recognize if Mom has been using drugs again. Evelyn and Bob will make the first visit together to be certain the step-by-step process of care and reporting is followed. In this way, the mother will know what to expect from both Evelyn and Bob in the ensuing weeks. Evelyn will be able to tell Bob how quickly he or the caseworker (or 911) should be notified if problems occur, and will report to Bob after each visit for at least the first month. On each visit, Bob will evaluate the babies, the mother, and the care that Evelyn is doing.

In this case we've reviewed some of the basic principles of evaluation on a continuous basis; of discussing the parameters, timelines, and checkpoints for reporting. Bob will have given and received feedback (clinical data reporting) from a clinical situation based on Evelyn's data gathering and his own personal assessment.

Periodic Evaluation: Beginning on a daily basis, then moving to a weekly, biweekly, and monthly basis, Bob completed a more long-term, periodic evaluation of the plan of care and outcomes, and how the team's process was proceeding. At the end of one month, which proceeded rather smoothly, Bob and the rest of the interdisciplinary team discussed the case. Bob evaluated the plan against the goals and projected outcomes: Is the mother able to cope with the twins, given the support she has been given? This is being measured by whether or not the twins are gaining weight and thriving, a lack of evidence of abuse or neglect, and the mother's self-report of being in control. The assessment of all the support professionals agrees with the mother's statement that she has been able to care for the babies and herself without incident. Despite all the concerns of the staff, periodic evaluation yields positive results. Based on our evaluation model, what two questions does Bob need to ask himself at this point?

_____

_____

_____

Discussion:

1. How is the system working? (So far, so good. We'll need to keep up the continuous evaluation and communication, however. We seem to have matched the right person with the right work, and our communication in the delegation process has been effective.)
2. How is the personnel performance affecting the results of this case? (The people involved have been doing an excellent job! It's time for positive feedback for all the professionals that have been so deeply concerned and involved in this case!)

Specific Incident Evaluation: The twins seemed to be consuming formula at a faster rate, and this meant Evelyn had to pick up groceries more often. One day, on returning home from the market, she noted that their mother was fast asleep on the couch, a cigarette burning in the ashtray, while the twins were howling from hunger. It was difficult to arouse Mom, so Evelyn fed and changed the twins. The mother stated she had been up late the night before trying to get them settled and was exhausted. Evelyn, having been an exhausted new mother herself, decided not to report this incident as a possible problem unless it occurred again. Several days later, the twins were again screaming as Evelyn arrived, but this time Mom had left the used syringe out on the kitchen table. How would you, as a supervising RN, evaluate this incident? Use the questions in the table in Checkpoint 11–6 to guide your evaluation.

DOCUMENTATION AND THE DELEGATION PROCESS

As we travel the country talking to nurses during and after seminars and consulting projects, we are often asked "How do I document the delegation process?" We have several recommendations, based on the particular situation and the degree of seriousness of the problem. Many nurses voice concerns about creating visible "proof," in the form of documentation, to demonstrate that they have indeed completed their responsibility as a supervisor of a delegated act.

In order to record the process of evaluation and feedback, many facilities have developed policies, procedures, or forms to be completed: For example, if a specific problem or error has occurred, you may be asked to fill out an "Unusual Occurrence Report" or "Incident Report." In these cases, follow the guidelines you've been given at your workplace. Generally, the actual observable problem is recorded in the chart objectively, but any interpersonal performance feedback is *not documented* on the patient record. (For example, if a medication was omitted, record that it was omitted, and what you did to care for the patient. The facility incident report is generally a form that is used for communication to the health care agency's insurance company and often asks who was responsible for the incident and what form of follow-up was done.) Personnel feedback and evaluation is documented on such forms as interim performance progress notes, performance appraisal forms, or other anecdotal notes that are often kept by managers. As a delegating nurse, you may be asked to give written information to your manager about what you've discussed with your delegate when performance has been exceptional in either direction.

CHECKPOINT 11–6

Answer each question in the space provided.

1. What signs tell you something is wrong here?	The potential problem could have been reported earlier.
2. What's good about this incident?	The twins are okay. The drug abuse evidence will help get the children ultimately to a safe foster home. This is a great teaching example to use for future.
3. What should be happening?	
4. Do I need to do something about it?	
5. What is the exact nature? Objective criteria to know if solved?	
6. What can be done?	
7. Positives and negatives for each solution.	
8. Plan steps and implement short/long-term solutions.	
9. Evaluate short-term results by objective criteria.	
10. Evaluate long-term. Solved?	
(Are new/additional strategies needed?)	

See the end of the chapter for the answers.

Documentation of the matching of the jobs to the delegate is often completed through assignment sheets or daily task lists. We recommend that you check to find out whether these are saved, and for what time period, in your department. We also recommend that you keep notes on your daily activities. Whatever method you currently use to keep track of your work for the case, or the shift, is an acceptable place to make that notation that you talked to Pam about the difficulty she was having in performing a task, but if the problem continues or becomes more serious, you will want to use a more formal method of documentation and alert the appropriate management person.

When you've done the delegation process well, following all the steps, and a delegate makes an error, how can you support your decision to delegate that given task? Your decision is endorsed by delegating according to state statutes, your facility job description, and validated competencies or skills checklists. You will save your notes from the day that record you did instruct and verify competency. (This information is *not* charted in the patient record, however.) Many organizations have established guidelines and policies about delegating that may also support your decision. Your follow-up and feedback given to the delegate will be documented in some way by your manager, and an "Unusual Occurrence Report" will be completed according to specific agency rules.

An excellent example of documentation of delegation by unlicensed care providers has been proposed by the Department of Health and Social Services in the state of Washington. As Harris points out,

> Specific policy and procedures must be written by a facility to delineate the scope of responsibilities to be delegated.... The successful completion of training and/or competency evaluation as required under [Medicare regulations of 1989] would be the minimum requirement for delegation of additional responsibilities to a home health care aide. Additional criteria include demonstration of ability to perform instructions from professional nurse; demonstrated successful interaction with home care team; interest and initiative for this responsibility; and additional training and supervision for a delegated responsibility (Harris, 1993).

A sample form, similar to The Proposed Unlicensed Care Provider Registration/Documentation Form by the Washington Department of Health and Human Services (1993) is shown in Exhibit 11–3.

Exhibit 11–3 Documentation of Unlicensed Care Provider Skills

Name _____ Social Security Number_____

Name of Client Receiving Care _____

Type of Setting (Adult Family Home, Children's Foster Home, etc.)_____

Training Completed by Caregiver: yes _____   no _____

Procedures To Be Delegated:

___ Oral Medication

___ Topical Medication

___ Tube Medication

___ Inhalants

___ Changing Sterile Dressings

___ Suppositories and Unit Dose Enemas

___ Home Blood Glucose Testing and Monitoring

___ Injectable Insulin

___ Gastrostomy Tube Feedings

___ Clean Intermittent Catheterization

___ IV Therapy

Date of Initial Nursing Assessment _____

Date of Task/Client Specific Training by RN _____

Dates of Reassessment _____

Remarks _____

_____

   "I have delegated nursing tasks and provided necessary training as documented above pursuant to RCW 18.88A and RCW_____."

RN Signature _____ Date _____

Courtesy of the Washington State Department of Health and Human Services, Olympia, Washington.

As delegation to unlicensed health care personnel becomes even more widespread in the future, documentation such as this will be adopted across the health care continuum. If you are concerned about the absence of adequate job descriptions or competency checklists, or you feel you need a form such as the one above, begin now to identify how you can be involved in planning documents that can be initiated to record your professional practice.

CELEBRATE THE SUCCESS OF THE TEAM!

Whether you work in an acute care ICU, a public health department, or any other health care arena, health care is a serious business. Supervising other people and delegating work to them is a complex and often anxiety-laden proposition. But when you learn to delegate properly, using the skills we have been presenting in this handbook, you'll gain the confidence needed to grow professionally, and safe, effective, high quality patient care can be delivered.

Due to the stressful nature of working with others, we may focus only on the potential for error and the actual problems that occur. It sometimes seems we have little time to do anything else. However, as a registered nurse and as a leader of your health care team, you are in the very best position to help your coworkers focus also on the most wondrous work you are doing! The outcomes of your efforts are evidence of the existence of all that is good and full of light in this harried, violent, and often frightening world.

Think of what you have accomplished, not alone, but together with the members of your team, you and your delegates.

You have helped create a new family, a haven for love and nurturing, because you and your team provided family planning information or infertility therapy and prenatal care; you taught the mother about nutrition and sexually transmitted diseases and made sure she received financial assistance. Or you may have been the nursing care team who helped birth the baby and gave him his first bath, or supervised and supported the new family as they attempted a sleepy adjustment at home.

Perhaps you were a part of the nursing care team who helped keep another disabled child in school, teaching the teachers to suction, providing therapy in the rehabilitation setting, or nudging him once again out of a crisis in the pediatric intensive care. Maybe you are one of the group of health care professionals who is intent on finding the answer to preventing this child's disability through research or public health measures.

Maybe it was your team who helped someone's grandmother to come to terms with Grandfather's inability to recognize her or his past. Or you may have been the ones who treated grandfather when his suicide attempt followed the first diagnosis of his disease. From the emergency room to the psychiatric long-term care unit, you have been there for them, working together as a team.

Victories are continual, each day, in all settings of the health care continuum, whether you've saved a life during a "code" or whether you gently cared and supported as a peaceful, sheltered death ensued. Nurses are there, in the most challenging, difficult, joyful, or tragic episodes of human life. And you are not alone.

So recognize your unique contribution to this world, and recognize all the people that help make it happen. And celebrate the success of the team!

CHECKPOINT 11–7

1. Think of all the people that help you when you are in an emergency (or other challenging) situation in your health care setting. List them and what they do.
   Example: A "code" in an acute care facility:

   a) secretary: called the needed MD, called for stat labs
   b) unit runner: ran specimens to lab
   c) lab technician: took the stairs to get to the patient more quickly to draw blood
   d) nursing assistant: reported the bloody stools, BP drop, and stayed to get supplies
   e) student nurse: answered other call bells
   f) pastoral care: got coffee and gave support to family
   g) LPN: gave medications to other patients while code progressing
   h) a new nurse: recorded during code
   i) code team: all did their jobs
   j) housekeeping: cleaned room for quick transfer

continues

CHECKPOINT 11–7 *continued*

k) admitting clerk: found room for patient
l) supervisor: called in staff for ICU to help save patient

2. Discuss with your coworkers the successes you have enjoyed in the last week.

_____

_____

_____

3. How can you and your team plan to celebrate your successes more often?

ANSWERS TO CHECKPOINTS

11–5. Using the questions preceding the checkpoint, consider possible alternatives. Evaluation of this shift may show that the following could have occurred. Personal barriers of the nurses could have been in the way; perhaps they did not assign all the work they could have to the aides, consistent with their job descriptions. Perhaps the RNs did not know the extent of responsibilities that could be assigned, or did not trust Marty and Joe. Checkpoints did not reveal that RNs were behind and that the others were getting work completed so that tasks could be reassigned. Marty and Joe may not have been asked to do things they could have done, or perhaps their job descriptions are too limited and need to be reevaluated. Did all RNs communicate their needs assertively and clearly and ask for help? It doesn't seem that feedback of a clinical nature flowed freely in all directions. Other issues could be part of the problem: disorganization, people unfamiliar with the department, emergencies, inaccurate acuity system, performance of the RNs and/or the delegates.

11–6. (Refer to steps as given in Exhibit 11–2.) 1. What signs tell you something is wrong? Evelyn could have reported the first problem so that Bob could have visited to determine whether drug abuse was a problem. 2. What is good? Evelyn reported it now and was very observant. The twins are still intact. 3. If all had gone well, she might have reported this earlier, or one of the other professionals could have seen other signs. 4. Should we do something? Yes, this may be a good chance to give more instruction to Evelyn. It will help other patients in the future. 5. The objective criteria we'd use to determine whether the problem was solved are that any and all possible symptoms of drug abuse or child abuse or neglect in the home would be reported to further follow-up. 6. What should Bob do? Bob should talk with the manager about his plan but will probably give feedback to Evelyn and determine if this is a learning need or if Bob should have communicated his expectations more clearly, or if there is a system glitch. Is it to be expected that a new mother would be difficult to rouse? This is certainly difficult to tell, and Bob should be careful to be positive about all that Evelyn did well in this situation. Also, he should determine whether she left him a message about this that was not given to him. First Bob must secure emergency care for the mother and the twins; then he must *look at how the incident occurred and how to avoid it in the future, using his feedback model to let Evelyn know about his concerns.*

REFERENCES

Anderson, C. 1990. *Patient teaching and communicating in an information age.* Albany, N.Y.: Delmar.

Hansten, R. 1991. Delegation: Learning when and how to let go. *Nursing* 91 (April): 126.

Hansten, R., and M. Washburn. 1993. *The nurse manager answer book.* Gaithersburg, Md.: Aspen Publishers, Inc.

Harris, M. D. 1993. Competent, supervised, unlicensed personnel will contribute to high-quality, in-home health care. *Home Healthcare Nurse* 11(6): 55.

Washington Department of Health and Human Services. 1993. *Unlicensed care provider registration/documentation, Attachment J* (DSHS 00-000(X) 1/93).

Addresses and Telephone Numbers for State Boards of Nursing

Alabama Board of Nursing
RSA Plaza, Suite 250
770 Washington Ave.
Montgomery, AL 36130-3900
205/242-4060

Alaska Board of Nursing Licensing
Dept. of Commerce and Economic
   Dev.
Division of Occupational Licensing
PO Box 110806
Juneau, AK 99811-0806

Arizona Board of Nursing
1651 E. Morten, Suite 150
Phoenix, AZ 85020
602/255-5092

Arkansas State Board of Nursing
University Tower Building
1123 South University Ave., Suite 800
Little Rock, AR 72204
501/686-2700

California Board of Registered Nursing
PO Box 944210
400 R Street, Suite 4030
Sacramento, CA 95814
916/322-3350

Colorado Board of Nursing
1650 Broadway, Suite 670
Denver, CO 80202
303/894-2430

Department of Health Services
Conn. Board of Examiners for Nursing
150 Washington St.
Hartford, CT 06106
203/566-1041

Delaware Board of Nursing
Margaret O'Neill Building
Federal and Court St.
PO Box 1401
Dover, DE 19903-1401
302/739-4522

District of Columbia Board of Nursing
Dept. of Consumer and Regulatory
   Affairs
614 H Street, NW, Room 904
PO Box 37200
Washington, DC 20001
202/727-7461

Florida State Board of Nursing
111 East Coastline Dr., Suite 516
Jacksonville, FL 32202
904/359-6331

Georgia Board of Nursing, Registered
    Nurses
166 Pryor Street, SW, Suite 400
Atlanta, GA 30303
404/656-3943

Guam Board of Nurse Examiners
PO Box 2816
Agana, GU 96910
001/671/477-8766 or 8517

State of Hawaii Board of Nursing
PO Box 3469
Honolulu, HI 96801
808/548-3086

Idaho Board of Nursing
280 North 8th St., Suite 210
Boise, ID 83720
208/334-3110

Illinois Department of Professional
    Regulation
320 West Washington St., 3rd Floor
Springfield, IL 62786
217/785-0800

Indiana State Board of Nursing
Health Professions Service Bureau
402 West Washington St., Room 041
Indianapolis, IN 46204
317/232-2960

Iowa Board of Nursing
1223 East Court
Des Moines, IA 50319
515/281-3255

Kansas Board of Nursing
Landon State Office Building
900 SW Jackson, Room 551
Topeka, KS 66612-1230
913/296-3929

Kentucky State Board of Nursing
312 Whittington Parkway, Suite 300
Louisville, KY 40222-5172
502/239-7000

Louisiana State Board of Nursing
150 Baronne Street, Room 912
New Orleans, LA 70112
504/568-5464

Maine State Board of Nursing
State House Station
PO Box 158
Augusta, ME 044333-0158
207/624-5275

Maryland Board of Nursing
Metro Executive Center
4201 Patterson Ave.
Baltimore, MD 21215-2299
410/764-4747

Massachusetts Board of Registration in
    Nursing
100 Cambridge St., Suite 1519
Boston, MA 02202
617/727-9961

Michigan Board of Nursing
PO Box 30018
Lansing, MI 48909
517/373-1600

Minnesota Board of Nursing
2700 University Ave. West, Suite 108
St. Paul, MN 55114
612/642-0567

Mississippi Board of Nursing
239 North Lamar, Suite 401
Jackson, MS 39201
601/359-6170

Missouri State Board of Nursing
3605 Missouri Blvd.
PO Box 656
Jefferson City, MO 65102
314/751-0681

Montana State Board of Nursing
Arcade Building, Lower Level
111 North Jackson
PO Box 200513
Helena, MT 59620-0513
406/444-4279

Nebraska Board of Nursing
State House Station
PO Box 95007
Lincoln, NE 68509-5007
402/471-2115

Nevada State Board of Nursing
1281 Terminal Way, Suite 116
Reno, NV 89502
702/786-2778

New Hampshire Board of Nursing
Division of Public Health Services
Health and Welfare Building
#6 Hazen Dr.
Concord, NH 03301-2657

New Jersey Board of Nursing
124 Halsey St., 6th Floor
PO Box 45010
Newark, NJ 07101
201/504-6493

New Mexico Board of Nursing
4253 Montgomery NE, Suite 130
Albuquerque, NM 87109
505/841-8340

New York State Board of Nursing
State Education Department
Cultural Education Center
Albany, NY 12230
518/474-3843

North Carolina State Board of Nursing
PO Box 2129
Raleigh, NC 27602-2129
919/782-3211

North Dakota Board of Nursing
919 South 7th St., Suite 504
Bismarck, ND 58504-5881
701/224-2974

Ohio Board of Nursing
77 South High St., 17th Floor
Columbus, OH 43266-0316
614/466-3947

Oklahoma Board of Nursing
Registration and Nursing Education
2915 North Classen Blvd., Suite 524
Oklahoma City, OK 73106
405/525-2076

Oregon State Board of Nursing
800 NE Oregon St. #25, Suite 465
Portland, OR 97232
503/731-4745

Pennsylvania State Board of Nursing
PO Box 2649
Harrisburg, PA 17105-2649
717/783-7142

Colegio de Proffesionales de la
    Enfermeria de Puerto Rico
Board of Nurse Examiners
Call Box 10200
Santerce, PR 00908-0200

Rhode Island Board of Nursing
Registration and Nursing Education
Cannon Health Building, Room 104
#3 Capitol Hill
Providence, RI 02908

State Board of Nursing for South
    Carolina
220 Executive Center Dr., Suite 220
Columbia, SC 29210
803/731-1648

South Dakota Board of Nursing
3307 South Lincoln Ave.
Sioux Falls, SD 57105-5224
605/335-4973

Tennessee State Board of Nursing
283 Plus Park Blvd.
Nashville, TN 37427-1010
615/367-6232

Board of Nurse Examiners, State of
    Texas
9101 Burnet Rd., Suite 104
PO Box 140466
Austin, TX 78714-0466
512/835-4880

Utah State Board of Nursing
Division of Occupational and
    Professional Licensing
Heber M. Wells Building, 4th Floor
160 East 300 St., PO Box 45802
Salt Lake City, UT 84145-0801

Vermont State Board of Nursing
109 State St.
Montpelier, VT 05609-1106
802/828-2396

Virgin Islands Board of Nurse Licensor
Kongens Gade #3 PO Box 4247
St. Thomas, VI 00803
809/776-7397

Virginia State Board of Nursing
6606 West Broad St., 4th Floor
Richmond, VA 23230-1717
804/662-9909

Washington State Board of Nursing
Division of Professional Licensing
PO Box 47864
Olympia, WA 98504-7864
206/453-2686

West Virginia Board of Examiners for
    Registered Nurses
101 Dee Dr.
Charleston, WV 25311-1620
304/558-3692

Wisconsin Board of Nursing
Room 174
PO Box 8935
Madison, WI 53708-8935
608/266-0145

Wyoming State Board of Nursing
Barrett Building, 2nd Floor
2301 Central Ave.
Cheyenne, WY 82002
307/777-7601

National Council of State Boards of
    Nursing
676 North Saint Clair St.
Suite 550
Chicago, IL 60611-2921
312/787-6555

Index

289